Study Guide
with Worked Examples

Study Guide
with Worked Examples

for use with

international
trade

Robert C. Feenstra   Alan M. Taylor

Stephen Ross Yeaple
University of Colorado at Boulder

WORTH PUBLISHERS

Study Guide with Worked Examples
by Stephen Ross Yeaple
for use with *Feenstra / Taylor: International Trade*

ISBN 13: 978-1-4292-0931-1
ISBN 10: 1-4292-0931-3

First Printing

Printed in the United States of America

Worth Publishers
41 Madison Avenue
New York, NY 10010
www.worthpublishers.com

CONTENTS

PREFACE

Robert Feenstra and Alan Taylor have written an excellent textbook that identifies the important issues in international economics and presents and explains a wide range of microeconomic and macroeconomic models that can be used to analyze these issues. This ***Study Guide with Worked Examples*** complements the textbook by providing students additional opportunities to develop their knowledge of international economics through active learning. Active learning strategies are useful not only in academics but also in sports, music, or the arts. A good coach or teacher (1) *identifies* an important skill for a player or student to develop, (2) *demonstrates* that skill to the player or student, (3) *confirms* that the player or student is executing the technique properly, and finally (4) *drills* the player or student until the skill becomes second nature. In most higher education settings, materials are made available to you that can take you through these steps, but it is up to you to take those steps.

The strategy employed in the ***Study Guide with Worked Examples*** has two components. First, for each section of each chapter in the textbook, the essential concepts are reviewed and key terms are presented in order to make students aware of what material they need to know. In places, fundamental economic principles from introductory microeconomic and macroeconomics courses are reviewed. Students are also invited to provide the definition of the key terms that form the basic vocabulary of international economics.

The second component involves problem solving. For each section of each chapter questions are asked (1) that test students' knowledge of essential concepts and (2) that help reinforce the logical structure of economic analysis. The problems vary considerably in difficulty, occasionally asking students to extend the uses of economic principles beyond the applications discussed in the textbook. Although space is provided for answers directly after each question, students are encouraged to use additional space to provide careful explanations because most of the value created from answering stimulating questions is in the practice of writing detailed answers. Tips are provided immediately following questions that delve into particularly important or difficult topics to identify common mistakes and demonstrate common features of different types of economic problems. Finally, detailed answers for every study guide question are provided at the end of the book.

The more time and effort that you put into your studies, the more rewarding your experience will be and the more you will appreciate the quality of the textbook that Robert Feenstra and Alan Taylor have written.

ACKNOWLEDGMENTS

I would like to thank Rob Feenstra, Alan Taylor, and Sarah Dorger, Acquisitions Editor at Worth Publishers, for encouraging me to write this study guide. I thank all of the people at Worth Publishers who gave me direction and helped in putting this book together, especially Marie McHale, Development Editor, and Stacey Alexander, Production Manager. I am deeply grateful to my wife, Katherine, for proofreading much of the book. Thanks also to the students in my International Trade class at Princeton University for commenting on the earliest drafts of the manuscript. Finally, I thank my children for their enthusiasm.

Stephen Ross Yeaple
University of Colorado at Boulder

Study Guide

with Worked Examples

Trade in the Global Economy

Overview

The term "globalization" means many things: the flow of goods and services across borders; the movement of people and firms; the spread of culture and ideas between countries; and the tight integration of financial markets around the world. In this book we analyze the flows of goods and services, people, and capital between countries and the policies that governments use to influence these flows. The volume of these flows is huge and is growing very rapidly. In addition to attempting to understand the forces that drive these flows, we will also delve deeply into the impact of these flows on welfare. How does trade affect a nation's material well-being? Does international trade increase the gap between the rich and the poor? What is the impact of immigration on workers?

This chapter presents a broad view of the flows in goods and services, people, and capital across borders. We will see that these flows are complex and difficult to summarize, but there are patterns in these flows that can be explained.

1 International Trade

ESSENTIAL CONCEPTS

International trade occurs when the residents of one country sell *merchandise goods* or *services* to residents of another country. The volume of international trade between countries is huge. In 2000 the total value of exports of goods was $10.2 trillion and the total volume of exports of services was $2.4 trillion. This chapter presents a large amount of information on the size and direction of international trade flows that may be hard to digest. We attempt to boil down some patterns in the international trade data.

- Countries with large *gross domestic product* (GDP) account for most international trade.
- Small countries engage in proportionately more trade relative to their GDP than do large countries.
- The volume of trade between two countries falls off rapidly in the distance between the two countries.

- Trade occurs between very similar countries and between very different countries.
- Two-way trade between countries is common; for example, the largest market for U.S. exports is Canada, and Canada is the largest source country for U.S. imports.
- Trade volumes have increased more rapidly than gross domestic product since the 1950s.
- Tariffs have fallen steadily since the 1950s.
- Technological progress in shipping has dramatically reduced international trade costs.

Why do countries engage in international trade? What affect does international trade have on the wealth of nations? What impact do these trade volumes have on the distribution of income? These are the big questions within the field of international trade, and various answers to these questions are given in Chapters 2 to 7. Chapters 2 to 4 and Chapter 7 present models that explain the motive for trade between countries with different characteristics, such as access to technology and natural resource abundances. Chapter 6 presents a model that explains why very similar countries, perhaps even identical countries, can gain from engaging in international trade and why most international trade between countries occurs between large developed countries that are in close proximity to each other.

Government policies toward trade have a big impact on the volume of trade. During periods when trade barriers, such as tariffs and quotas, have been low, international trade has flourished, whereas during periods of high trade barriers, such as the years between World War I and World War II, trade volumes have contracted. The effect of trade policies on the volume of international trade and on welfare are the subject of Chapters 8 to 11. Throughout this section of the book, we discuss the role of an important international institution, the World Trade Organization (WTO), in coordinating trade policies among its member countries and facilitating the growth of international trade.

KEY TERMS

Use the space provided to record your notes on the following key terms.

Exports _____

_____

_____

Imports _____

_____

_____

Merchandise goods _____

_____

_____

Service exports _____

_____

_____

Trade balance _____

_____

_____

Trade surplus _____

_____

_____

Trade deficit _____

_____

_____

Bilateral trade balance _____

_____

_____

Gross domestic product _____

_____

_____

Trade barriers _____

_____

_____

Import tariffs _____

_____

_____

Import quota _____

_____

_____

REVIEW QUESTIONS

Problem 1: Why is a bilateral trade balance often a misleading measure? Explain.

_____

_____

_____

Problem 2: Table 1-2 in the textbook shows the share of trade in gross domestic product. What characteristics appear to be important in explaining how reliant a country is on international trade?

_____

_____

_____

Problem 3: According to Table 1-2 in the textbook, the international trade volumes of Hong Kong and Malaysia exceed their GDP. How is this possible?

_____

_____

_____

Problem 4: Consider the following assertion: "Globalization is an irresistible force drawing countries together." Does the historical record support this assertion?

_____

_____

_____

The statistics presented in the chapter are "aggregate" volumes, lacking any detail about the types of goods and services traded. The actual motives for trade are obscured. In later chapters we will see that there are patterns in the composition of trade between countries.

Problem 4 is meant to point out that trade barriers between countries affect the volume of international trade. Historically, tariffs and quotas have occasionally increased rather than decreased. This is one reason for the fact that the two "golden eras" of globalization are separated by many years.

2 Migration and Foreign Direct Investment

ESSENTIAL CONCEPTS

International *migration* is a contentious topic in many countries. Many concerns raised by immigration are economic in nature. How does immigration affect wages? Do immigrants take jobs away from native-born residents? Given these fears, it is not surprising that all countries have restrictions on inward migration, and it is a safe bet that in the absence of these restrictions there would be substantially more international migration of labor. Chapter 5 presents an economic analysis of the effects of migration and shows that from the perspective of theory, immigration's effect on wages is primarily a short-run phenomenon. In the long run, the economy can absorb an increase in labor force without major changes in wages. The trade models presented in Chapter 4 also demonstrate that international trade acts as a substitute for immigration: A worker may not be able to enter the U.S. labor market, but the goods produced by the worker can.

Foreign direct investment occurs when a firm in one country owns a company in another country. Flows of foreign direct investment (FDI) between countries are substantial. A common perception is that multinational companies primarily invest in low-wage countries in order to reduce their costs of production. Although this type of foreign direct investment does occur, most foreign direct investment is between developed countries. A key example is the vast network of assembly plants in the United States owned by the Japanese firm Toyota. This type of foreign direct investment is often called *horizontal FDI* because it involves replicating the same production activity in many locations. The motive for this type of FDI is typically explained by the desire of firms to produce near their customers. *Vertical FDI* occurs when a multinational opens a plant in a low-wage country. Much of the vertical FDI of U.S. multinationals is in Mexico. Although the numbers for vertical FDI are considerably smaller than the numbers for horizontal FDI, vertical FDI is more controversial.

KEY TERMS

Use the space provided to record your notes on the following key terms.

Migration _____

_____

_____

Foreign direct investment _____

_____

_____

Horizontal FDI _____

_____

_____

Vertical FDI _____

_____

_____

Reverse-vertical FDI _____

_____

_____

Exchange rate _____

_____

_____

REVIEW QUESTIONS

Problem 5: Worker migration between countries is almost entirely from the lowest-wage countries to the highest-wage countries. True or false? Explain.

_____

_____

_____

Problem 6: Why might a multinational produce the same good in many different countries? Explain.

_____

_____

_____

Problem 7: Foreign direct investment can affect the volume of trade. Would you expect that vertical and horizontal FDI have a different or similar impact on trade volumes? Explain.

_____

_____

_____

TIPS

The book measures migration by the number of foreign-born people in a country, and it measures foreign direct investment by the change in the level of foreign ownership of companies in a given time period. The first is a "stock"; the second is a "flow." The actual sales of the foreign companies owned by multinationals are much larger than the flow of new investments.

Problem 7 points out that the flows of trade and foreign direct investment are interrelated.

2

Trade and Technology: The Ricardian Model

Overview

Trade patterns between countries display regularities that can be explained using economic theory. Different facts suggest different economic mechanisms. This chapter introduces a model developed by the nineteenth-century economist David Ricardo that relates a particular country characteristic, its technology, to its trade pattern. Ricardo showed that a country could be technologically "backward" in every industry and still gain from trading with more productive countries. The analysis of Ricardo's model illustrates the principle of *comparative advantage,* one of the most fundamental concepts in economics. Many of the economic mechanisms found in Ricardo's model are also to be found in the more complicated models discussed later in the book. For this reason, it will pay to be especially vigilant in your study of this chapter!

The next four chapters explore various other models that offer explanations for particular regularities in the pattern of trade across countries. In addition to providing some explanation for these trade patterns, the models can also be used to understand the impact of international trade on welfare.

1 Reasons for Trade

ESSENTIAL CONCEPTS

The pattern of trade between countries, both in the aggregate statistics presented in Chapter 1 and in the example of U.S. imports of snowboards presented at the beginning of this chapter, suggests that there are a range of explanations for why countries trade with each other. Many of these explanations involve differences across countries in terms of the characteristics of their economies. For instance, countries may differ in their access to *technology* or in their supply of productive *resources.* Differences in technology will lead some countries to have *absolute advantages* in the production of some goods. That is, in the production of some goods they may be the world's productivity leaders. The actual explanation for trading patterns lies not in a country's absolute advantage, however, but rather in its *comparative advantage.* A country has a comparative advantage in the good that it is relatively better able to produce. Comparative advantage can be due to differences in technology, but it can also stem from a country's endowment of *resources,* be those resources natural (such as arable land or coal) or artificially created (such as capital).

Finally, geography matters for the structure of trade in many ways. Aside from geography's impact on a country's endowments of natural resources, geography also determines the distances between countries. A key regularity in the data is that the amount of trade between two countries falls in the distance between them. Trading relationships that are fostered by *proximity* are often strengthened by government policy. Canada, Mexico, and the United States have traditionally traded a great deal with each other because of the ease of transport and communication. A *free trade area* agreed to by these countries has also deepened their trading ties.

KEY TERMS

Use the space provided to record your notes on the following key terms.

Exports _____

_____

_____

Imports _____

_____

_____

Proximity _____

_____

_____

Resources _____

_____

_____

Natural resources _____

_____

_____

Labor resources _____

_____

_____

Capital _____

_____

_____

Factors of production _____

_____

_____

Absolute advantage _____

_____

_____

Comparative advantage _____

_____

_____

Technology _____

_____

_____

Free trade area _____

_____

_____

Foreign direct investment _____

_____

_____

Outsourcing _____

_____

_____

2 The Ricardian Model

ESSENTIAL CONCEPTS

This chapter uses a simple general equilibrium model developed by David Ricardo to illustrate the principle of *comparative advantage*. In a general equilibrium model, an economy has a supply of *factors,* or resources used to produce goods. *Technology* determines how factors are turned into goods. Demand for these goods is determined by consumers' income, which depends on the economy's output; by consumers' preferences, which are represented by *indifference curves;* and by *relative prices*. Finally, a general equilibrium model specifies how people and firms compete. In this chapter, *perfect competition* prevails in every market.

The economy's *production possibility frontier* (PPF) summarizes what the economy can produce given its technology and factor endowment. In Ricardo's model, the marginal product of labor (MPL) in each industry is constant so that an industry's output is just its marginal product of labor multiplied by the number of workers employed in the industry. By moving labor between industries, we can trace out a country's PPF. The slope of this PPF tells us the *opportunity cost* of expanding the output of the good on the X axis in terms of the good on the Y axis. A country has a comparative advantage in a good if its opportunity cost of production of that good is lower than the opportunity cost of that good in other countries.

The level of consumer demand for goods depends on (1) consumers' budget constraints, (2) consumers' tastes, and (3) relative prices. Because these concepts are used in many of the book's chapters, it is worth reviewing them. Suppose a consumer has income I to spend on apples and shirts. The number of apples she demands is D_A and the number of shirts she demands is D_S. The price of apples is P_A and the price of shirts is P_S. If she spends all her income, then

$$I = P_A \cdot D_A + P_S \cdot D_S \Rightarrow D_S = \frac{I}{P_S} - \frac{P_A}{P_S} \cdot D_A.$$

Note that P_A / P_S is called the *relative price* of apples. The relative price tells us the *opportunity cost* of an apple to a consumer given the prices of the two goods, or how many shirts need to be given up to buy an additional apple. For simplicity, the country is treated as one consumer that has its own budget constraint. Where on the budget constraint a consumer chooses to purchase depends on her preferences, which are represented by *indifference curves* as shown in Figure 2-1.

There are two assumptions behind the way that indifference curves are drawn: (1) consumers want *more* of all goods, and (2) *ceteris paribus* consumers get diminishing returns out of consuming more of the same good. From these assumptions it follows that indifference curves are convex (as shown) and higher indifference curves imply greater utility. Changes in income and relative prices change a consumer's budget constraint but have no impact on the consumer's tastes. That is, the map of indifference curves never changes, just which curve we can reach. The tastes of the entire country are represented using a single set of indifference curves that tell us which bundle on their budget constraint consumers choose and how well off they are.

Finally, we assume that there is perfect competition. Because firms take prices and wages as given in making their hiring decision, the relative prices that they charge exactly reflect the opportunity cost of production facing the economy. Because firms make

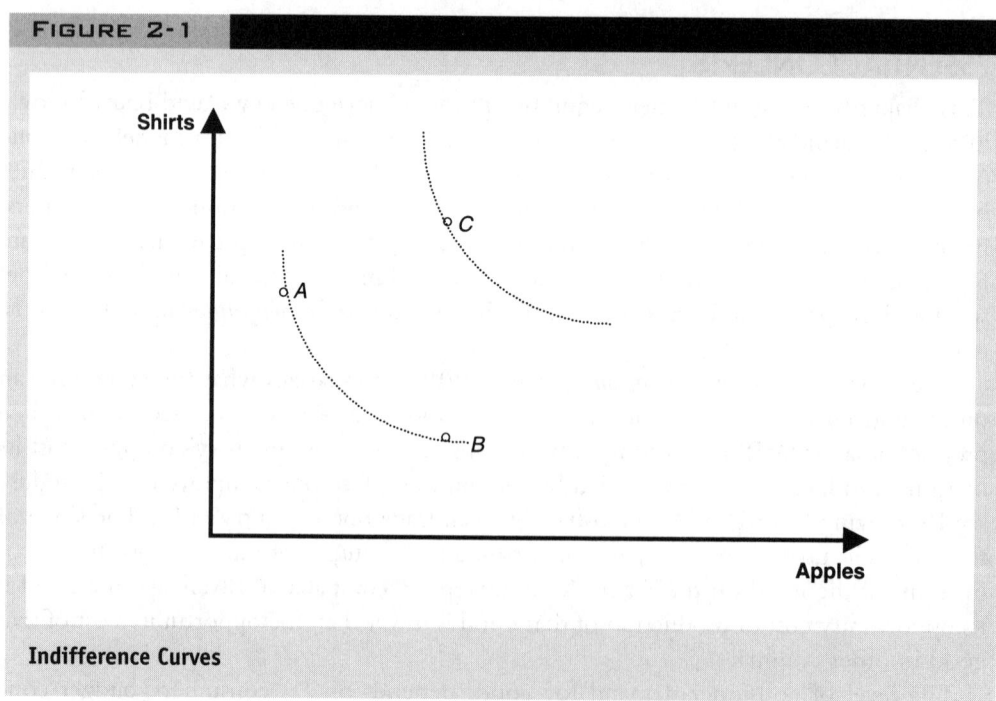

FIGURE 2-1

Indifference Curves

zero profits, their earnings are passed on to workers so that workers can consume what is produced.

An equilibrium occurs when firms supply goods and hire workers to maximize their profits, consumers demand goods to maximize their utility, and supply equals demand. In a "no-trade equilibrium" there is only domestic demand, so the level of domestic production must equal the level of domestic demand. When international trade is allowed, foreign demand and supply must be taken into account.

KEY TERMS

Use the space provided to record your notes on the following key terms.

Factors _____

_____

_____

Marginal product of labor _____

_____

_____

Production possibilities frontier _____

_____

_____

Opportunity cost _____

_____

_____

Perfect competition _____

_____

_____

Relative price _____

_____

_____

Indifference curves _____

_____

_____

Utility _____

_____

_____

REVIEW QUESTIONS

Problem 1: Home is endowed with 100 workers who can produce two goods: shirts and apples. Worker's *marginal product* of labor in shirts (MPL_S) is 2. (One worker can produce 2 shirts.) The marginal product of labor in apples is 5.

1a. Graph Home's PPF with output of shirts (Q_S) on the Y axis and apples (Q_A) on the X axis; label the intercepts and the slope.

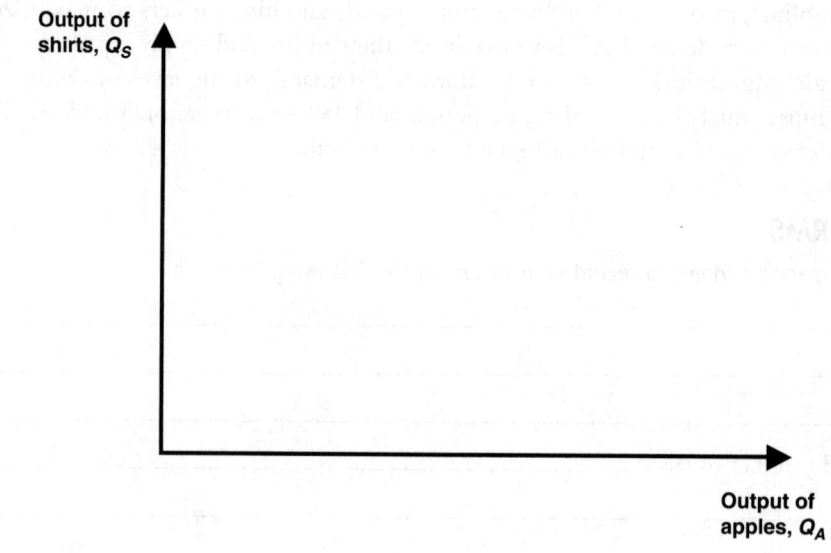

1b. Explain why the PPF is a straight line. _____

_____

_____

1c. What is the opportunity cost of apples in terms of shirts? _____

_____

1d. What is the opportunity cost of shirts in terms of apples? _____

_____

1e. How would you change the graph that was the answer to 1a if the number of workers in the country fell to 50? Show in the axes provided below.

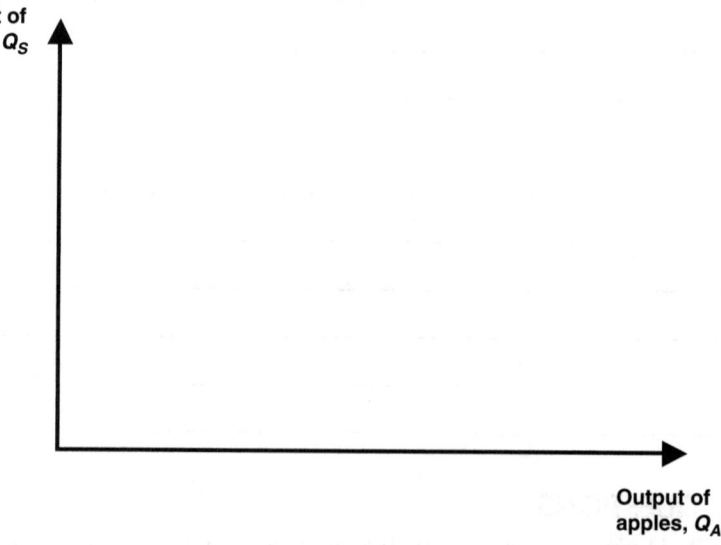

1f. Does this change the opportunity costs of the goods? _____

_____

1g. Suppose that the workers wake up feeling sick one day and their marginal product in both goods is half as much as it was before ($MPL_S = 1$ and $MPL_A = 5/2$). How would this change the PPF relative to your answer in 1a? Show in the axes provided below.

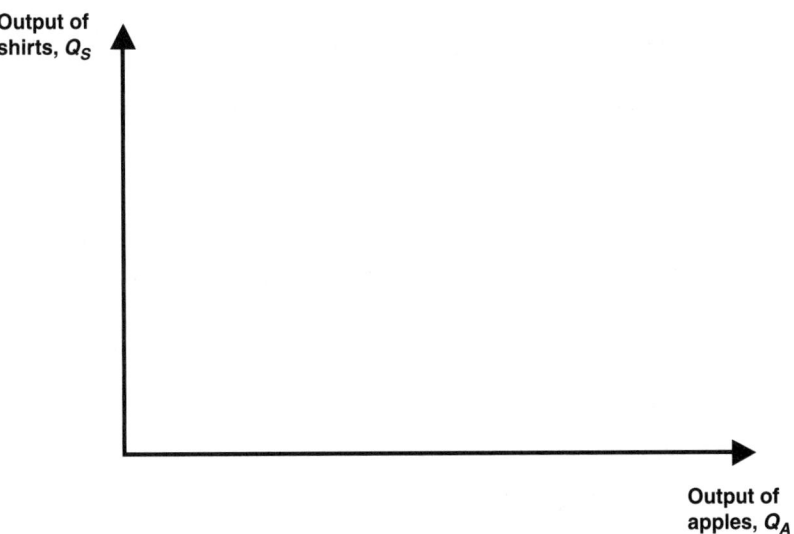

1h. Now suppose that the bumblebees in Home become depressed and so are less able to pollinate the apple trees. As a result, the MPL_A falls from 5 to 2. How does this change affect Home's PPF? Show the "before" and "after" cases in the axes provided below.

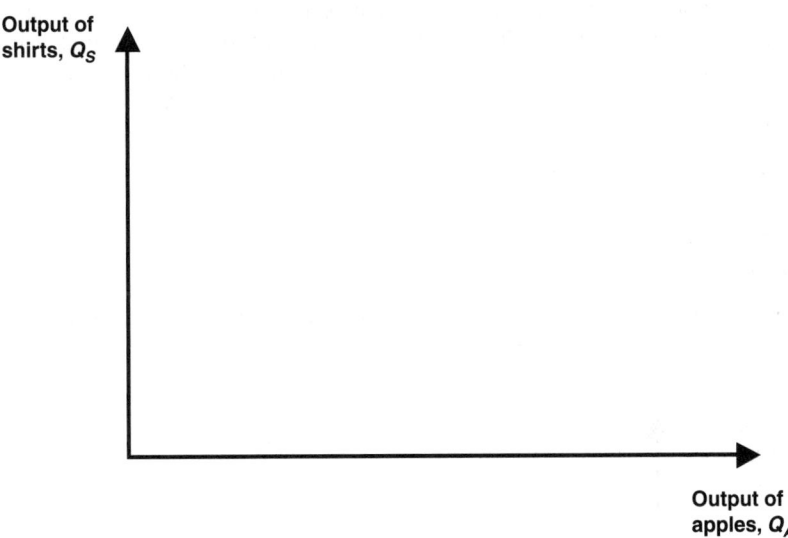

1i. How does "the great bee depression" affect the opportunity cost of apples in terms of shirts? _____

_____

_____

TIPS

In the Ricardian model the PPF is always straight, never curved. This is because there is only one factor and its marginal product in each industry is assumed to be constant. Later we will see models with "curved" PPFs.

The opportunity cost of good *A* in terms of good *B* is only equal to the slope of the PPF if good *A* is on the X axis.

The problems above can be used as a "cookbook" for other problems. Experiment with different numbers for stock of factors and for technology to get more practice.

Problem 2: Home is endowed with 100 workers. The marginal product of labor in shirts (MPL_S) is 2. The marginal product of labor in apples is 5. Suppose the price of a shirt is $5 and the price of an apple is $2.

2a. Given the information provided in problem 2, where on the PPF will the economy produce?

_____

_____

2b. Suppose the price of an apple rises to $4. What will firms produce?

_____

_____

TIPS

There is perfect competition. Given prices, firms adjust output to maximize their profits and in the process generate demand for factors. Prices of factors then adjust to guarantee that firms make zero profits.

Because marginal products are constant in Ricardo's model, firms are willing to supply *any* level of output along the PPF as long as relative prices are equal to the slope of the PPF.

For any other relative price, the economy *must* specialize in one good.

Problem 3: An apple costs 20¢ ($P_A = \$1 / 5$), a shirt costs 50¢ ($P_S = \$1 / 2$), and the consumer's income is $100.

3a. What is the equation for the budget constraint? Graph this budget constraint, being careful to label all the relevant information.

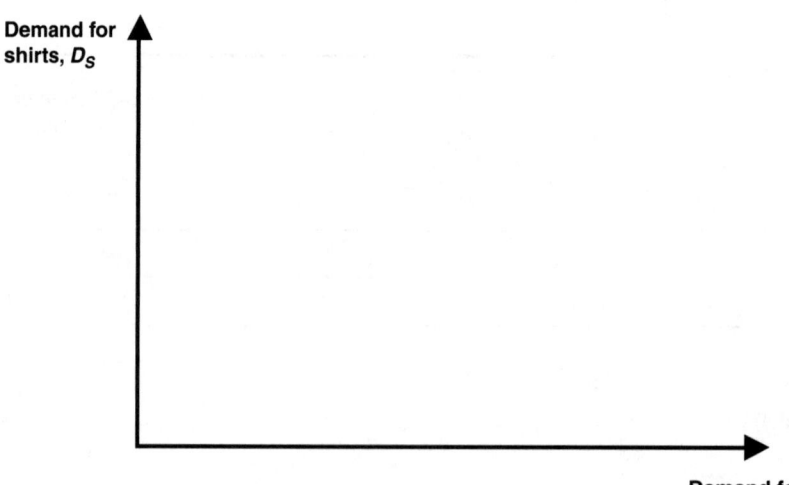

Demand for shirts, D_S

Demand for apples, D_A

3b. How would your graph change if income is $200, the price of apples is 40¢, and the price of a shirt is $1?

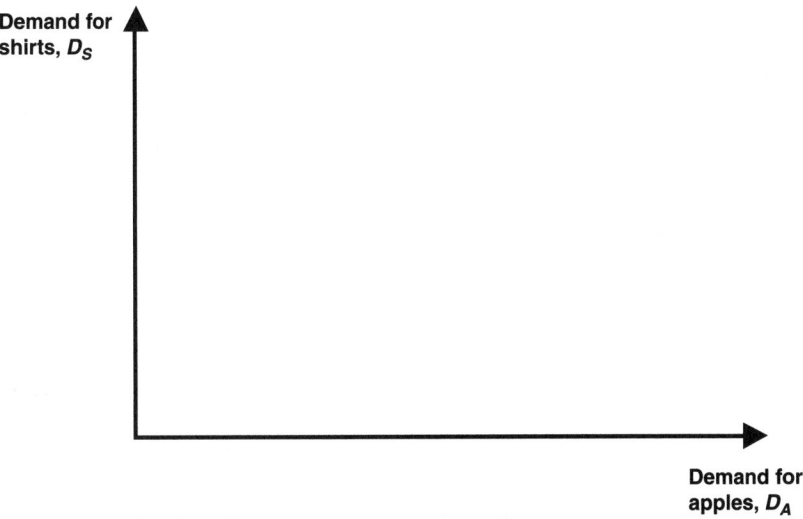

3c. Starting from the case in which income is $200, the price of apples is 40¢, and the price of shirts is $1, show how the graph changes when the price of shirts falls to 50¢ and everything else stays the same. How has the opportunity cost of apples been affected by the change in the dollar price of shirts? _____

_____

_____

3d. Show how the graph changes when the price of shirts is $1 and the price of apples falls to 20¢. How has the opportunity cost of shirts been affected by the change in the price of apples? _____

_____

_____

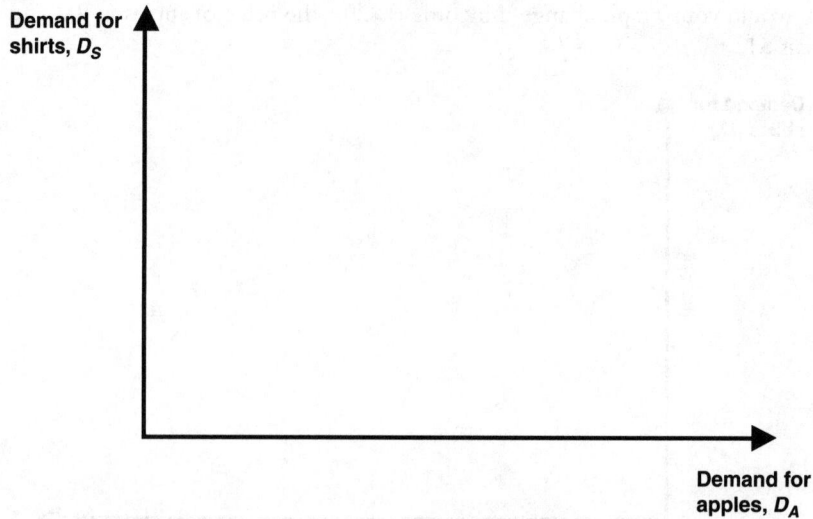

....

TIPS

It is important to remember that the slope of the budget constraint is the price of the good on the *X* axis divided by the price of the good on the *Y* axis.

Relative prices do *not* involve dollar signs! They are "real" in the sense that they tell us the tradeoff facing consumers in actual goods.

In the Ricardian model, international trade will be like a change in relative prices as shown in problems 3c and 3d. Consumers can afford more of both goods as long as the consumer spends his income on both goods.

....

Problem 4: Consider the information in Figure 2-1. The dotted lines are indifference curves, and *A, B,* and *C* are three different bundles of goods.

4a. Given the choice of *A, B,* or *C,* which bundle would the consumer select? _____

_____

_____

4b. Given the choice of *A* or *B,* which bundle would the consumer select? _____

_____

_____

4c. A consumer's income is $200, the price of apples is 40¢, and the price of a shirt is $1. Graph the consumer's budget constraint. Draw an indifference curve that determines the consumer's demand. Label this demand.

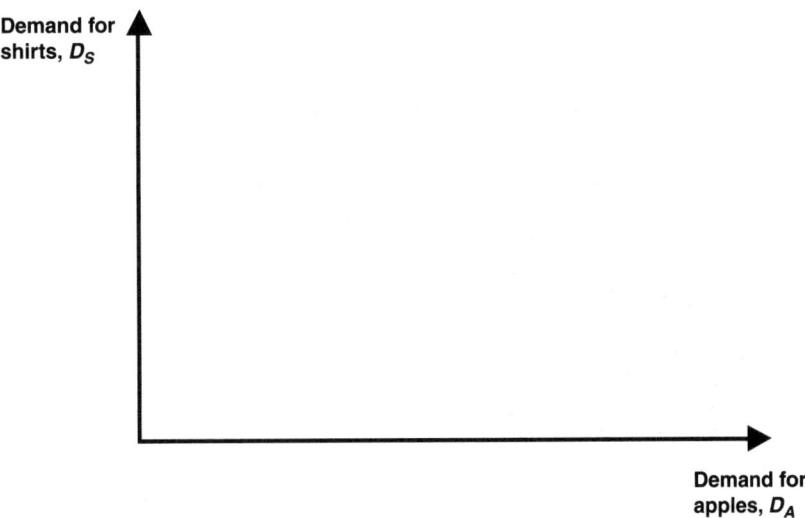

4d. Show how the graph changes when the price of shirts falls to 50¢ and everything else stays the same. Show the new indifference curve and demand levels.

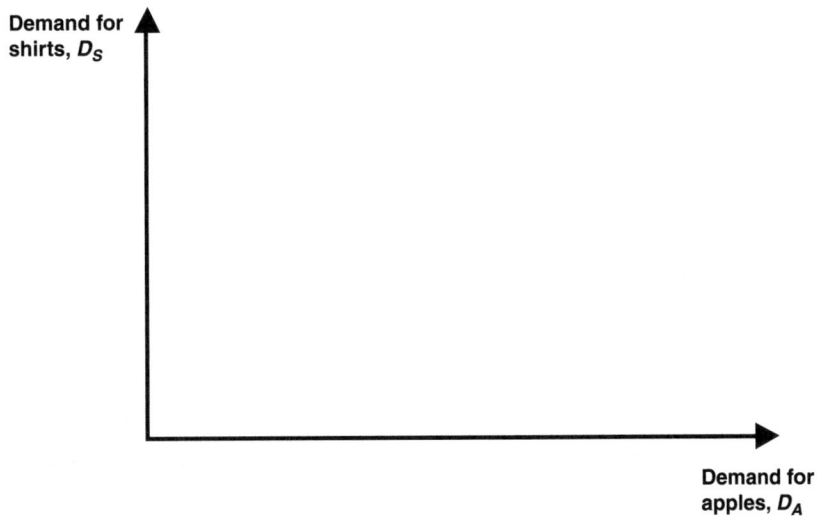

....

It is imperative not to draw indifference curves so that they appear to cross. Indifference curves *cannot* cross because otherwise they could not involve different levels of "utility."

We often draw two indifference curves, one representing utility before a change and one representing utility after a change. In principle, there are an infinite number of indifference curves corresponding to all other possible levels of utility, but we don't draw them to avoid cluttering up the picture.

TIPS

....

Problem 5: Home's stock of factors is 100 workers. Two goods are produced: shirts and apples. Workers' marginal product of labor in shirts is 2, and the marginal product of labor in apples is 5.

5a. Graph a no-trade equilibrium for this economy that shows the country's PPF (with axes labeled) and an indifference curve that shows demand levels. Indicate the relative prices.

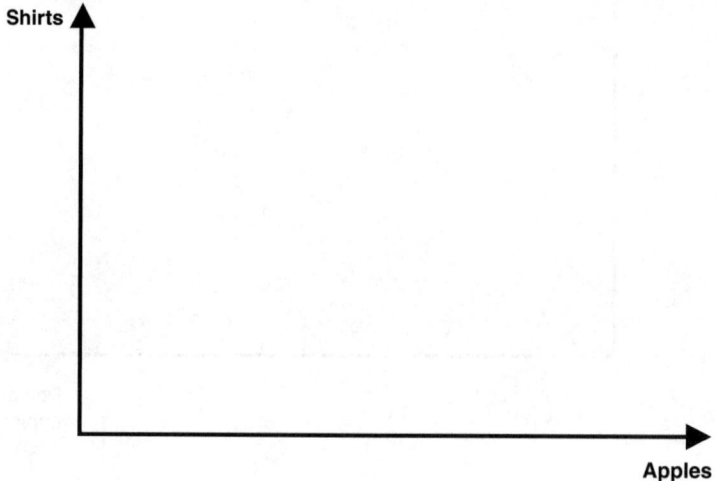

5b. Suppose that a technology improvement leads to an increase in the marginal product of labor in apples to 10. Show how the equilibrium changes.

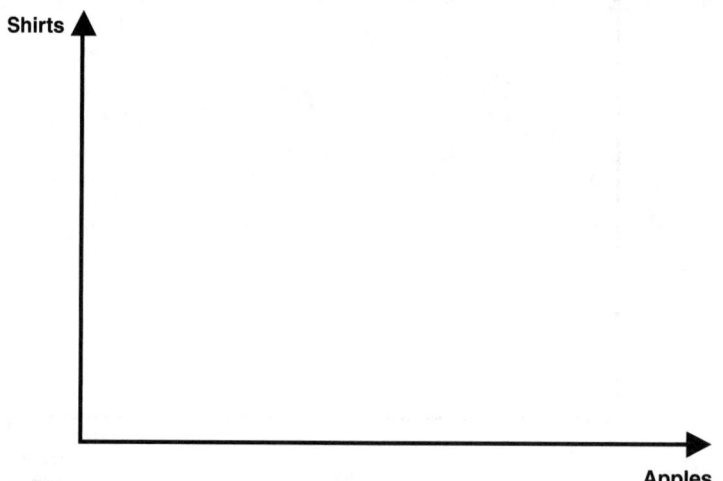

5c. Going back to the initial information, suppose the economy is given the opportunity to trade as much as it wants with the outside world at the *fixed* international relative price of apples of 1. On the next page, draw a figure showing how producers and consumers respond to this opportunity.

Problem 5c demonstrates a general feature of the Ricardian model. Being allowed to trade with the outside world at *any* relative price that is different than the no-trade equilibrium price must make the country better off.

You should notice a similarity in the answers to problems 5b and 5c. Technical progress and the ability to trade at fixed world prices have the same effect: They shift out the consumption possibilities frontier.

TIPS

3 Determining the Pattern of International Trade

ESSENTIAL CONCEPTS

To analyze how different technologies across countries affect the trading pattern, the model includes two countries. One of these countries will have an *absolute advantage* in both goods. That is, it will have a better technology for producing both goods. A country has an *absolute advantage* in a good if its marginal product of producing that good is higher than in another country. A country has a *comparative advantage* in a good when it has a lower opportunity cost of producing it than does another country. Because the relative price of a good in a no-trade equilibrium reflects the opportunity cost of producing that good, the country with a lower relative price for a good in a no-trade equilibrium has a comparative advantage in that good.

Consider the following example. Suppose that Home worker's *marginal product* of labor in shirts (MPL_S) is 2, and the marginal product of labor in apples is 5. Foreign worker's marginal product of labor in shirts is 8, and the marginal product of labor in apples is 8. Hence, Foreign has an absolute advantage in the production of both goods. The opportunity cost of apples in Home is 2 / 5 shirts, whereas the opportunity cost of apples in Foreign is 1 shirt. By definition, then, Home has a comparative advantage in apples and Foreign has a comparative advantage in shirts.

By reorganizing production toward their comparative advantage, countries increase the quantity of world output. To see this, suppose that the two countries are producing both goods. If Home expands production of apples by 1 unit, it has to cut shirt production by 2 / 5 units. If Foreign cuts apple production by 1 unit, it will free enough labor to produce another shirt. Apple output is unchanged, while shirt output has *risen* by 1 − 2 / 5 = 3 / 5 units. Reorganizing production toward countries' comparative advantage and allowing international trade give rise to *gains from trade* due to the more efficient use of the world's resources. The distribution of these gains between countries depends on the *terms of trade* on world markets.

KEY TERMS

Use the space provided to record your notes on the following key terms.

Absolute advantage _____

_____

_____

Comparative advantage _____

_____

_____

International trade equilibrium _____

_____

_____

Gains from trade _____

_____

_____

World price line _____

_____

_____

REVIEW QUESTIONS

Problem 6: Suppose that Home has a marginal product of labor of 4 making apples and a marginal product of labor of 4 making shirts.

6a. Foreign has a marginal product of labor of 6 making apples. Choose a number for the marginal product of labor in Foreign for shirts that gives Foreign a comparative advantage in apples. _____

_____

_____

6b. Choose numbers for the marginal product of labor in apples and in shirts in Foreign so that the wage rate is twice as high in Foreign, but there are no gains from trade. _____

_____

_____

Problem 7: Explain why a country will export the good in which it has a comparative advantage and import the other good if trade is balanced. _____

_____

_____

Problem 8: Suppose that Home has 100 workers, a marginal product of labor of 4 making apples, and a marginal product of labor of 4 making shirts. Foreign has 100 workers, a marginal product of labor of 8 making apples, and a marginal product of labor of 6 in shirts.

8a. What range of relative prices could be observed in a trading equilibrium? Explain.

_____

_____

8b. Draw the production possibilities frontier, world price line, and indifference curves for each country for a trading equilibrium when the relative price on world markets is halfway between their autarky relative prices. Label the intercepts of the world price line and PPF.

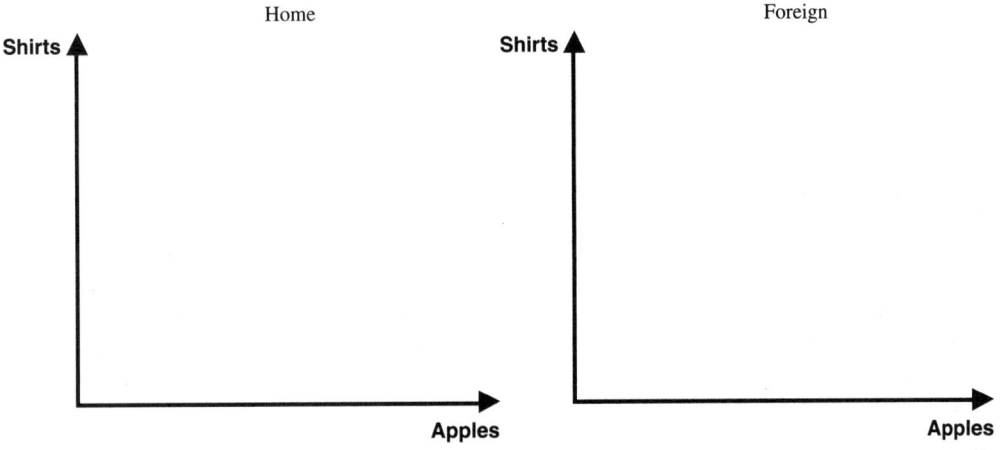

Home   Foreign

....

Gains from trade have nothing to do with wage differences between countries. Wage differences are due to absolute advantage, but it is comparative advantage that creates gains from trade.

   From your work with production and budget constraint you should notice that the greater the difference between world relative prices and relative prices in a no-trade equilibrium, the more the country gains from trade.

TIPS

....

4 Solving for International Prices

ESSENTIAL CONCEPTS

International prices are determined by international supply and demand for goods. The model includes two goods, but it is sufficient to think about just one good for determining the *one* relative price. If trade is balanced, then the value of Home's exports is equal to the value of its imports of the other good *and* to the value of Foreign's imports. Exports are domestic production minus domestic consumption. By varying the relative price of the good, we observe how a country's production and consumption change and so predict how the country's desire to trade is affected. The relative price that makes one country's export supply equal the other country's import demand is the equilibrium international price, or the *terms of trade*.

KEY TERMS

Use the space provided to record your notes on the following key terms.

Export supply curve _____

_____

_____

Import demand curve _____

_____

_____

Terms of trade _____

_____

_____

REVIEW QUESTIONS

Problem 9: Suppose that Home has 100 units of labor with a marginal product of 4 making apples and a marginal product of 4 making shirts. In the no-trade equilibrium, suppose that consumers in Home demand 175 apples. Foreign has 100 units of labor with a marginal product of 8 making apples and a marginal product of 6 in shirts. In a no-trade equilibrium Foreign consumes 400 apples. It may help you to consult your answers to problem 8 for the following problems.

9a. Draw Home's export supply curve.

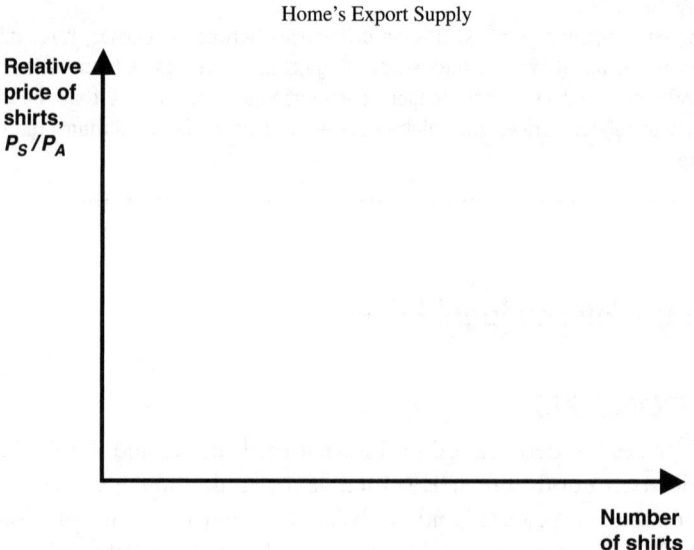

Home's Export Supply

9b. Add Foreign's import demand curve to the diagram so that the world relative price of shirts is between the two countries' no-trade relative prices.

9c. Suppose the number of workers in Home were to double. How would this change shift Home's export supply curve? Show in your original diagram.

If instead the problem had asked about Foreign's export supply and Home's import demand, the graph would have looked different but the information would be the same!

The answer to 9c displays a general result in trade models: Larger countries are less likely to gain from trade. Relative prices in the international trade equilibrium are not much different for the large country than in a no-trade equilibrium. This is because Foreign demand is small relative to Home supply. As we saw in earlier problems, countries gain more the bigger the difference is between no-trade and trade relative prices.

TIPS

3

Who Gains and Who Loses from Trade?

Overview

Chapter 2 demonstrated that there are gains from trade in the sense that countries that engage in international trade can consume more than countries that do not. This chapter analyzes the way that international trade affects the actual spending power, or real income, of individuals rather than countries. As the title of the chapter suggests, it is possible for a country to gain from trade while some (but not all!) individuals living in that country are made poorer by international trade.

International trade affects the welfare of individuals through its effects on the real earnings of the factors that they own. Some people get most of their income by working, whereas others get income from their ownership of land or of capital. International trade increases the earnings of some factors and lowers the real earnings of other factors. As a result, some individuals will gain from international trade and others will lose. To get at these issues, it is critical to use a model that has more than one type of factor.

The *specific-factors model* that is introduced in this chapter features three factors. This model shows that there are clear winners and clear losers from international trade. The idea that a country gains from trade has a very specific meaning: The gains to those that benefit from international trade exceed the losses of those that are harmed by international trade.

1 Specific-Factors Model

ESSENTIAL CONCEPTS

The model assumes that one industry (agriculture) uses labor and land and the other industry (manufacturing) uses labor and capital. This model is called the specific-factors model because land is *specific* to the agriculture sector and capital is *specific* to the manufacturing sector; labor is used in both sectors, so it is not specific to either one. Labor is sometimes referred to as the *mobile factor* because it can move freely between the two industries.

Adding a specific factor to production in each industry gives rise to the key feature of the specific-factors model: *diminishing returns.* To produce agricultural products, a firm needs land and labor. Land is in fixed supply, so output can only be expanded by adding labor (i.e., moving it out of manufacturing). As more workers are put to work using the same amount of land, the marginal product of labor in agriculture decreases. In the manufacturing industry the same assumption applies. Because the amount of capital is fixed, the marginal product of labor in manufacturing is decreasing in the level of manufacturing employment because as the number of workers in manufacturing rises there are fewer machines for each worker to use.

One important implication of diminishing returns is that it causes a country's PPF to be bowed out (or concave). This means that when the country goes to trade with the outside world, it will increase the output of the good whose relative price has risen and decrease the output of the other good, but it will not completely specialize in the production of either good. This is because moving labor from one industry to another causes the marginal product of labor to fall in the expanding industry and rise in the contracting industry. For example, if the relative price of manufacturing goods rises because of international trade, the opportunity cost of manufacturing goods will also rise as the country expands the production of manufacturing goods (falling MPL_M) and contracts the production of agricultural goods (rising MPL_A).

When countries are not engaged in international trade, the opportunity costs of production differ across countries. Trade allows the countries to expand the production of the goods in which they have a lower opportunity cost in the no-trade equilibrium and contract production of the goods in which they have a higher opportunity cost. Hence, there are gains from trade.

KEY TERMS

Use the space provided to record your notes on the following key terms.

Specific-factor model _____

_____

_____

Diminishing returns _____

_____

_____

Embargo _____

_____

_____

Autarky _____

_____

_____

REVIEW QUESTIONS

Problem 1: Suppose that the technology for creating manufacturing goods is $Q_M = \sqrt{\overline{K} \cdot L_M}$, where Q_M is manufacturing output; $\overline{K}$ is the country's endowment of capital, the factor specific to manufacturing; and L_M is the amount of the mobile factor, labor, used in manufacturing.

1a. How much does Q_M rise if both inputs $(\overline{K}, L_M)$ are doubled? _____

1b. Now suppose that $\overline{K}$ is fixed at 100. How much does Q_M rise if L_M is doubled? _____

_____

1c. Is the cost of lost manufacturing output associated with reducing manufacturing employment by one employee larger or smaller when the initial level of employment is 100 or 10? _____

_____

_____

Problem 2: Suppose that there are two goods: Agriculture (*A*) and Manufacturing (*M*). Agriculture is produced with Land and Labor and Manufacturing is produced with Capital and Labor. Labor is mobile between industries. The next two questions refer to Figure 3-1.

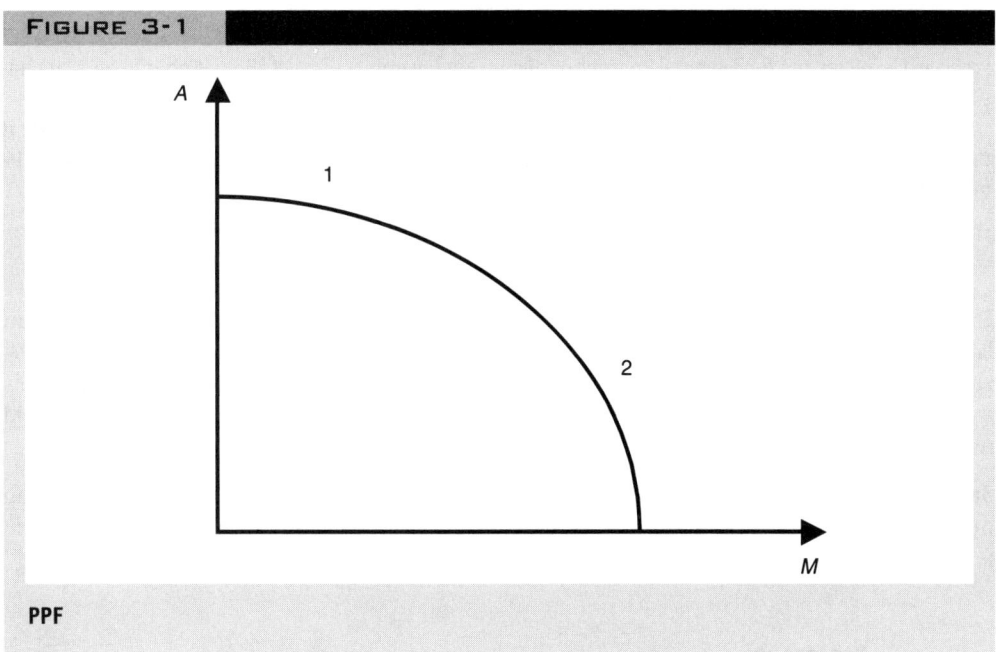

FIGURE 3-1

PPF

2a. Is the opportunity cost of *M* in terms of *A* higher at point 1 or point 2 in Figure 3-1?

_____

2b. Provide an intuitive explanation for why the PPF is "bowed out" in Figure 3-1.

_____

_____

2c. If the price of a manufactured good is $P_M = \$10/$unit and the marginal product of labor in manufacturing is 2 units per worker, what must the wage paid to a unit of labor be?

_____

_____

2d. If $P_M > P_A$, in which industry is the marginal product of labor higher? _____

_____

_____

2e. Suppose you own a manufacturing firm. If $P_M = \$10$/unit, the wage is \$25, and the marginal product of labor is 4 units per worker, are you hiring too many, too few, or the right amount of labor? _____

_____

_____

2f. Suppose the price of manufactured goods in terms of agricultural products falls. What would we expect to happen to the marginal product of labor in agriculture?

_____

_____

Problem 1 explores the fundamental concept of diminishing marginal product. Do not go into an exam until you are completely comfortable with this concept!

An important implication of the diminishing marginal product of labor in the specific-factors model is that the PPF displays increasing opportunity costs. That is, the more of a good that is produced, the higher the opportunity cost of producing more.

Problem 3: An economy called Home makes autos from capital and labor and bananas from land and labor. Labor is mobile between the two industries. Home is in a no-trade equilibrium, but it is considering opening to international trade with the rest of the world. The relative price of autos in terms of bananas is higher in Home than the fixed price on world markets.

3a. Create a diagram with a PPF, indifference curves, and an international price line showing how production and consumption in Home changes from its no-trade levels to its post-trade levels. Indicate the trade pattern on the diagram.

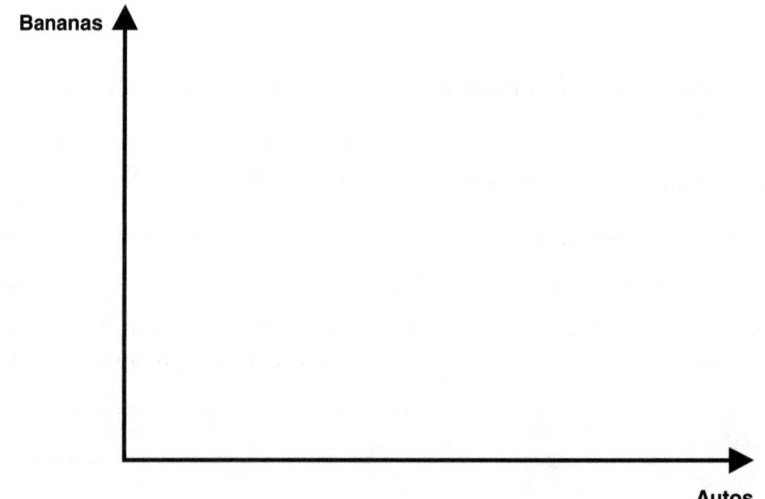

3b. Explain how your diagram shows how the country as a whole is better or worse off with trade than without trade. _____

_____

_____

3c. Now suppose that there are two countries in the world, Home and Foreign. The countries are not initially engaged in international trade and the relative price of autos is higher in Foreign than in Home. If the countries engaged in international trade, which country would export bananas? _____

_____

_____

3d. Once the two countries are engaged in trade, in which country is the opportunity cost of producing autos higher in terms of bananas? _____

_____

_____

_____

TIPS

Make sure that you can correctly identify production and consumption on a PPF-indifference curve diagram. This is fundamental!

Study carefully how the indifference curves are drawn in the answer to problem 3a. Trade allows the country to get to a higher indifference curve. It is *not* shifting indifference curves.

Care must be taken in drawing the diagram to avoid the suggestion that the indifference curves would ever cross.

The answers to problems 3c and 3d illustrate an important point. Without trade, the opportunity cost of production is different in the two countries, whereas with trade it is the same. When the opportunity cost of production is the same in both locations, world resources are being used efficiently: No country is "low cost" or "high cost."

2 Earnings of Labor

ESSENTIAL CONCEPTS

How does trade affect the livelihoods of people who get their income from their labor? To answer this question, one needs to understand how trade affects the buying power of a worker's wage (W). This is known as the *real wage*. There are two ways to measure the buying power of the wage. If the two goods being produced are agricultural products and manufacturing products, we can measure the buying power of the wage in terms of agricultural products (W/P_A) or in terms of the buying power of the wage in terms of manufacturing products (W/P_M).

To see this, consider a worker's budget constraint. The worker earns nominal income (in dollars) W and pays P_A for autos and P_B for bananas. Her budget constraint is then

$$W = P_A D_A + P_B D_B,$$

which is plotted in panel (a) of Figure 3-2. If both W/P_A and W/P_B were to increase, then the worker's budget constraint shifts out and the worker can afford more of both

FIGURE 3-2

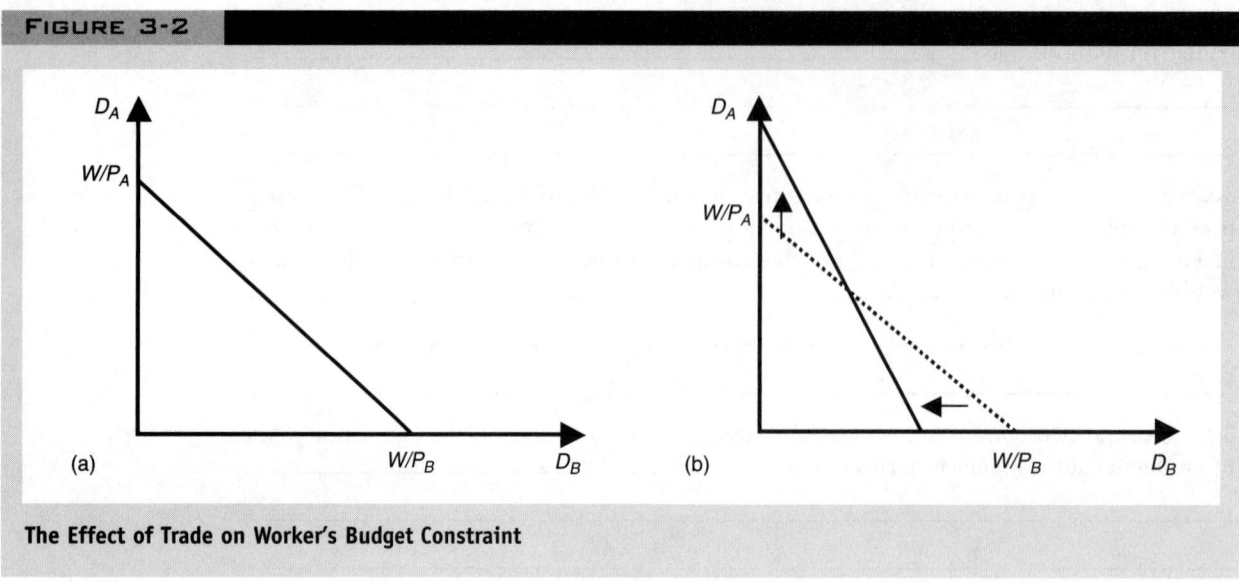

The Effect of Trade on Worker's Budget Constraint

goods. The opposite is true if W/P_A and W/P_B were to decrease. The case where these two measures of welfare do not move in the same direction creates complications. This case is shown in panel (b) of Figure 3-2, where W/P_A increases but W/P_B decreases.

The dotted line is the budget constraint before the price change, and the solid line is the budget constraint after the change. If the worker spends all her income on autos, she is better off. If the worker spends all her income on bananas, she is worse off. The actual impact depends on how much the consumer values autos relative to bananas.

The effect of international trade on the real income of a worker can be determined by the profit-maximizing equation for firms and the knowledge of how labor moves from one industry to another. For instance, the hiring equation for agriculture is $P_A \cdot MPL_A = W$, which can be rewritten $W/P_A = MPL_A$. If employment in agriculture went up, then MPL_A went down and so too did the earnings of a worker relative to the price of agricultural goods. If employment in agriculture went down, then the opposite conclusion is reached. The real wage in terms of manufacturing goods can be analyzed in the same way.

KEY TERMS

Use the space provided to record your notes on the following key terms.

Real wage _____

_____

_____

Trade adjustment assistance _____

_____

_____

Services _____

_____

_____

REVIEW QUESTIONS

Problem 4: A country called Home makes autos from capital and labor and bananas from land and labor. Labor is mobile between the two industries. The country is in a no-trade equilibrium, but it is considering opening to international trade with the rest of the world. The relative price of autos in terms of bananas is higher in Home than the (fixed) price on world markets.

4a. The diagram below shows the real wage in terms of bananas (how many bananas a unit of labor can buy) and the allocation of labor across industries in the no-trade equilibrium. Use this diagram to show these variables in a trading equilibrium.

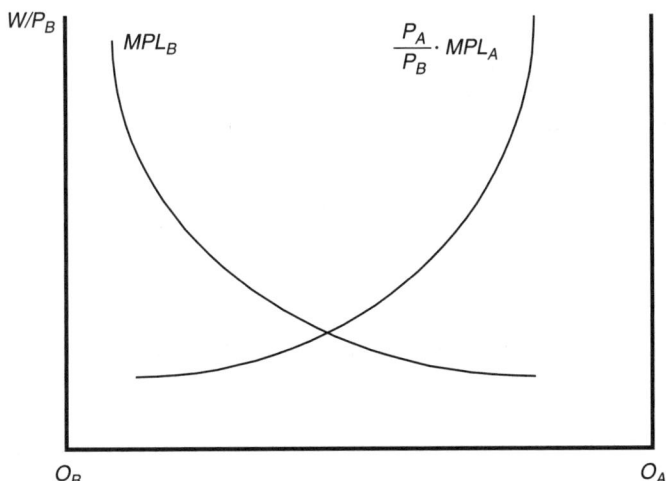

4b. If workers spend all their income on autos, does trade make workers better off or worse off? _____

_____

4c. If workers spend all their income on bananas, does trade make workers better off or worse off? _____

_____

4d. If workers spend their income on both goods, what can you say about the effect of trade on workers' well-being? _____

_____

....

The effect of trade on the real income of the mobile factor (labor) must always be ambiguous in the specific-factors model because the movement of labor between industries raises the marginal product in the contracting industry and lowers it in the expanding industry.

Notice that the marginal products diagram in problem 4 has been reformulated by dividing all the nominal variables (wage, value of marginal products, etc.) by P_B. A change in the relative price has exactly the same effect on real variables as a change in the nominal price of one, holding fixed the other price. In other words, an increase in P_A holding P_B fixed has the same consequences as a decrease in P_B holding P_A fixed. The key difference is in how the diagram works when drawn this way. Either type of price change affects only the curve that is "attached" to the relative price P_A/P_B. A good exercise would be to redo problem 4 with all prices in terms of autos.

TIPS

....

Problem 5: Consider the following questions concerning worker mobility.

5a. Suppose that wages in a country were $15 per hour in one industry and $12 per hour in another. Is labor perfectly mobile in this country? Explain. _____

_____

_____

5b. Provide an explanation for why it is often the case that displaced workers earn less in their new jobs than they did in their previous job. _____

_____

_____

Problem 6: Suppose a country makes computers with capital and labor and tulips with land and labor. When the country goes from a no-trade equilibrium to a trade equilibrium, the price of computers rises while the price of tulips stays the same. Suppose that labor is not allowed to move between industries.

6a. What is the effect of trade on the real income of computer workers? _____

_____

_____

6b. What is the effect of trade on the real income of tulip workers? _____

_____

_____

TIPS

Both problems 5 and 6 illustrate the role that labor mobility plays in the specific-factors model. It is important to understand that there is only one wage because workers can move freely between industries. If there were some reason labor couldn't move, such as a trade union or government-imposed barrier to entry, then there would be two wages.

3 Earnings of Capital and Land

ESSENTIAL CONCEPTS

Although the specific-factor model makes "wishy-washy" predictions about the effect of international trade on the real income of the mobile factor, it makes strong predictions about the effect of international trade on the real income of specific factors. International trade increases the real income of the factor specific to the export industry and decreases the real income of the factor specific to the import industry. This has a very intuitive explanation. Trade induces the export sector to expand and the import sector to contract. Because the amount of the specific factor is fixed in the export sector, the only way to expand production is to increase the amount of labor in that sector. As more labor enters the export sector and there are more workers using the fixed quantity of the specific factor, the specific factor becomes more valuable. As labor leaves the import sector, the specific factor has fewer workers using it and that factor becomes less valuable. In terms of the marginal product of a specific factor, an increase in the amount of labor using that fixed factor increases the marginal product of that factor. The higher the marginal product of the factor, the greater the real income of that factor when measured in terms of the output of that sector.

KEY TERMS

Use the space provided to record your notes on the following key terms.

Rental on capital _____

_____

_____

Rental on land _____

_____

_____

Nominal protection coefficient _____

_____

_____

REVIEW QUESTIONS

Problem 7: Two countries, Home and Foreign, produce autos from capital and labor and bananas from land and labor. Labor is mobile between the two industries. The no-trade equilibrium in the two countries is illustrated in the diagram below.

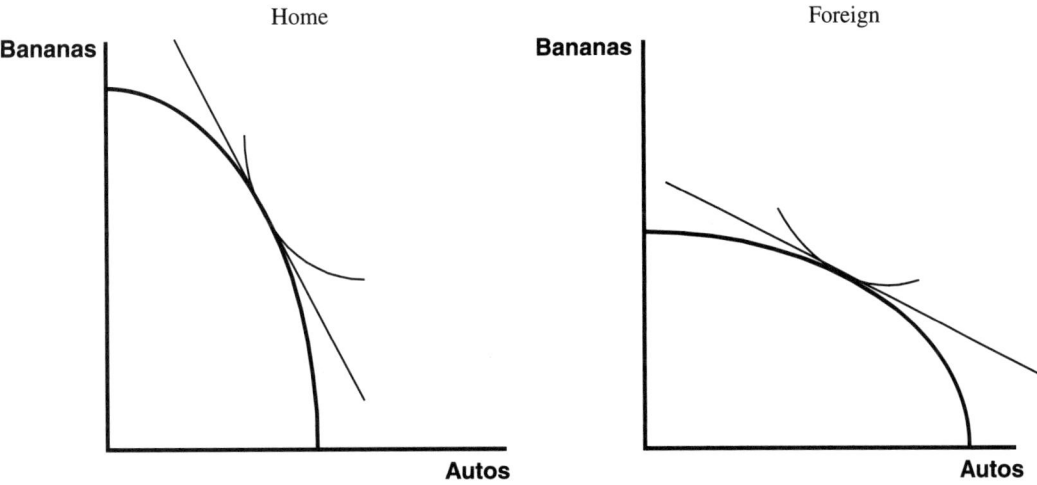

7a. In the diagram above, show a candidate equilibrium if the two countries are trading with each other. Indicate how production and consumption have changed in the two countries.

7b. How has the real rental to capital changed in Home? Explain. _____

_____

_____

7c. How has the real rental to capital changed in Foreign? _____

_____

_____

7d. What happens to the demand for land in Home? _____

_____

_____

7e. If the winners could without cost compensate the losers, would the countries engage in free trade?

_____

_____

TIPS

When the ratio of factors used in production changes, it means (1) that the marginal products of each factor has changed and (2) that the change of the marginal product of one factor moves in exactly the opposite direction as the marginal product of the other factor. If capital and labor are used in production and the capital/labor ratio increases, then the marginal product of labor goes up (more machines per worker) and the marginal product of capital goes down (fewer workers per machines).

Because the marginal products of different factors used in production move in opposite directions in response to changes in the price of goods, the incomes of factors move in opposite directions. Trade is always controversial in the specific-factors world.

A specific factor is just an input into production that is used only in that industry. In the textbook, Land is specific to agriculture and Capital is specific to Manufacturing. In reality, there are many inputs into production that are specific to an industry. Machines are designed for uses that are specific to an industry. Worker skills can also be industry specific (pastry cooks have skills that do not translate well into law enforcement).

4

Trade and Resources:
The Heckscher-Ohlin Model

Overview

This chapter outlines the structure of a "long-run" model of international trade that relates a country's factor endowment to its trade pattern. This model is called the Heckscher-Ohlin model after the economists Eli Heckscher and Bertil Ohlin, who sought to understand the rapid increase in international trade in the late nineteenth century. The model predicts a country's trade pattern on the basis of its endowments, and it predicts how international trade affects the real income of the owners of a country's capital and labor. As in the specific-factor model, a country gains from trade in the sense that it can consume more goods, but some (perhaps many!) individuals within the country will find that their real income has fallen. The chapter concludes with an assessment of the model's ability to explain world trading patterns and a discussion of how the model can be extended to improve its predictive ability.

1 Heckscher-Ohlin Model

ESSENTIAL CONCEPTS

The classic *Heckscher-Ohlin model* is a world in which there are two countries, two goods, and two factors. For convenience we call the factors capital and labor and the countries Home and Foreign. Both goods use capital and labor in their production and both factors are free to move from one industry to another. This is the sense in which this is a "long-run" model. (In the short run it is easy to imagine that factors are stuck in their industry.) The key way that the two goods are different from each other (aside from how consumers use them) is in their *factor intensity*.

Factor intensity is a key concept that merits some review. Suppose that computers and shoes both use capital (K) and labor (L) in their production. The going market rate for a unit of capital is R and the going rate for a unit of labor is W. The relative demands for labor in the computer and shoe industry are shown in Figure 4-1.

FIGURE 4-1

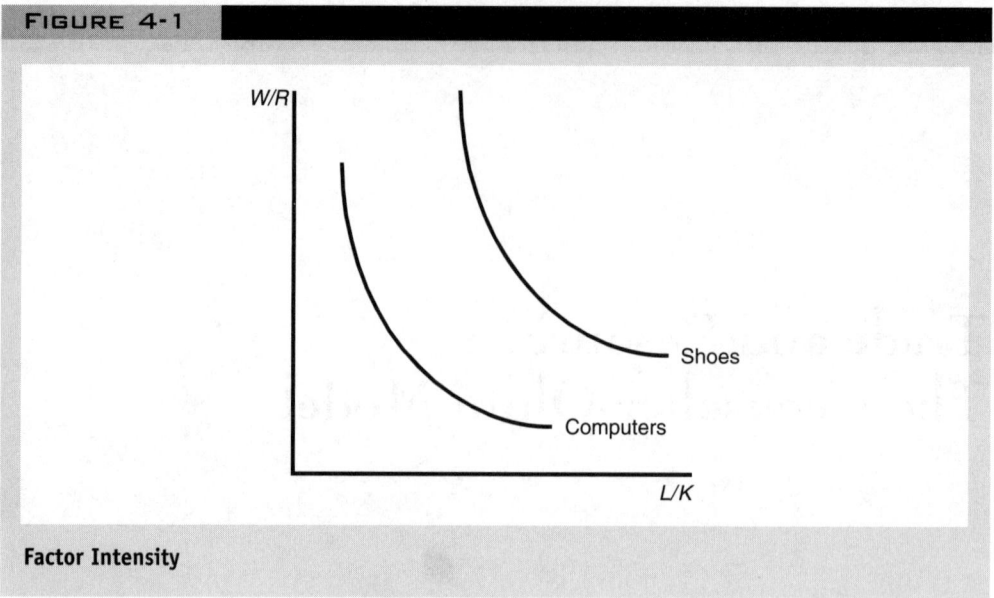

Factor Intensity

The technology used to produce these goods allows producers some degree of substitutability between these factors. Hence, as W rises relative to R, firms in both industries use a mix of inputs that features relatively less L and relatively more K, as Figure 4-1 shows. We say that shoes are *labor intensive* compared with computers because whatever level of W/R prevails in factor markets, the firms that produce shoes use a higher ratio of labor to capital than the firms that produce computers. Alternatively, we could say that computers are *capital intensive* relative to shoes.

The assumption that goods differ in their factor intensity is important because it tells us something about the shape of a country's PPF. First, because goods differ in their factor intensity, the PPF is concave (or bowed out), as shown in Figure 4-2.

FIGURE 4-2

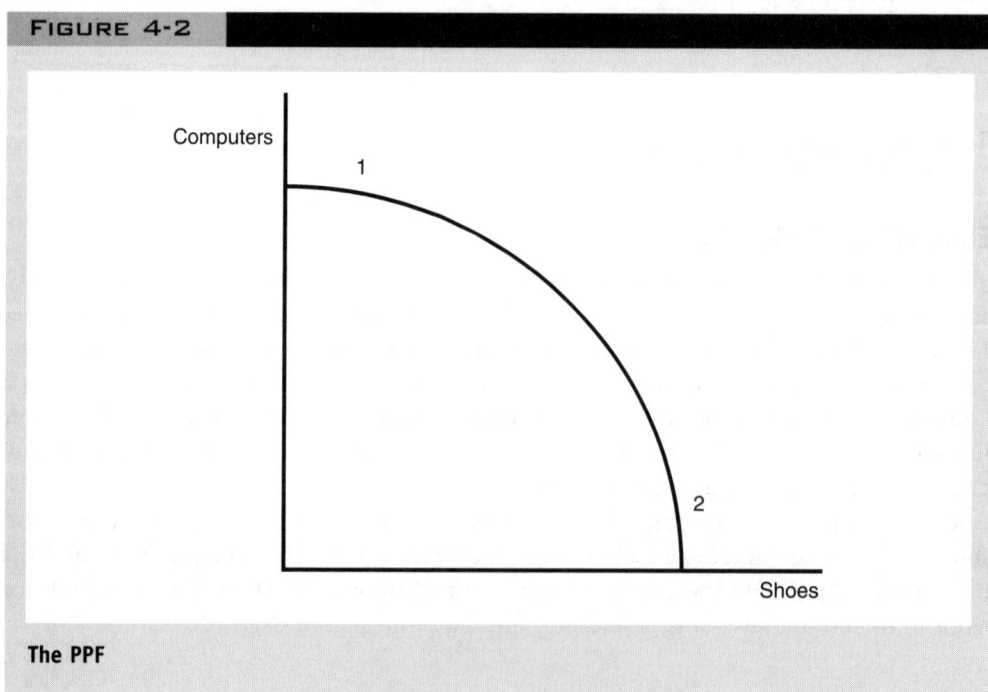

The PPF

To see why the PPF is concave, consider the effect of reallocating capital and labor across industries. At a point such as 1 in Figure 4-2, nearly all the country's factors are being used to make the capital-intensive good, computers. The opportunity cost of shoe production is very low at point 1 because a lot of labor and a little capital can be pulled out of computer production to produce a substantial quantity of shoes with only a little reduction in computer production. As we move from point 1 to point 2, most of the labor has been extracted from the production of computers so that the expansion of shoe production can only be accomplished by extracting a lot of capital and a little labor from computer industry. This results in a small increase in the output of the labor-intensive shoe industry and a large drop in the output of the capital-intensive computer industry.

The second important implication of goods that differ in their factor intensity is the effect on the shape of the PPF of changing a country's endowment. Suppose that we were to add capital to a country's endowment. Because the country has a larger stock of factors and because both goods use both factors, the PPF shifts outward: More of both goods can be produced. However, because computers are capital intensive and shoes are labor intensive, the PPF shifts out in favor of computers, as shown in Figure 4-3.

The two countries are identical in every dimension except in terms of their endowments. They have identical tastes and technologies, but they have different *factor abundances.* Factor abundance is measured as the ratio of capital to labor (or its inverse). The *capital-abundant* country has a higher ratio of capital to labor in its endowment than the *labor-abundant* country, which has a higher ratio of labor to capital. From our discussion in the previous paragraph, this means that the two countries have systematically different PPFs: The capital-abundant country has a PPF skewed out toward the capital-intensive good, whereas the labor-abundant country has its PPF skewed out toward the labor-intensive good. Faced with the same relative price of computers, the capital-abundant country will supply relatively more computers and fewer shoes than the labor-abundant country, which will supply relatively more shoes than computers. Because the two countries have the same tastes, they will consume the two goods in the same ratio. This means that in a trading equilibrium, the capital-abundant country will export the capital-

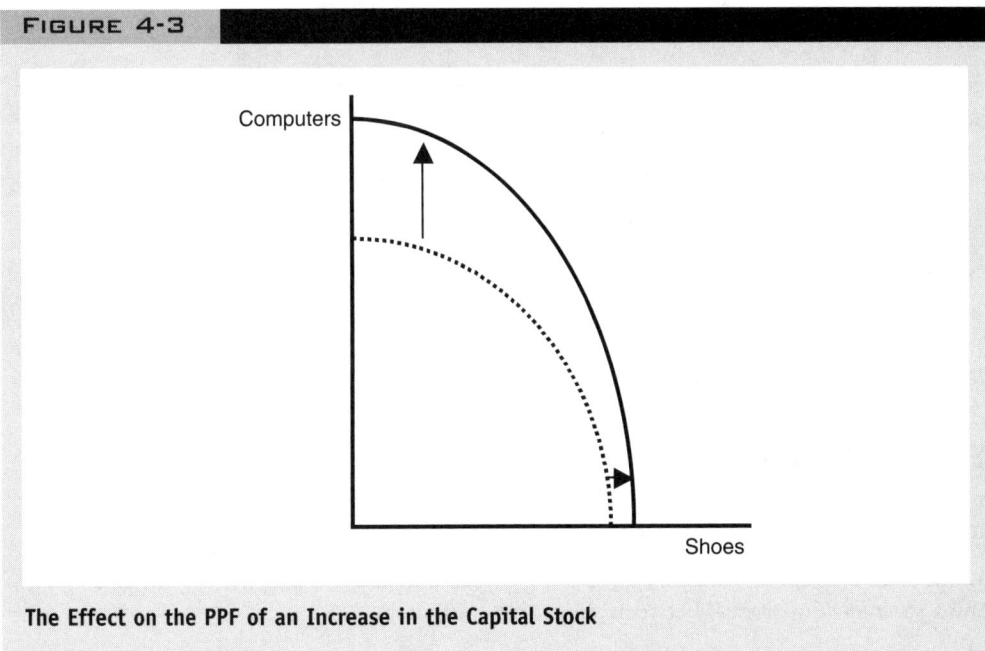

FIGURE 4-3

The Effect on the PPF of an Increase in the Capital Stock

intensive good and the labor-abundant country will export the labor-intensive good. This is the *Heckscher-Ohlin theorem*.

As intuitively sensible as the prediction of the Heckscher-Ohlin model sounds, it actually has some difficulty explaining trade patterns. A number of empirical studies have shown that the two-country, two-good, two-factor model does a poor job predicting trade patterns. The most famous of these studies is the *Leontief paradox*. Keep in mind that the model is designed to isolate one possible reason for international trade: unequal distribution of the world's factors. When the model fails to capture pieces of the trading pattern between countries, it suggests that the model ignores important features of the actual world in which we live.

KEY TERMS

Use the space provided to record your notes on the following key terms.

Heckscher-Ohlin model _____

_____

_____

Free-trade equilibrium _____

_____

_____

Reversal of factor intensity _____

_____

_____

Abundance in that factor _____

_____

_____

Scarce in that factor _____

_____

_____

Heckscher-Ohlin theorem _____

_____

_____

Leontief paradox _____

_____

_____

REVIEW QUESTIONS

Problem 1: The two countries are Home and Foreign, the two factors are capital and labor, and the two goods are shoes and computers.

1a. Shoes and computers are produced using capital and labor. Using the following diagram, draw a *factor intensity reversal* between shoes and computers.

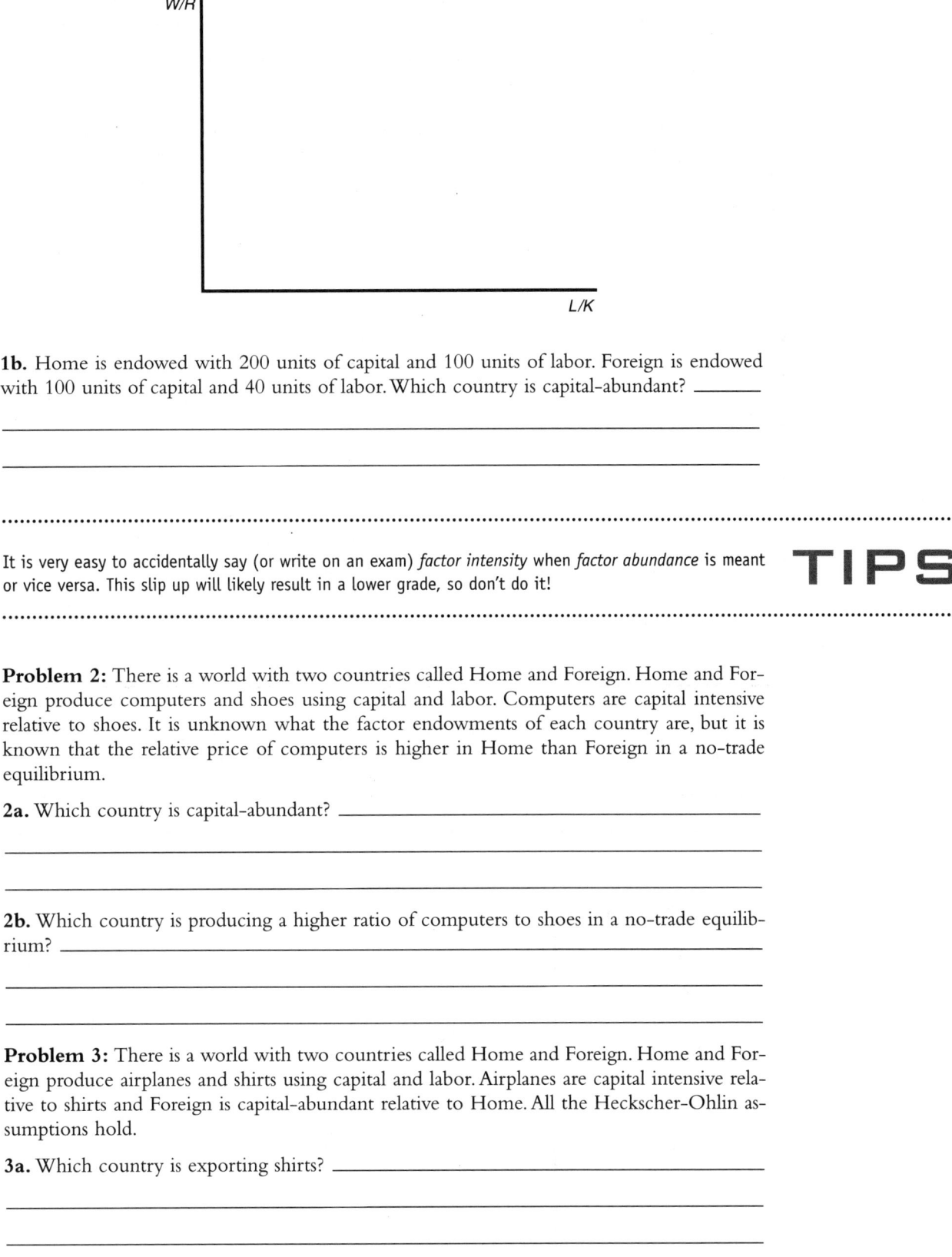

1b. Home is endowed with 200 units of capital and 100 units of labor. Foreign is endowed with 100 units of capital and 40 units of labor. Which country is capital-abundant? _____

_____

_____

....

It is very easy to accidentally say (or write on an exam) *factor intensity* when *factor abundance* is meant or vice versa. This slip up will likely result in a lower grade, so don't do it!

TIPS

....

Problem 2: There is a world with two countries called Home and Foreign. Home and Foreign produce computers and shoes using capital and labor. Computers are capital intensive relative to shoes. It is unknown what the factor endowments of each country are, but it is known that the relative price of computers is higher in Home than Foreign in a no-trade equilibrium.

2a. Which country is capital-abundant? _____

_____

_____

2b. Which country is producing a higher ratio of computers to shoes in a no-trade equilibrium? _____

_____

_____

Problem 3: There is a world with two countries called Home and Foreign. Home and Foreign produce airplanes and shirts using capital and labor. Airplanes are capital intensive relative to shirts and Foreign is capital-abundant relative to Home. All the Heckscher-Ohlin assumptions hold.

3a. Which country is exporting shirts? _____

_____

_____

3b. The consumers in Home are buying twice as many shirts as airplanes. What is the ratio of shirt to airplane consumption in Foreign? _____

_____

_____

3c. Suppose that Foreign's endowment of capital is increased. What happens to the relative price of airplanes in terms of shirts on world markets? Use the diagrams below in answering your question. _____

_____

_____

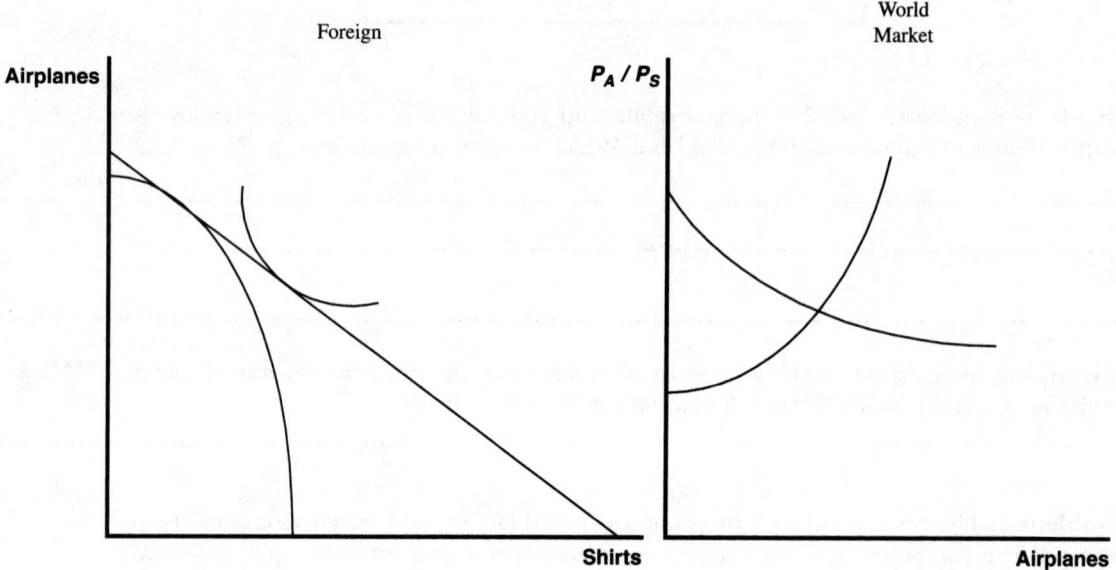

3d. Suppose that Foreign's endowment of capital is increased. What happens to the level of national welfare in Home (can it reach a higher indifference curve)? _____

_____

_____

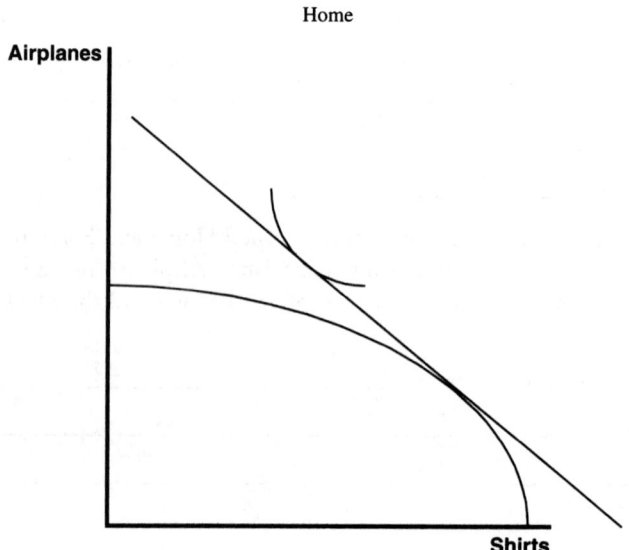

Problem 4: An important assumption in the Heckscher-Ohlin model is that the tastes are the same in both countries. Suppose that tastes are different in the Home and Foreign. Is it possible for a capital-abundant country (Foreign) to export the labor-intensive good (shirts) if tastes are different? If so, draw a PPF–indifference curve diagram for Home and a PPF–indifference curve diagram for Foreign that illustrates this case in the following space.

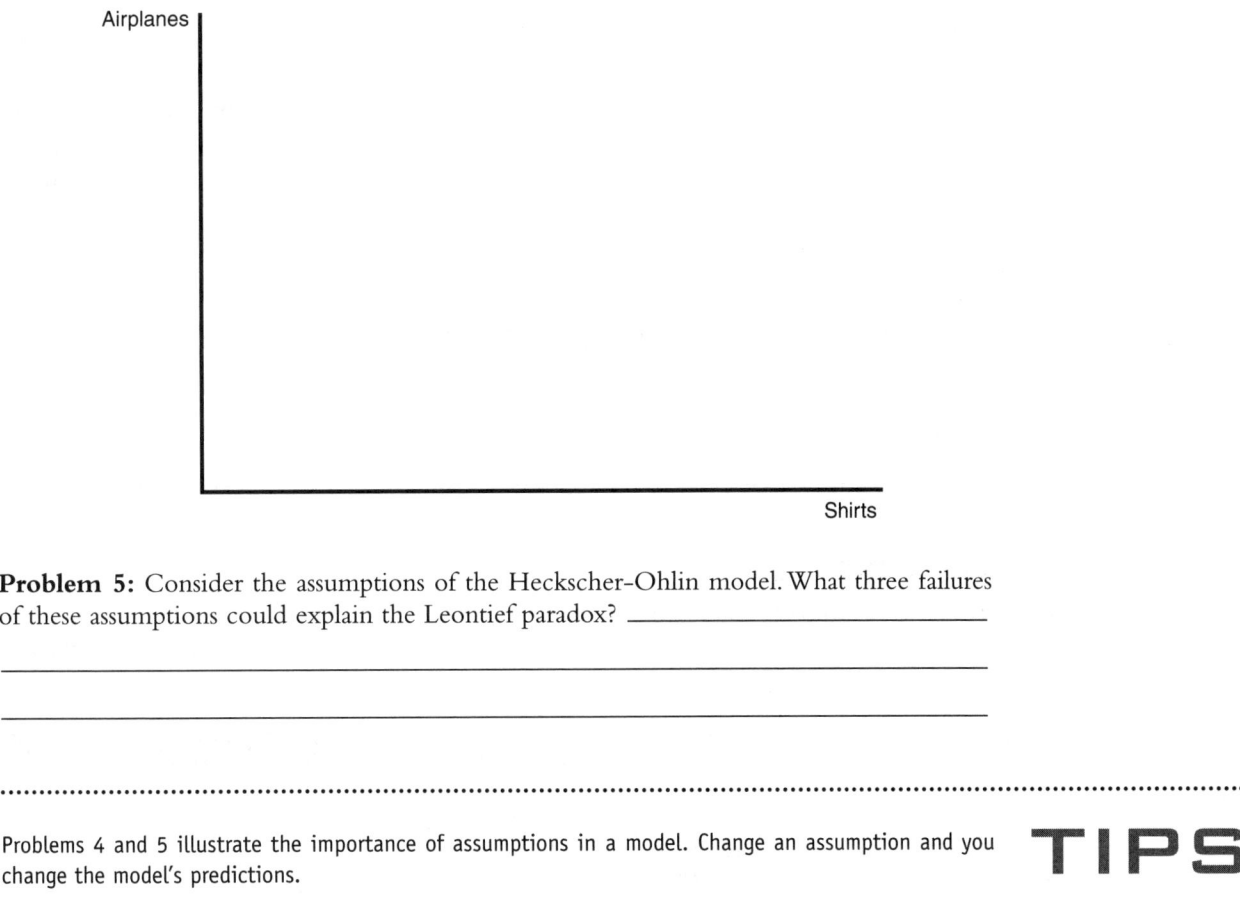

Problem 5: Consider the assumptions of the Heckscher-Ohlin model. What three failures of these assumptions could explain the Leontief paradox? _____

_____

_____

....

Problems 4 and 5 illustrate the importance of assumptions in a model. Change an assumption and you change the model's predictions.

TIPS

....

2 Effects of Trade on Factor Prices

ESSENTIAL CONCEPTS

We now consider the effect of changes in goods prices induced by international trade on the prices of factors in the long-run Heckscher-Ohlin model. As in the specific-factors model, international trade causes the real incomes of factor owners to change, with some factors seeing their real incomes rise and others seeing their real incomes fall. The types of predictions are very different in the long-run Heckscher-Ohlin model than in the specific-factors model. In the specific-factors model, we see that there is a divide across industries in the effect of international trade on real income: The factor specific to the export industry sees its real income rise with trade, whereas the factor specific to the import industry sees its real income fall. In the Heckscher-Ohlin model there is no specific factor. Instead, the *Stolper-Samuelson theorem* has the key implication that the owners of the factor in which the country is abundant gain from international trade, whereas the owners of the factor in which the country is scarce are hurt by international trade. It becomes possible then that an individual could see her real income fall in the short run (factor specific to import industry) and rise in the long run (abundant factor).

To think about the economics of the Stolper-Samuelson theorem, consider Figure 4-2. An increase in the relative price of shoes shifts production away from point 1 and toward point 2. An increase in shoe production requires a decrease in computer production. But because shoe producers demand a lot of labor and a little capital and computer producers demand a lot of capital and a little labor, shutting down computer output releases "too much" capital and "too little" labor. This is why W/R has to rise to get firms to use less labor and more capital. Because firms in both industries increase the ratio of capital to labor that they use in production, the marginal product of labor rises and the marginal product of capital falls in *both* industries. A decrease in the relative price of shoes has exactly the opposite effect.

KEY TERMS

Use the space provided to record your notes on the following key term.

Stopler-Samuelson theorem _____

_____

_____

REVIEW QUESTIONS

Problem 6: Consider the relative demand curve for a country shown in Figure 4-4. *RD* stands for relative demand and *RS* stands for relative supply. The two industries are computers and shoes.

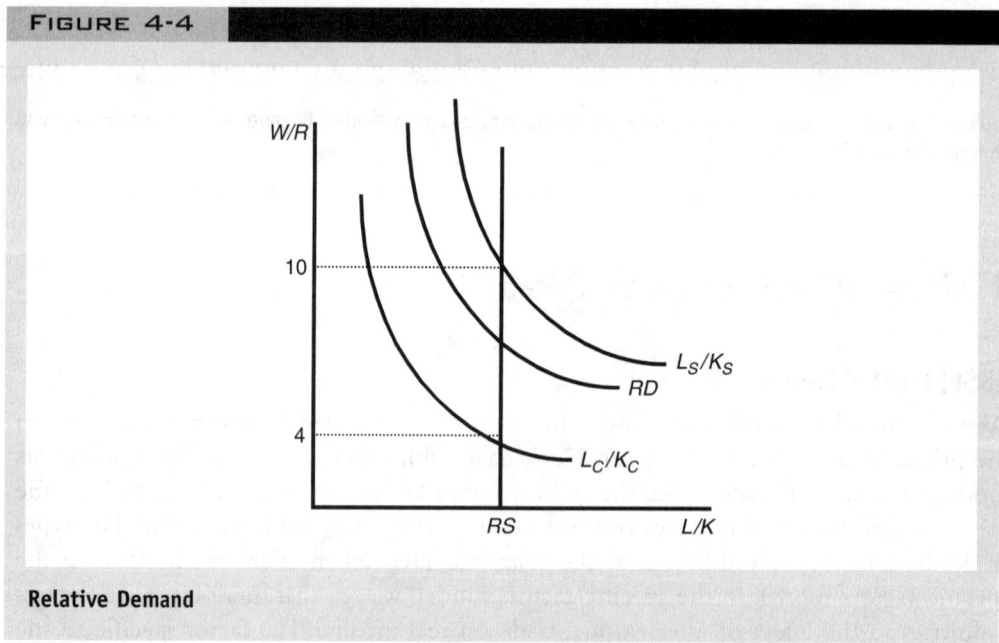

FIGURE 4-4

Relative Demand

6a. What is the highest relative wage that we could observe in this economy? _____

_____

_____

6b. What causes the relative demand curve for labor in a country to shift up? _____

_____

_____

6c. Suppose there is an upward shift in the relative demand curve for labor. What happens to the ratio of labor to capital used in production in each industry? _____

_____

_____

Problem 7: Consider the real-sounding but fictional country of Ubetcha. Ubetcha produces two goods, autos and hats, using capital and labor. Autos are capital intensive relative to hats. The country has long enjoyed its isolation from the world but is now considering free trade. The top Ubetchan economist traveled abroad and noticed that the relative price of autos is lower on world markets than it is in Ubetcha. All Heckscher-Ohlin assumptions hold.

7a. Suppose the country were to institute free trade with the rest of the world. How would the capital/labor ratio used by Ubetchan's producers of autos and hats change? _____

_____

_____

7b. If Ubetcha engages in free trade with the rest of the world, how will the marginal product of capital change in the auto and hat industries? _____

_____

_____

7c. Suppose there is an organization in Ubetcha, the Union of Ubetchan Capitalists, or UUC for short, which represents the interests of capital owners in the country. Would that organization support or lobby against the free-trade idea? Explain. _____

_____

_____

Problem 8: The National Election Study (NES) survey in the United States in 1992 found that workers with higher levels of education were more likely to support free trade than less educated workers.

8a. Assuming that the United States is a relatively skill-abundant country, is this result consistent with the Heckscher-Ohlin model? Explain. _____

_____

_____

8b. Suppose that the same questionnaire were asked in a skill-scarce country. What would the Heckscher-Ohlin model predict about the responses of workers? _____

_____

_____

Problem 9: Suppose that the world was one large, happy country that produced doughnuts and sofas using capital and labor. Sofas are capital intensive relative to doughnuts. International trade is *not* allowed. The following questions build on one another.

9a. Suppose that the world is divided into two identical countries (Home and Foreign); that is, they receive the same amount of labor and capital. Would there be any motive for immigration (i.e., would laborers want to move) between the two countries? Explain. _____

_____

_____

_____

9b. Now suppose that some of the capital is moved from Foreign to Home so that Home is capital-abundant relative to Foreign. Trade is still not allowed. What happens to the real income of labor in each of the two countries? _____

_____

_____

9c. If laborers are free to move internationally, which way do they move?

_____

_____

9d. What does the migration do to real incomes of laborers in Home and Foreign?

_____

_____

9e. If you were a capitalist in Home, would you be in favor of immigration? Explain.

_____

_____

_____

TIPS

Note that in problem 9, international trade is not allowed but immigration is. The problem shows that trade and immigration have similar effects on income distribution.

Problem 10: Your well-meaning but excessively enthusiastic relative, Bob, wants you to sign a petition to ban trade with a developing country. He claims that trade will encourage the expansion of labor-intensive "sweatshop" industries in the developing country and so will reduce the welfare of workers (the abundant factor) in that developing country. Does the Heckscher-Ohlin model necessarily imply that developing country workers will be hurt by trade? _____

_____

_____

Problem 11: What kind of result could Leontief have found that would have not been called a paradox? _____

_____

_____

3 Extending the Heckscher-Ohlin Model

ESSENTIAL CONCEPTS

A world where there are two goods, two factors, and two countries is relatively easy to analyze. Unfortunately, the world is not so simple, and we need to be careful taking what we can learn from the Heckscher-Ohlin setting considered earlier to the real world. Fortunately, it is not that hard to extend the Heckscher-Ohlin model to many goods, many factors, and many countries. To do so, we need a new concept of factor abundance. A country's relative abundance in a factor can be measured as its share of the world's endowment of that factor relative to its share of the world's income. If every country has the same tastes, then every country consumes goods in the same ratio. A factor's *services* can be thought of as *embodied* in the goods that we consume in the sense that a certain number of worker and machine hours "went in" to the finished product. Hence, consumers can be thought of as consuming factor services indirectly through their consumption of goods, and because goods can be traded, so too can factor services.

For example, if the United States has 26.6% of the world's GDP, it should consume 26.6% of the world's goods, and 26.6% of all the services of capital (i.e., the time the capital was used to make the goods), and 26.6% of all the services of land, and so on. If the U.S. has 50.7% of the world's research and development (R&D) scientists, then the goods that the United States exports to the rest of the world should have more R&D services embodied in them than the goods that the United States imports from the rest of the world.

One can measure the factor content of trade by measuring the inputs into the production of all goods and then use trade data to infer how much of each factor service is embodied in each. This is the idea of the *extended Heckscher-Ohlin theorem,* and it is this concept that is most appropriate for thinking about actual world trading patterns.

Another problem with the Heckscher-Ohlin model that we have discussed is its assumption that technologies are the same everywhere. It is clearly not true that factor prices are the same everywhere or that technologies are the same everywhere, and these two discrepancies are probably linked. If workers from country A can produce twice as much as workers from country B, then we need to be careful in how we measure a country's endowment of labor. This is the idea of measuring a country's *effective labor force,* and the idea occurred to Leontief many years ago. More generally, the productivity of all factors may vary across countries in such a way as to confound the predictions of the extended Heckscher-Ohlin model. By controlling for a factor's productivity in a given country, the model can be made to fit the data better.

KEY TERMS

Use the space provided to record your notes on the following key terms.

Extended Heckscher-Ohlin theorem _____

_____

_____

Factor content of exports _____

_____

_____

Factor content of imports _____

_____

_____

Effective labor force _____

_____

_____

Effective factor endowment _____

_____

_____

Abundant in that effective factor _____

_____

_____

Scarce in that effective factor _____

_____

_____

Sign test _____

_____

_____

REVIEW QUESTIONS

Problem 12: Suppose Home has 15% of the world's capital, 7% of the world's labor, 5% of the world's arable land, and 10% of the world's GDP.

12a. What does the extended Heckscher–Ohlin model predict about the labor content of Home's net exports? _____

_____

12b. Suppose that Home's workers are much better paid than workers in the rest of the world. Why might you expect the sign test to fail when measuring the labor content of Home's net exports? _____

_____

12c. Is it possible for a country to appear scarce in all factors? _____

_____

TIPS

A model that fails to predict reality is not necessarily a "failure." Even if a model doesn't predict reality well, it can be very useful if one can identify the assumptions that are the culprit for the model's poor performance! Empirical studies of the extended Heckscher-Ohlin model suggest that the assumption that technologies are the same across countries is inappropriate.

5

Movement of Labor and Capital between Countries

Overview

This chapter analyzes the effects that movements in factors between countries have on (1) factor rewards (wages, rental, etc.), (2) the pattern of production across countries, and (3) the size of global output. Two kinds of factor flows are considered: immigration (the movement of labor) and foreign direct investment (movement of capital). To analyze the short-run effects of immigration and foreign direct investment we use the specific-factors model introduced in Chapter 3. To analyze the long-run effect of factor movements we use the Heckscher-Ohlin model introduced in Chapter 4. To keep the analysis simple, we assume that in both the short run and the long run the international prices of goods are fixed.

A key point made in this chapter is that the short-run and long-run effects of factor movements on factor rewards are very different. Immigration and FDI alter the distribution of income across factors in the short run but have no effect on real income in the long run. The effects of factor flows on the pattern of production are also very different in the short run than in the long run. The chapter concludes by considering the gains from factor flows. Both immigration and foreign direct investment lead to a more efficient use of the world's resources and therefore to greater output given the same world resources.

1 Movement of Labor between Countries

ESSENTIAL CONCEPTS

Immigration causes the supply of labor to fall in one location and to rise in another. Hence, the effects of immigration on the real incomes of different factors and the output of each industry are treated as changes in countries' endowments of labor. How does the economy absorb the new workers, and what effect does it have on the people living in that country? The answer to this question depends on whether one considers the short run, when factors are limited in their ability to move across industries, or the long run, when factors are perfectly mobile across industries.

Because the specific-factors model is built upon the assumption of limited factor mobility across industries, it is appropriate for analyzing the short-run effects of immigration. To be consistent with Chapter 3, the specific factors are called land and capital and the mobile factor is called labor. (Of course, the specific factors could be different types of capital or labor.) To keep things as simple as possible, we assume that the country is trading freely with the rest of the world at fixed prices.

In the specific-factors model, new workers must be absorbed into both industries. When a worker is hired in an industry, the marginal product of labor in that industry must fall because there is now less of the specific factor per worker. Because prices are fixed, the decline in the marginal product of labor must be accompanied by a decline in the real wage in that industry. If workers were to enter only one industry, then the wage in that industry would fall below the wage level in the other industry. Hence, labor must be absorbed in both industries. Changes in the remaining economic variables are driven by the increase in labor employed in both industries. First, output of both industries must increase because there are more factors being used in production. Second, because there is more labor and the same amount of specific factor, the marginal products of both specific factors must rise. Hence, immigration increases the real income of the specific factors.

How does a country absorb an increase in its labor endowment in the long run? There are two possible channels that we will discuss in the context of a specific example. Suppose there are two industries, A and B. Industry A is labor intensive relative to industry B. The country is endowed with $\overline{K}$ units of capital and $\overline{L}$ units of labor. Because all factors are used, we have $\overline{K} = K_A + K_B$ and $\overline{L} = L_A + L_B$. In Chapter 4, we learned that the condition that the relative supply of labor $\overline{L}/\overline{K}$ must be equal to the relative demand for labor (a weighted average of relative demand in each industry) can be written

$$\frac{\overline{L}}{\overline{K}} = \left(\frac{K_A}{\overline{K}}\right)\left(\frac{L_A}{K_A}\right) + \left(\frac{K_B}{\overline{K}}\right)\left(\frac{L_B}{K_B}\right).$$

From this expression, we see that an increase in the endowment of labor $\overline{L}$ due to immigration can be absorbed either (1) by increasing the labor-to-capital ratio in each industry (L_A / K_A and L_B / K_B) or (2) by increasing the weight of the labor-intensive industry A (with its higher labor/capital ratio) in relative demand (increasing $K_A / \overline{K}$ and decreasing $K_B / \overline{K}$).

It turns out that the first channel plays *no* role in absorbing new workers in the long run. The labor/capital ratios used in each industry cannot change as long as the prices of goods are held fixed. This is hard to show formally, but we provide some intuition. The key insight follows from the fact that for a fixed set of goods prices, there is only *one capital-to-labor ratio* for each industry that makes (1) the value of the marginal product of labor the same in both industries, and (2) the value of the marginal product of capital is the same in both industries. In the short run, the rental on capital can be different across industries (think specific-factors model) so that employment can increase in both industries. This is not so in the long run. In the long run labor is absorbed into the economy exclusively through an increase in the output of the labor-intensive good and a decrease in the output of capital-intensive good.

To see how changing the mix of output can absorb the increase in labor, consider the following numerical example as an alternative to the *box diagram*. Suppose that the production of good A requires 1 unit of labor and 1 unit of capital, whereas the production of good B requires 1 unit of labor and 5 units of capital. If Q_A is the output of good A and Q_B is the output of good B, then if all factors are being used we have

$$\overline{K} = 5 \cdot Q_B + 1 \cdot Q_A$$

and

$$\overline{L} = 1 \cdot Q_B + 1 \cdot Q_A.$$

Doing a little algebra, we find that

$$Q_A = \frac{5\overline{L} - \overline{K}}{4} \text{ and } Q_B = \frac{\overline{K} - \overline{L}}{4}.$$

From these two expressions, it is clear that an increase in the labor endowment, $\overline{L}$, increases the output of the labor-intensive good A and decreases the output of the capital-intensive good B. This example illustrates the *Rybczynski theorem* and the *Factor price insensitivity result*. A change in endowments for whatever reason leads to a change in the mix of the country's outputs rather than a change in the country's factor prices when the prices of goods are held fixed.

KEY TERMS

Use the space provided to record your notes on the following key terms.

Specific-factors model _____

_____

_____

Rybczynski theorem _____

_____

_____

Factor price insensitivity _____

_____

_____

REVIEW QUESTIONS

Problem 1: Consider a country called Home that produces manufactured goods (M) and agricultural products (A). M is produced using capital and labor. A is produced using land and labor. (Hence, this is a short-run problem.) Labor is perfectly mobile between industries. Suppose that the country is trading with the rest of the world at fixed prices (P_M and P_A). Initially, the country has the same wages as the rest of the world.

1a. Suppose that the country's endowment of land expands. What impact does this expansion of land have on the wage (W)? Use the diagram provided below to support your answer.

_____

_____

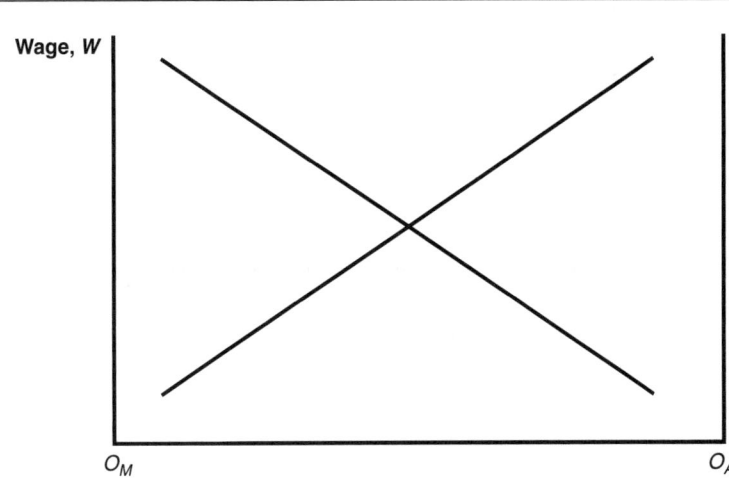

1b. Suppose that the wage is higher in Home than in the rest of the world so that Foreign labor will move to Home. What is the impact of the increase in labor for the wage in Home? Use the diagram provided below to support your answer. _____

_____

_____

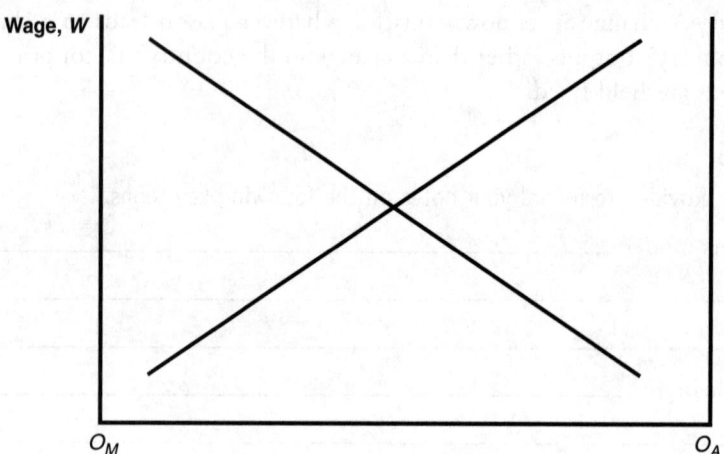

1c. What is the impact of the immigration to Home on the real earnings of a unit of capital in Home and on the real earnings of a unit of land in Home? _____

_____

_____

1d. Using the axes below, show how the output of both goods is affected by the immigration into the country. Explain your diagram. _____

_____

_____

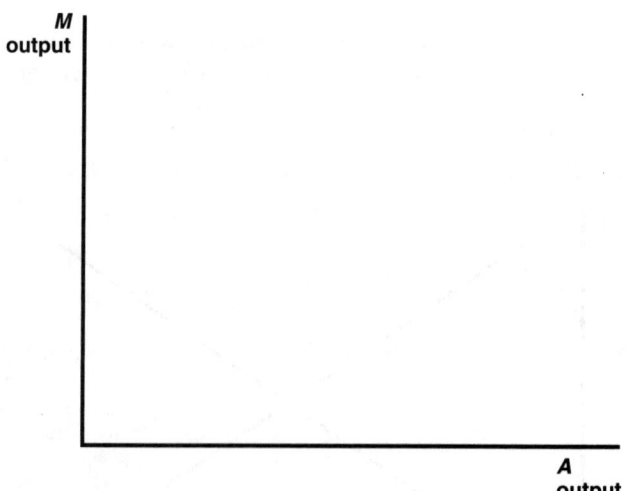

TIPS

It is important to understand why adding more of a specific factor shifts up the marginal product of labor in the industry using that factor.

When the stock of the endowment of the mobile factor changes, it is always the case that in the short run the output of both goods and the real return to both specific factors must change in the same direction. It is not possible without additional information, however, to say which industry is affected the most.

It does not matter whether one shifts the axes O_M or O_A when increasing the size of the labor force.

To convince yourself that you know the material well, run all the questions in problem 1 in reverse (consider an outflow of labor). All the answers should be reversed.

Problem 2: Consider a country that produces two goods: airplanes and shirts. The country is trading with the rest of the world at fixed goods prices. Airplane producers are using 5 units of capital and 3 units of labor to produce one unit of airplanes and shirt producers are using 2 units of capital and 2 units of labor to produce one shirt. Both factors are mobile between industries.

2a. Which good is capital intensive? _____

_____

_____

2b. Suppose there is a sudden emigration (outflow of labor). What happens to the level of employment in the airplane industry in the long run? Show using the box diagram below.

_____

_____

_____

2c. Can you derive an equation that relates the country's output to its endowments? _____

_____

_____

2d. Use the axes below to show how the emigration of labor alters the shape of the production possibilities frontier in the long run. Indicate the level of production of both goods before and after the outflow of labor.

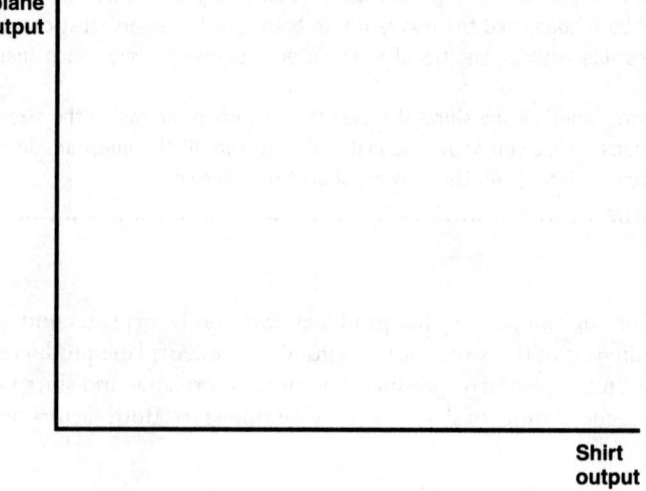

TIPS   The Rybczynski theorem can be used to explain why a country's PPF is skewed toward the good that is intensive in the country's relatively abundant factor. It would be helpful to convince yourself that this is so.

Problem 3: Consider a country that produces two goods, computers and shirts, using capital and labor. In the short run, labor is specific to its sector because workers need particular skills to be productive in the industry. In the long run, labor is perfectly mobile between industries. Capital is perfectly mobile in both the short and long run. The country is engaged in free trade at fixed world prices.

3a. Suppose there is an inward flow of computer workers into the country. What is the short-run impact of the immigration on the real incomes of both computer and shirt workers already in the country? Explain using the axes below. _____

_____

_____

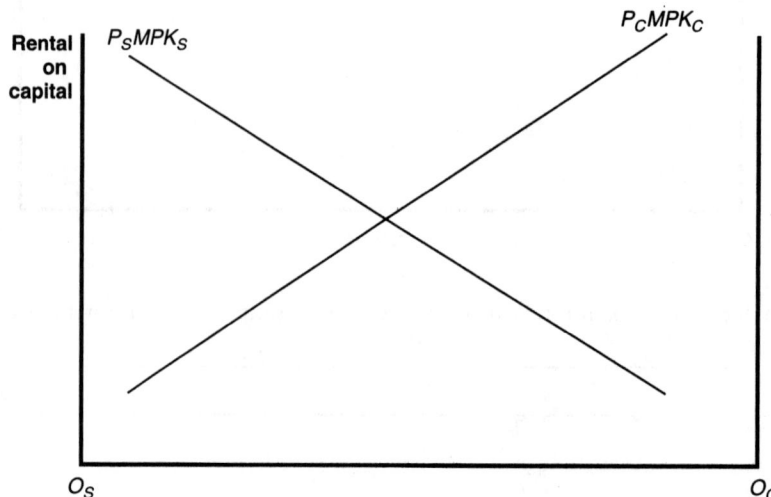

3b. What is the impact of the influx of computer workers on real wage in the long run (i.e., when workers are free to move between industries)? _____

_____

_____

3c. What is the effect of the immigration in the short and long run on the real income of capital? _____

_____

_____

··

TIPS

The assumptions that economists make regarding the nature of technology have important implications for how they perceive the effects of immigration. To answer any problem correctly, you must identify what factors are assumed to be mobile.

The contrast between the short-run and the long-run implications of immigration on factor prices is important. Any calculation of the impact of immigration on factor prices depends on the assumptions that were made to generate those estimates!

In the example considered here, workers have skills that are specific to particular industries. This is probably closer to truth than assuming that workers are perfectly mobile between sectors. By giving factors different names, we can use the same framework to think about other real-world cases.

··

Problem 4: Answer the following questions "true," "false," or "uncertain," and **explain** your answer.

4a. Most immigrants into the United States enter the country legally. _____

_____

_____

4b. Almost all immigrants (both legal and illegal) into the United States are very low skilled.

_____

_____

4c. The response of Miami's output to the Mariel boat lift is consistent with the Rybczynski theorem. _____

_____

_____

2 Foreign Direct Investment

ESSENTIAL CONCEPTS

Foreign direct investment (FDI) occurs when a company from one country obtains a production plant in a foreign country. If the plant is built from scratch, it is a greenfield investment. If instead the plant already existed under a different firm's ownership, the investment is called acquisition FDI. The chapter focuses mostly on greenfield investment because this type of FDI better fits the way FDI is modeled. In the short run, FDI is modeled as an increase in a country's endowment of one of the specific factors, capital. The key result is that an increase in the endowment of one of the specific factors drives up the demand for labor and its real wage. The real rental to both specific factors must fall. With respect to the outputs of goods, in the short run an increase in the stock of one specific factor increases the output of that specific factor and reduces the output of the other industry. The reduction in the output of the other industry occurs because the growth in the industry receiving FDI attracts workers out of agriculture.

In the long run, we assume that all factors are perfectly mobile between industries and that industries are characterized by their factor intensity; therefore, the effect of an inflow of capital is symmetrical to the case of an inflow of labor. Both the Rybczynski theorem and the factor price insensitivity result are still valid. FDI changes the country's output but has no impact on its factor prices in the long run.

KEY TERMS

Use the space provided to record your notes on the following key term.

Foreign direct investment _____

_____

_____

REVIEW QUESTIONS

Problem 5: Agricultural products (*A*) are produced with land and labor, and manufacturing products (*M*) are produced using capital and labor. Labor is perfectly mobile between industries but cannot move internationally.

5a. Suppose there are two countries, Home and Foreign, that are identical except that Home has a larger endowment of labor than Foreign. The two countries are engaged in free trade. Given this scenario, is there any motive for capital to move internationally? If so, which direction would it move? _____

_____

_____

5b. Assume that the international prices of *A* and *M* do not change and that capital moves from Foreign to Home. What will FDI do to Home's level of production of *M* and of *A*? Show using the following diagram. _____

_____

_____

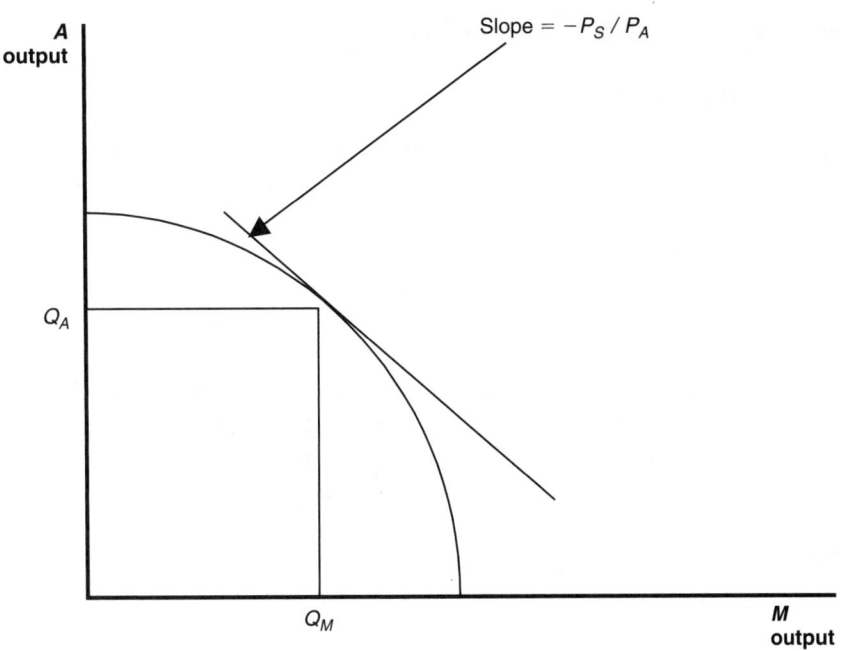

5c. What is the impact of this inward FDI on the real wage of labor, the real rental of capital, and the real rental of land in Home? _____

_____

_____

5d. How does the outward investment affect the real earnings of labor in Foreign? _____

_____

_____

....

Note the difference in the answers to problems 5c and 5d. The factors that are helped in Home are the factors that are hurt in Foreign and vice versa.

TIPS

....

Problem 6: Consider a country that produces airplanes and shirts using capital and labor. Shirts are labor intensive relative to airplanes. Labor and capital are perfectly mobile between industries. The country is engaged in free trade at fixed world prices. Suppose that some of the capital used to make shirts is transferred abroad via outward foreign direct investment.

6a. What is the impact of the transfer of capital abroad on the production of shirts in the long run? _____

_____

_____

6b. What is the long-run impact of the outward foreign direct investment on the real wage?

_____

_____

_____

3 Gains from Labor and Capital Flows

ESSENTIALS CONCEPTS

Thus far, the analysis has highlighted how changes in endowments due to labor and capital flows alter real incomes of various factors and the output of different goods. How do these flows affect the national welfare of the country that is the source of these flows and the national welfare of the country that is the destination for these flows? To answer this question, keep in mind that labor moves from the low-wage country to the high-wage country and capital moves from the low- to the high-rental country. Because factor prices reflect the value of the marginal product, factors move from countries with low marginal products to countries with high marginal products. This means that factor flows increase world output: There are gains from factor movement. In general, both source and destination countries share in the gains, but the disruptive effect of the change in income distribution can be very large relative to the total welfare gain.

KEY TERMS

Use the space provided to record your notes on the following key term.

Real value added _____

_____

_____

REVIEW QUESTIONS

Problem 7: There are two countries, Home and Foreign. The two countries are identical except that Home has a labor force of 100 and Foreign has a labor force of 200. Given this allocation of labor across Home and Foreign, the value of the marginal product of labor in Home is 30 and the value of the marginal product of labor in Foreign is 20. If labor were to be free to move, the wage in both countries would be 25. Figure 5-1 summarizes this situation.

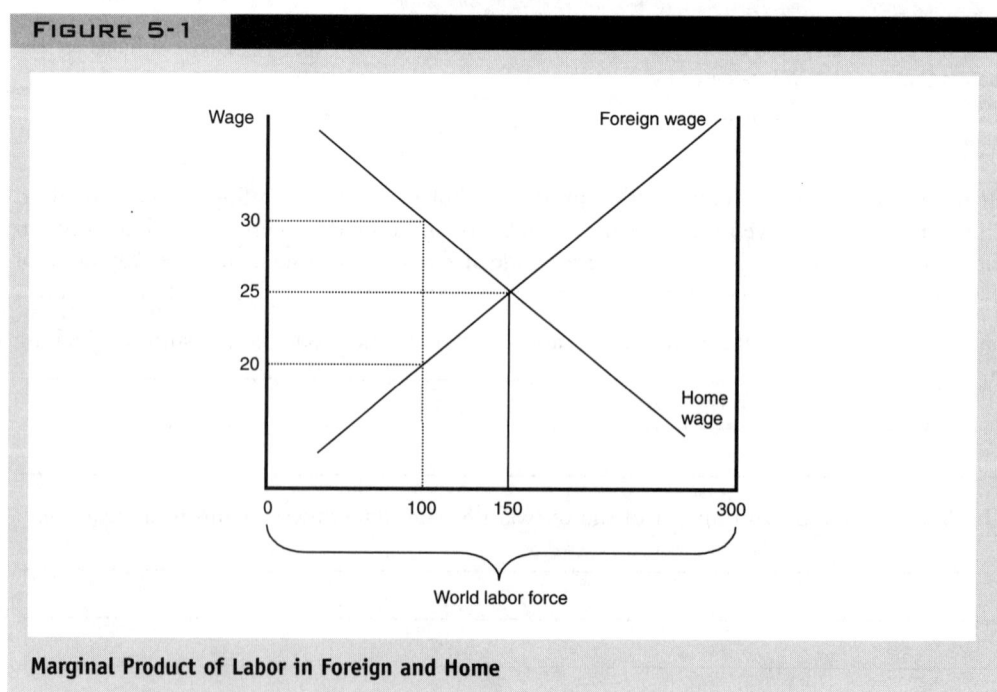

FIGURE 5-1

Marginal Product of Labor in Foreign and Home

7a. If immigration were free between countries, how much would the value of output change in Home? _____

_____

_____

7b. What is Home's national gain in allowing immigration? _____

_____

_____

7c. Who benefits from this immigration in Home and how much? _____

_____

_____

· ·

The analysis of the gains from FDI is conceptually identical to that of immigration. The marginal product of capital and the rental are considered instead of the marginal product of labor and the wage. One could repeat problem 7 for FDI renaming all the variables appropriately.

TIPS

· ·

Problem 8: Why are younger people more likely to immigrate than older people?

_____

_____

_____

6

Increasing Returns to Scale and Imperfect Competition

Overview

This chapter begins with an example of actual trading patterns, U.S. imports and exports of golf clubs. Two aspects of this trading pattern cannot be explained by the models of comparative advantage presented in earlier chapters. First, the United States simultaneously imports golf clubs from a wide range of countries at very different prices. Second, the United States exports golf clubs to many of the same countries from which it is also importing golf clubs! This kind of *intra-industry trade,* or "two-way" trade in the same good between countries, is pervasive, occurring between many trading partners in many goods.

This chapter shows that models built on the assumption of *imperfect competition* improve our understanding of trade patterns and provide additional insight into the gains from trade. The centerpiece of the chapter is the model of trade under *monopolistic competition.* Firms in a monopolistically competitive industry have a monopoly over their own particular brand or "variety" of a *differentiated* good. There is an element of competition, however, in the sense that the demand for a firm's variety depends on the actions of other firms. Firms produce their variety using an *increasing returns to scale* technology. Firms face fixed product development cost and constant marginal costs of production, so their average cost falls as they produce larger volumes of output.

The monopolistic competition model makes predictions that are distinct from those of a comparative-advantage–based model. With respect to trade patterns, the model predicts intra–industry trade between similar countries and gives rise to the *gravity equation,* which is an accurate predictor of the volume of trade between countries. With respect to the gains from trade, the model identifies two channels through which trade affects welfare. International trade expands the range of variety available to consumers and allows firms to better exploit economies of scale by expanding the size of their operations.

The chapter concludes with an alternative model built on imperfect competition. Rather than assume that products are differentiated, the model assumes that goods are homogeneous. It shows that imperfect competition can explain a common phenomenon known as *dumping,* in which a firm charges a lower price in the foreign market than in

59

its home market. Finally, it shows that imperfect competition alone can give rise to intra-industry trade even in the absence of product differentiation and economies of scale.

1 Basics of Imperfect Competition

ESSENTIAL CONCEPTS

The first section is designed (1) to review the theory of monopoly and (2) to introduce the concept of *product differentiation* in the context of a *duopoly*. A monopolist faces a downward-sloping demand curves and chooses its output (and hence the price of its product) to maximize its *economic profits*. A firm's profit is equal to the difference between its sales revenue and its total costs of production. By choosing to sell one more unit, the firm increases its revenue by the value of its *marginal revenue* and increases its total cost by its marginal cost. Suppose a firm is selling Q units at a price of P. The additional revenue raised by this firm if it sells one more unit is

$$P - \Delta P \cdot Q.$$

The firm earns P from selling one more unit but because the firm has to cut its price by ΔP on all the units it had been selling, it loses $\Delta P \cdot Q$. If the marginal revenue exceeds marginal cost, then the firm can increase its revenue by more than its cost by selling one more unit. If the marginal revenue is less than marginal cost, a firm can raise its profits by selling one less unit of its good because cutting production by one unit lowers revenue by less than it lowers total cost. Hence, a profit-maximizing firm chooses output so that marginal revenue is equal to marginal cost.

In the case of duopoly with differentiated products, there is a single demand curve for an industry's output, D, but each firm faces a demand curve that is specific to its variety of that industry's good. When the two firms charge the same price, industry demand is divided equally among varieties so that each firm sells $D / 2$. Because products are differentiated, a firm cannot grab the entire market by lowering its price below that of its competitor. Instead, a firm that reduces its price attracts new customers to its product, some of whom would have chosen to purchase the product of the firm's competitor. The demand curve for the firm, d, is flatter than the demand curve $D / 2$, because the firm can steal some of its competitor's customers by lowering its price.

KEY TERMS

Use the space provided to record your notes on the following key terms.

Imperfect competition _____

_____

_____

Duopoly _____

_____

_____

Marginal revenue _____

_____

_____

Marginal cost _____

_____

_____

Differentiated goods _____

_____

_____

Economic profits _____

_____

_____

Monopoly profits _____

_____

_____

REVIEW QUESTIONS

Problem 1: After extensive market research a firm discovers that it faces the demand curve recorded in the following table.

Quantity Sold	Price, $	Revenue, $	Marginal Revenue, $
1	7		
2	6		
3	5		
4	4		
5	3		
6	2		
7	1		

1a. Calculate the revenue and the marginal revenue associated with each output level and fill in the columns in the table.

1b. If the marginal cost is $2.5 per unit, what level of production should the firm choose to maximize its profits? Explain. _____

_____

_____

1c. Calculate the profits associated with this level of output. _____

_____

_____

Problem 2: A firm faces the demand curve, marginal revenue curve, and marginal cost curve shown in the following diagram. Add to this diagram the optimal level of output and show geometrically on this diagram the level of a firm's profits.

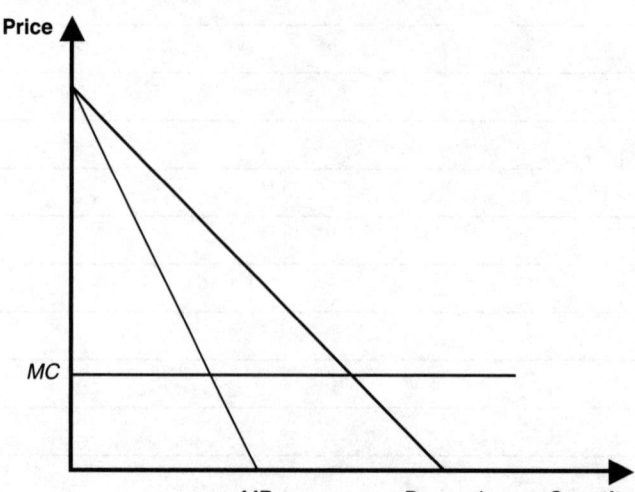

Problem 3: Consider a duopoly. In the diagram below, $D/2$ is industry demand divided by the two differentiated varieties in the market when each variety has the same price and d is the demand curve specific to each firm.

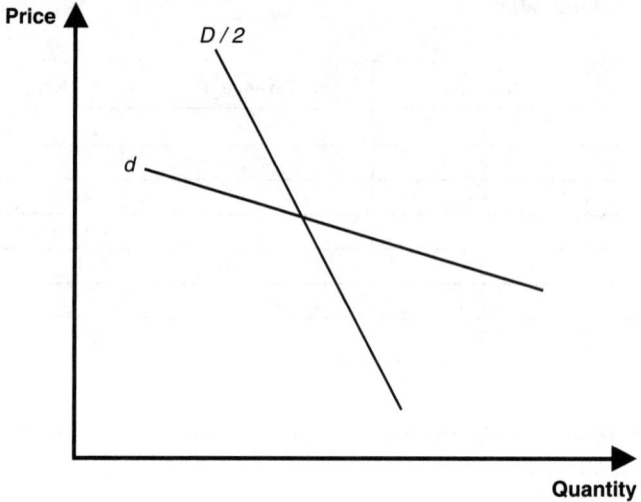

Why is the d curve flatter than the $D/2$ curve? _____

_____

_____

2   Trade under Monopolistic Competition

ESSENTIAL CONCEPTS

The model of monopolistic competition is based on four assumptions. First, each firm produces a good that is similar to but differentiated from the goods that other firms in the industry produce. Because each firm's product is somewhat different from the goods of the other firms, a firm can raise its price without losing all its customers to other firms; that is, each firm faces a downward-sloping demand curve for its product. Second, there are many firms in the industry. Third, firms produce using a technology with increasing returns to scale: average costs of production fall as the quantity produced increases. Fourth, firms can enter and exit the industry freely, so that monopoly profits are zero in the long run. In monopolistic competition, firms have some monopoly power, and yet in a long-run equilibrium each firm's profits are zero.

The model neatly captures two gains from trade that are very different than those due to comparative advantage: International trade results in (1) a wider variety of goods available and (2) lower prices due to the better exploitation of economies of scale. Opening to trade induces a rationalization effect: Some firms close when exposed to the increased competition in a larger global market, but the ones that remain produce at a larger scale. Increasing returns to scale mean that as a firm expands its output, its average costs are falling. The drop in average cost is passed on to consumers in the form of lower prices.

The model also allows us to better understand trade patterns between countries. Each variety is produced in one location but is demanded in all trading countries. Hence, there is one-way trade in each variety. Because each country produces distinct varieties, there is two-way or *intra-industry trade* within goods.

KEY TERMS
Use the space provided to record your notes on the following key terms.

Increasing returns to scale _____

_____

_____

Economies of scale _____

_____

_____

Monopolistic competition _____

_____

_____

Intra-industry trade _____

_____

_____

REVIEW QUESTIONS
Problem 4: A firm faces a fixed cost of $100 and a marginal cost of $2 per unit of output. If the firm is planning to sell 10 units, what is the lowest price that the firm can charge that will allow it to break even?

_____

_____

Problem 5: In the following diagram, D / N is industry demand divided by the number of differentiated goods when each good has the same price and d is the demand curve facing each individual producer of a differentiated good.

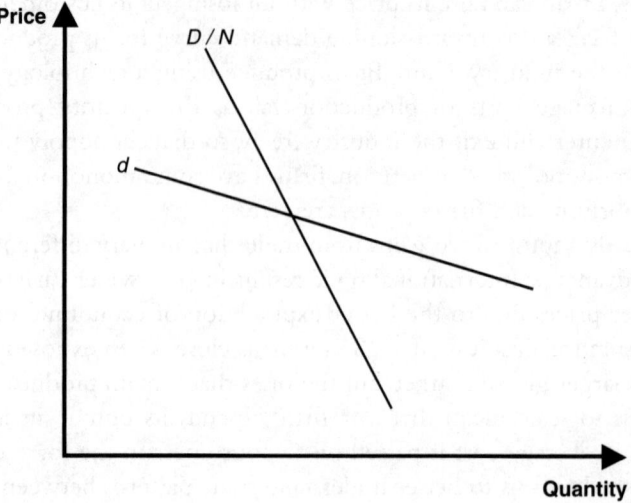

5a. Draw in the diagram the effect on *d* and *D / N* of an increase in *N*, the number of competing varieties.

5b. Explain why you drew the demand curves as you did. _____

_____

_____

TIPS Understanding the response of demand curves *D / N* and *d* is critical to understanding many of the key implications of the monopolistic competition model.

Problem 6: The marginal and average cost curves facing a firm are drawn in the following diagram.

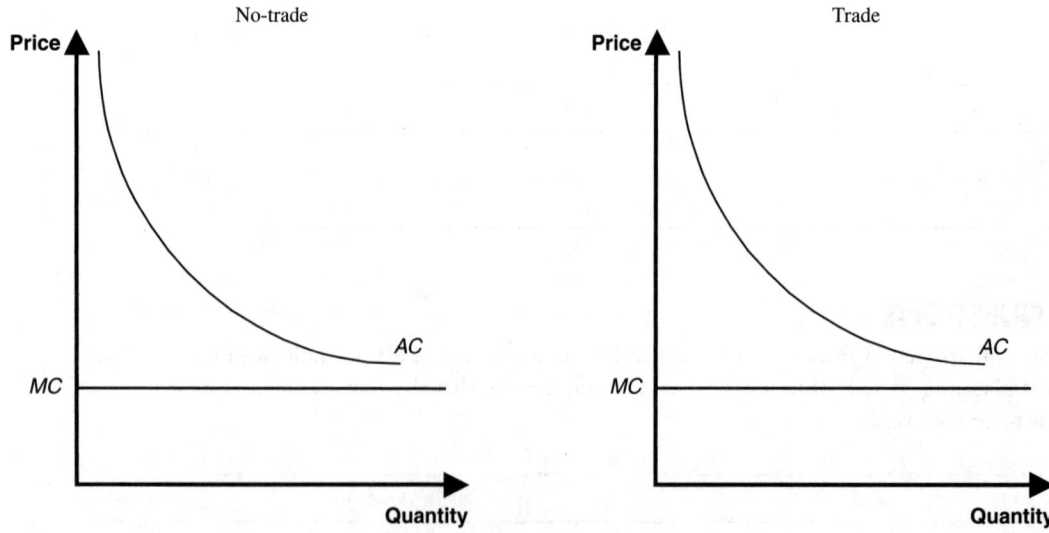

6a. In the left-hand panel, draw demand curves *D / N* and *d*, a marginal revenue curve, and the level of the optimal price and quantity for a firm in a long-run no-trade equilibrium.

6b. In the right-hand panel, draw demand curves D/N and d, a marginal revenue curve, and the level of the price and quantity for a firm in a long-run trading equilibrium for the case of two identical countries.

6c. Explain *how* the two panels are drawn differently. _____

_____

_____

6d. Explain *why* the two panels are different. _____

_____

_____

6e. What are the gains from trade, and how can they appear in the difference in the way the two panels were drawn? _____

_____

_____

6f. What are the adjustment costs associated with international trade, and how do they appear in the way the two panels were drawn in the previous diagram? _____

_____

_____

Problem 7: Consider a world with two countries. One of the countries is large and the other is small. There is one monopolistically competitive industry that uses labor as the only input.

7a. In autarky, in which country has the highest real wage? Explain. _____

_____

_____

7b. Which country gains the most from international trade? Explain. _____

_____

_____

Problem 8: Essentially only two producers in the world make wide-bodied aircraft. Would monopolistic competition be an appropriate model for this industry? Why or why not?

_____

_____

_____

TIPS

The monopolistic competition model is popular among economists because it is neat and tidy. Because the number of firms is large, we abstract from messy "strategic behavior" across firms. When the number of firms is small, however, we can no longer avoid thinking about strategic behavior.

A key observation is that the gains from trade are essentially gains to market size. Large markets allow for more variety at lower prices. The gains from trade come from consolidating two small markets into one large global market.

3 Empirical Applications of Monopolistic Competition and Trade

ESSENTIAL CONCEPTS

This section shows that the monopolistic competition model is helpful in understanding key parts of international trading patterns. First, the model helps to explain the gains from trade between similar countries, such as the United States and Canada. Evidence produced from the North American Free Trade Agreement (NAFTA) suggests that there are high short-term adjustment costs that are balanced by growth in the productivity and the employment of the surviving firms. Second, the monopolistic competition model predicts that intra-industry trade should be highest in industries in which there is a high degree of product differentiation. The *index of intra-industry trade* measures the extent to which trade is two-way between countries. As predicted by the monopolistic competition model, the index is high for goods that exhibit a high degree of product differentiation. Third, the monopolistic competition model predicts that international trade patterns should be well predicted by a *gravity equation,* which is given by

$$TRADE = \frac{GDP_1 \cdot GDP_2}{DIST^{\eta}}.$$

The gravity equation predicts that the volume of trade between two countries (here countries 1 and 2) is increasing in the gross domestic product of either country and is decreasing in their distance from each other. This relationship comes from the fact that each country produces a distinct set of varieties that are demanded in each country. The share of a country's GDP (the value of the output of its varieties) that is sold to a given foreign country is increasing in the foreign country's income or GDP and decreasing in distance between the two countries because transport costs rise with distance. The gravity equation is an accurate predictor of the volume of trade between countries.

KEY TERMS

Use the space provided to record your notes on the following key terms.

Free-trade agreements _____

_____

Regional trade agreements _____

_____

Trade adjustment assistance _____

_____

Index of intra-industry trade _____

_____

Gravity equation _____

_____

Border effects _____

_____

_____

Tariffs _____

_____

_____

Quotas _____

_____

_____

REVIEW QUESTIONS

Problem 9: Different soil conditions generate variation in the character of grapes and the wine that is made from them. Is it possible that intra-industry trade can be high in certain industries even in the absence of imperfect competition? _____

_____

_____

Problem 10: Consider a country that opens to trade with a neighboring country. The immediate effect of this opening is an increase in unemployment. Workers eventually find jobs, but most workers find themselves employed in a different industry. Is the main motive for trade between these two countries most likely to be monopolistic competition or comparative advantage? Explain. _____

_____

_____

Problem 11: Would you expect the gravity equation to explain trade patterns best between a set of countries that are similar in terms of their endowments or a set of countries that are different in their endowments? Explain. _____

_____

_____

Problem 12: How could you use data on international trade flows to assess which industries display a high degree of product differentiation and which ones do not? _____

_____

_____

As indicated in the answer to problem 9, product differentiation alone can give rise to high levels of intra-industry trade.

Problems 10 to 12 demonstrate that there are many things at work in trading patterns between countries. Because different models have different implications, it is important to know which model is appropriate for which phenomenon.

TIPS

Problem 13: Explain how the gravity equation can be used to measure the "border effect."

_____

_____

Problem 14: How has NAFTA affected the range of product variety available in the United States? _____

_____

_____

4 Imperfect Competition with Homogeneous Products: The Case of Dumping

ESSENTIAL CONCEPTS

This section shows that imperfect competition can explain the common phenomenon of _dumping_. Dumping occurs when a firm sells a product abroad at a price that is either less than the price it charges in its local market or less than its average cost of production. As we will learn later in the book, government policies toward dumping are the source of substantial friction between countries.

Two examples of dumping are considered. In the first example, a monopolist is choosing how much of its good to sell in its home market and in foreign markets. If it is difficult for consumers to arbitrage price differences across countries, then the firm can engage in _price discrimination_ across countries. The firm chooses output so that the marginal revenue in each market is equal to the marginal cost of production. Firms will often find that selling its product at a lower price abroad than at home is a profit-maximizing strategy.

The second example involves two firms located in two different countries. The firms produce identical profits under the same conditions, and it is costly to transport the good between countries. Under these circumstances _reciprocal dumping_ will arise: Each firm invades the other firm's domestic market, driving down the price in that market. Dumping arises in the model in the sense that the price charged in the foreign market is less than the price in the firm's home market plus the additional cost of transporting the good abroad. The two key points are (1) dumping is a natural phenomenon in many monopolistic and oligopolistic markets, and (2) intra-industry trade can result from imperfect competition even when there is no product differentiation.

KEY TERMS

Use the space provided to record your notes on the following key terms.

Price discrimination _____

_____

_____

Discriminating monopoly _____

_____

_____

Dumping _____

_____

_____

Antidumping duty _____

_____

_____

Oligopoly _____

_____

_____

Reciprocal dumping _____

_____

_____

REVIEW QUESTIONS

Problem 15: Suppose a monopolist located in Home has a constant marginal cost of $2 and can sell its good in two countries, Home and Foreign. Consumers are assumed to be unable to arbitrage any price difference across countries. Demand at Home is given by $P = 10 - Q$ and demand in Foreign is $P = 6 - Q$.

15a. What is the equation for the marginal revenue curve facing the monopolist in the Home and Foreign markets? _____

_____

15b. At what price is the firm selling its product in the two markets? _____

_____

15c. In the following diagrams, draw demand and marginal revenue curves in Home (its domestic market) and Foreign (its export market) so that the firm chooses to "dump" its product abroad.

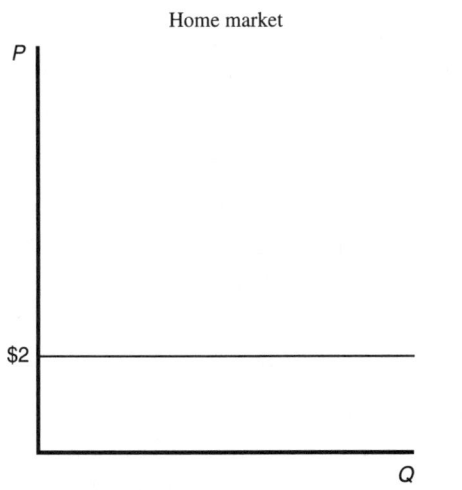

Home market

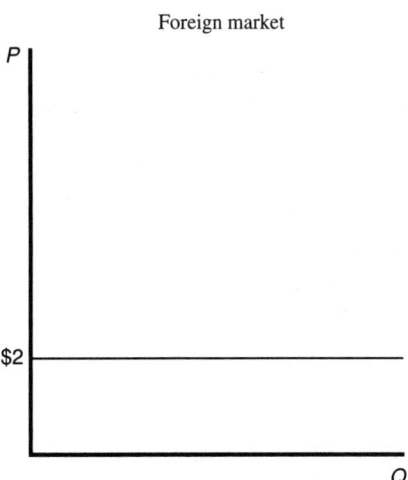

Foreign market

TIPS

It is important to know how to derive the marginal revenue equation from a linear demand curve. If you get stuck at this step, then you cannot answer fully any subsequent question! For a linear demand curve, the marginal revenue curve always has the same Y intercept and a slope that is twice as large (in absolute value) as the demand curve.

Problem 16: Suppose that a firm charges $10 for a good in its home market and $10 in its export market. Could this firm be accused of dumping? Explain. _____

_____

_____

Problem 17: A firm located in country H produces the sleep medication Beddybuy. The firm faces a downward-sloping (linear) demand curve in its home market. In the neighboring country F, the government imposes prices controls so that there is a ceiling on the price that the firm can charge for Beddybuy.

17a. Use the following axes to show the case where the firm is willing to sell Beddybuy in country F and charges a higher price for Beddybuy in H.

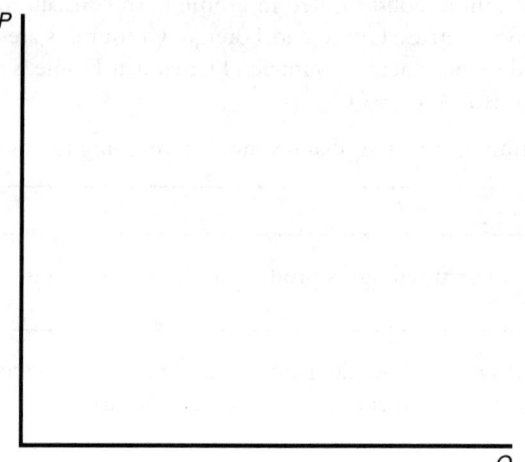

17b. Suppose some sleep-deprived consumers in country H learn that they can get Beddybuy in country F for the lower price from Internet pharmacies. Is it possible that this would cause the firm to stop selling its product in F? Explain. _____

_____

_____

Problem 18: A politician argues against free trade area in a particular industry that produces a homogenous good. She argues that because there is no difference in the cost of production in the two countries in the free trade area there are no gains from trade. Assess this argument.

_____

_____

Problem 19: Suppose that there are two countries. There is one producer of wheat in each country. Each producer has a marginal cost of $10. Demand in each country is given by $P = 95 - Q$, where P is the price and Q is the total amount sold in that country.

19a. Suppose the two countries are in autarky. Provide the equation for the marginal revenue curve facing each producer in its home market. _____

19b. What is the profit-maximizing price charged by firms in autarky? _____

19c. What is the economic profit earned by each firm? _____

Now suppose that the two firms can sell their product in each other's market but there are transport costs between countries so that each good costs $5 to ship.

19d. Provide an equation for the marginal revenue facing a firm in its home market and an equation for the marginal revenue facing a firm in its export market.

19e. Solve for the quantity sold by a firm in its home market and in the export market. _____

19f. In what sense, if any, are the firms engaged in dumping in the foreign market? _____

19g. What is the effect of the opening of international trade on firms' profits? _____

7

Foreign Outsourcing of Goods and Services

Overview

Outsourcing occurs when the production process for a *final good* is broken down into individual activities that are then relocated to different countries. As outsourcing becomes more pervasive, increasingly countries are specializing in parts of production processes, such as product development, *intermediate input* production, and assembly, rather than in final goods, such as computers and shirts. This phenomenon appears in trading patterns as an increase in the share of trade that is in intermediate inputs and business services and as a decrease in the share of trade accounted for by final goods.

The first goal of this chapter is to develop a model to analyze the role of outsourcing in the growing gap in the wages between skilled and unskilled workers. Firms in the model choose where to locate production activities given wage differences across countries. Changes in transport costs induce firms to outsource a larger set of production activities to low-wage countries. Because the additional activities that are being outsourced are low-skill intensive from the perspective of the high-wage country and high-skill intensive from the perspective of the low-wage country, outsourcing expands the relative demand for skilled labor in both countries.

The second goal of the chapter is to discuss the gains from trade associated with outsourcing. As in other models, outsourcing leads to a more efficient use of the world's resources and so makes it possible to produce more output with the same stock of factors. These gains from trade show up in the data as an increase in productivity. The model highlights the importance of a country's terms of trade across production activities in determining the size of the gains from trade.

The final goal of this chapter is to examine the newest form of outsourcing, the outsourcing of *business services* such as accounting, computer programming, and order processing. This form of outsourcing has led to growing consternation among professional workers in developed countries as jobs that had previously been insulated from international trade become vulnerable to outsourcing.

1 A Model of Outsourcing

ESSENTIAL CONCEPTS

The model of outsourcing is built upon the key concept of the *value chain*. The production process for making a final good involves many different activities (or steps) that can be done in different locations. Each activity requires some skilled and unskilled labor plus some additional factors (such as capital and infrastructure), but activities have different skill intensities. For instance, the production of a good may involve some high-technology parts that are very skilled-labor intensive and some low-technology parts that are very unskilled-labor intensive. The value chain is an ordering of these activities according to their relative skill intensity.

In the model, factor prices differ across countries. For instance, assume that Home has high wages for skilled and unskilled workers and low capital rentals relative to Foreign. Assume further that the relative wage for skilled workers is higher in Foreign than in Home. The difference in factor prices across countries and the difference in the skill intensity across activities (the ratio of skilled to unskilled workers used in the activity) mean that some activities will be cheaper to do in Home and other activities will be cheaper to do in Foreign.

An example is shown in Figure 7-1. The vertical axis in this diagram is the cost of an activity, and the horizontal axis is the value chain. Each activity in the value chain is a point on the horizontal axis. As we move right on the horizontal axis, the skill intensity of the activity is increasing so that assembly would be found near the bottom of the value chain and research and development (R&D) would be found near the top. In drawing the diagram, capital costs (and any transport costs) have been assumed to be uniform across activities.

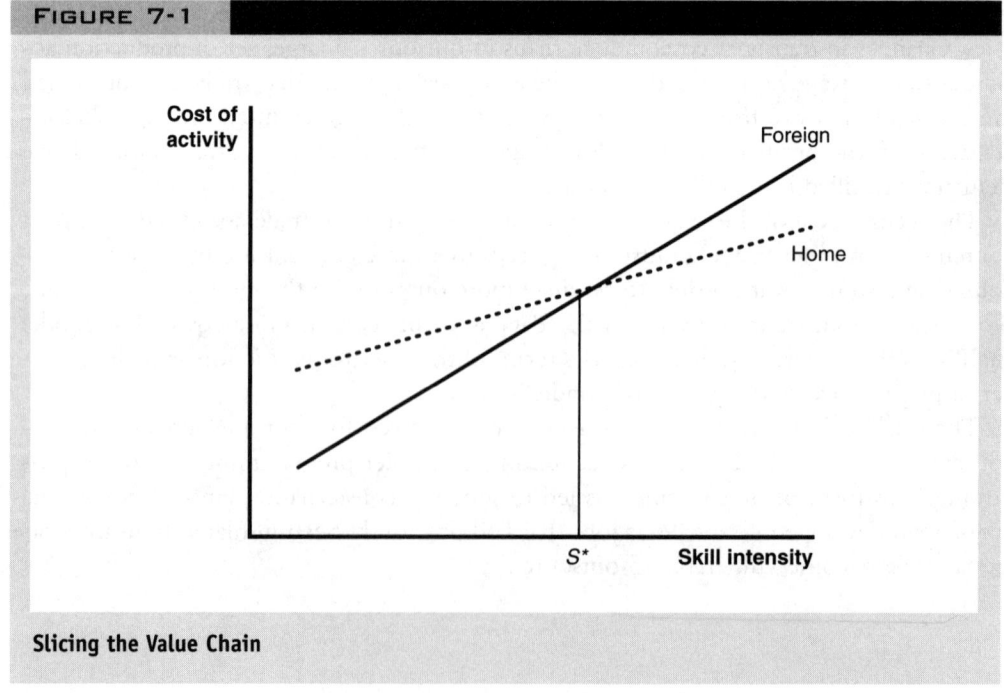

FIGURE 7-1

Slicing the Value Chain

The solid line shows Foreign's cost per activity, and the dotted line shows Home's cost per activity. Because the relative wage of skilled workers is higher in Foreign than in Home, Foreign's cost line is steeper than Home's cost line. Given the factor prices in each country, a Home firm would *slice the value chain* by producing all activities with a skill intensity less than S^* in Foreign and by producing all activities with a skill intensity greater than S^* in Home. In summary, the least skill-intensive activities are outsourced.

A reduction in transport or capital costs in Foreign induces additional outsourcing into Foreign. The downward shift in Foreign's cost line induces a rightward shift in S^* so that some activities that had previously been done in Home would be outsourced to the Foreign. The shift in S^* to the right raises the average skill intensity of activities done in both Home and Foreign. This implies that the relative demand for skilled labor and the relative wage of skilled labor rise in both countries.

The economic effects of an increase in outsourcing are very difficult to tell apart from the effects of *skill-biased technical change*. In both cases the relative demand for skilled labor rises in all countries, pushing up the relative wage of skilled workers. Recent empirical studies show that both outsourcing and technical change explain part of the growing wage gap between skilled and unskilled labor, but the exact contribution of each is hard to identify.

KEY TERMS

Use the space provided to record your notes on the following key terms.

Value chain _____

_____

_____

Foreign outsourcing _____

_____

_____

Offshoring _____

_____

_____

Skill-biased technical change _____

_____

_____

REVIEW QUESTIONS

Problem 1: A good is produced using three production activities (a, b, and c) that each use skilled and unskilled labor. The following table shows the number of skilled and unskilled workers needed to produce one unit in each production stage.

	a	b	c
Skilled labor	1	2	3
Unskilled labor	4	3	2

There are two countries: Home (H) and Foreign (F). The skilled worker wage is $4 in H and $5 in F. The unskilled worker wage is $2 in H and $1 in F. Transport costs of $2 per unit must be added to cost of a production stage if that production stage is outsourced to F.

1a. Given this information, which production activities are done in which country? _____

_____

1b. If the transport cost falls to zero, what happens to the location of production of each stage (assume that the wages don't change)? _____

_____

_____

1c. How has the reduction in transport cost in Foreign affected the relative demand for skilled labor in each country? _____

_____

_____

1d. If instead of activities, we renamed a, b, and c final goods, would there be any difference in the effect of a reduction in transport costs on relative wages? _____

_____

_____

TIPS

Problem 1d asks the question, "How different is outsourcing from traditional trade in goods?" The model presented in the chapter is designed to determine the impact of outsourcing, but it could equally have been applied to determining specialization in final goods production when the costs of production differ across countries. The effect on relative demand for labor would be the same, but the way it might appear to individuals in society would be very different.

Note that the analysis ignores the changes in the wages caused by the shift in activities across countries. The changes in wages caused by outsourcing would tend to shift the costs of doing activities in each country.

Problem 2: Suppose a low-wage country banned inward foreign direct investment. In the outsourcing model, how would such restrictions affect the range of production activities performed in the country? _____

_____

_____

Problem 3: The Heckscher-Ohlin model is built on the concept that goods can be ranked in terms of their factor intensity. What complications arise when activities can be outsourced?

_____

_____

Problem 4: It is a well-documented fact that the ratio of white collar jobs to blue collar jobs has risen in U.S. manufacturing over the last two decades.

4a. How could outsourcing explain this fact? _____

_____

_____

4b. Why does the Heckscher-Ohlin model have difficulty explaining this fact? _____

_____

_____

4c. Can there be explanations for this fact that do not involve international trade? _____

_____

_____

2 The Gains from Outsourcing

ESSENTIAL CONCEPTS

As in the more standard models of international trade discussed in the earlier chapters of the book, the ability of firms to relocate some production activities abroad leads to gains from trade through a more efficient allocation of world's resources. To make this point, we reinterpret the Heckscher-Ohlin model, which was developed in Chapter 4, in order to analyze the gains from outsourcing.

This reinterpretation occurs in three steps. First, label the axes of the production possibilities frontier as inputs into the production of the final good rather than the final goods. Examples of such inputs are research and development and components. Second, replace indifference curves with *isoquants*. The inputs in the PPF are used to produce a final good rather than utility. Third, imagine that a country's resources are divided over a number of identical firms so that each firm has an equal share of the country's resources and a PPF. Given this reinterpretation, countries have comparative advantages at stages of production rather than in final goods. The gains from trade in inputs are very similar to the gains from trade in final goods, only they show up as increases in productivity: Firms can produce more final good output with the same amount of inputs.

Although there are gains from outsourcing, changes in global market conditions can cause changes in the terms of trade. If developing countries become more adept at activities in which the developed world has a comparative advantage, then the developed world can experience a terms-of-trade loss. Any terms-of-trade loss is bad for a country because it means that the country's budget constraint has shifted inward. This is the point made by Professor Samuelson. The possibility that changes in the terms of trade on global markets could reduce the welfare of developed country workers does not mean that outsourcing is bad for a country. It just means that developed countries may someday gain less from trade than they are currently.

KEY TERMS

Use the space provided to record your notes on the following key terms.

Isoquant _____

_____

_____

Business services _____

_____

_____

REVIEW QUESTIONS

Problem 5: The country of Home has many identical firms that produce a single final good using R&D and components. R&D and components are in turn produced using skilled and unskilled labor. R&D is relatively skill intensive compared with components production. The country is initially in autarky.

5a. Suppose that Home is now able to trade with Foreign, which is relatively skilled-labor scarce. Show, using the following diagram, the impact of trade on the output of a typical firm in Home.

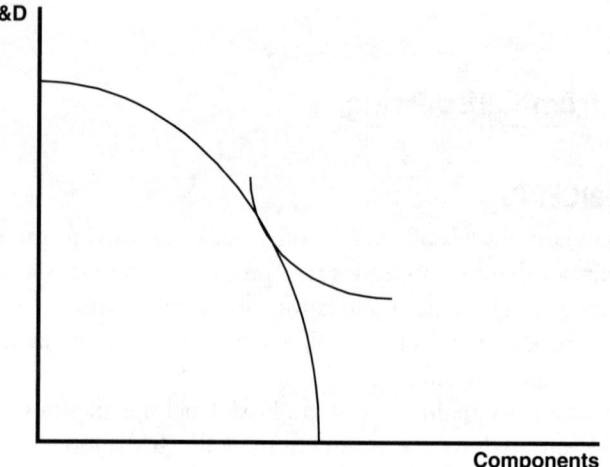

5b. Describe the pattern of trade between Home and Foreign. _____

_____

_____

5c. Describe the gains from trade for Home. _____

_____

_____

5d. What is the effect of trade on the relative demand for skilled labor in Home? _____

_____

_____

5e. Now suppose that Home's terms of trade improve. Show the effect of the terms of trade improvement in the following diagram.

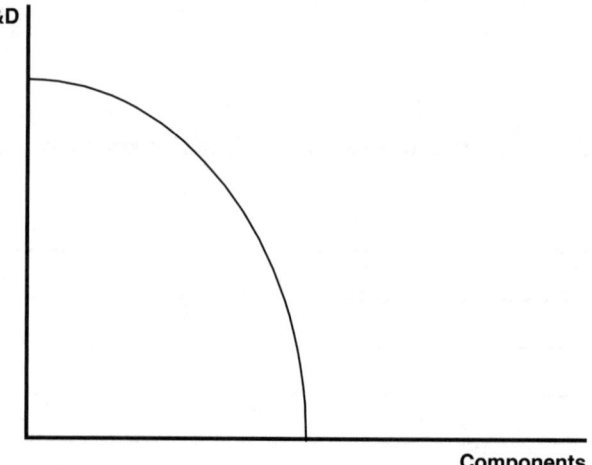

5f. What is the effect of a terms-of-trade improvement on the observed productivity of the typical firm in Home? Explain. _____

_____

_____

Problem 6: Output is produced from business services and components. Home has an absolute advantage in both business services and components and a comparative advantage in business services relative to Foreign.

6a. If Home could increase Foreign's productivity in components by giving some of its technology to Foreign, would this make Home better or worse off? Explain. _____

_____

_____

6b. If Home could increase Foreign's productivity in business services by giving some of its technology to Foreign, would this make Home better or worse off? Explain. _____

_____

_____

....

A deterioration in a country's terms of trade has negative implications for that country whether they involve the prices of intermediate inputs or the prices of final goods. The same analysis could have been applied in any of the models of comparative advantage.

It should be clear that this simplified model of outsourcing is just a reinterpretation of the Heckscher-Ohlin model.

TIPS

....

Problem 7: According to the study of Amiti and Wei cited in the textbook, what portion of U.S. productivity growth can be attributed to outsourcing? _____

_____

_____

3 Outsourcing in Services

ESSENTIAL CONCEPTS

Most workers in developed countries are employed in services industries. For years, these workers were not directly exposed to international trade because services were largely impossible to trade. Advances in information technology have meant, however, that many services workers have found that their jobs could be outsourced. As a result, there has been a general increase in the anxiety of service workers in developed countries regarding international trade.

In recent years skilled workers in developed countries have found that many skill-intensive activities are being outsourced to developing countries such as India. The value chain model introduced in this chapter can be used to think about this phenomenon with two slight adjustments. First, skilled workers in India are currently paid considerably less than their developed country counterparts (although skilled labor wages are rising rapidly in India). Second, the assumption is dropped that transport costs are uniform across activities. Instead, it is assumed that transport costs are very high in low-skill-intensive activities and very low in high-skill-intensive activities. This assumption is motivated by conditions in India, the largest destination for service outsourcing. In India, physical infrastructure such as roads is rudimentary, whereas information technology infrastructure is relatively advanced.

KEY TERMS

Use the space provided to record your notes on the following key term.

Business services _____

_____

_____

REVIEW QUESTIONS

Problem 8: The following diagram shows the cost per activity in Home and Foreign if transport costs were the same in both countries. By assumption the cost of activities in Foreign are lower for all activities (represented by the Foreign curve) than in Home (represented by the Home curve).

8a. Now suppose that there are transport costs in Foreign that are not uniform across activities: They are "high" for a set of the most unskilled labor activities and "low" for a set of the most skilled labor activities. Draw in the Foreign cost, inclusive of transport costs, so that the most highly skilled activities are outsourced from Home to Foreign.

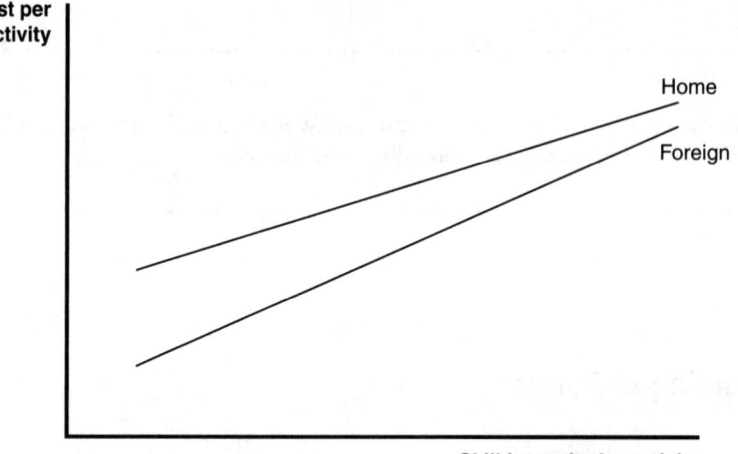

8b. Is it possible to construct an example in which both very high and very low skill-intensive activities are outsourced while the moderately skill-intensive activities are not? _____

_____

_____

Problem 9: Why might India's growing success in business services be potentially "bad news" for the United States? _____

_____

_____

Problem 10: Until recently, many services could not be traded internationally. Could the increased tradability of services result in a further decline in manufacturing employment in the United States? _____

_____

_____

....

As problem 8 demonstrates, it is possible to generate all kinds of different outcomes with respect to outsourcing if one is free to choose any pattern of transportation costs one wants.

   "Bad news" in trade models generally comes from a deterioration in a country's terms of trade.

TIPS

....

8

Import Tariffs and Quotas under Perfect Competition

Overview

As trade creates gains between countries and winners and losers within countries, a country's *trade policy* affects the welfare of other nations and redistributes income within its borders. Because one country's policies can negatively affect other countries, the *World Trade Organization* acts as a forum for countries to come to a collective agreement on trade policies and resolves disputes between countries when they arise. The structure and history of the WTO affect all relevant aspects of trade policy.

The chapter introduces a perfectly competitive, partial equilibrium model to analyze the welfare impact of two types of trade policies: the import *tariff* and the import *quota*. The tariff, which is a tax on imports, is the most common way that countries reduce the volume of their imports. The analysis suggests that import tariffs lower the welfare of *small* importing countries but can actually improve the welfare of *large* importing countries. Large countries' gain is at the expense of their trading partners, however, explaining some of the conflicts that arise between countries. The import quota is a direct restriction on the number of imports allowed into a country. In the perfectly competitive model, the welfare effects associated with import *quotas* are much like those of the import tariff. Like tariffs, quotas raise domestic prices above world price and so aid producers and harm consumers. Governments typically enforce quotas in a way that ensures that they lower national welfare.

1 A Brief History of the World Trade Organization

ESSENTIAL CONCEPTS

Prior to World War II the world was in a major economic slump commonly referred to as the Great Depression. During this period, countries used trade policies to aid domestic producers, but the collective effect of a simultaneous rise in tariffs across all major countries was to reduce the volume of trade for all countries. The loss of the gains from trade is generally thought to have contributed to the seriousness of the Depression.

In 1947, the General Agreement on Tariffs and Trade (GATT) was established, with the goal of reducing trade barriers. In addition to providing a forum for negotiating the reduction of trade barriers, the GATT contained 24 articles that regulated countries' use of trade policies. Under the GATT, countries met periodically for negotiations, called *rounds,* with the purpose of lowering trade barriers and introducing rules for the conduct of trade policy.

In 1994 the GATT was replaced by the World Trade Organization. The articles of the GATT were written into the WTO agreement. Unlike the GATT, the WTO is a formal institution that has a mechanism, or procedure, for settling disputes that arise when countries are accused of violating the rules. This subsection introduces some of the key rules of the WTO and the GATT before it.

KEY TERMS

Use the space provided to record your notes on the following key terms.

Trade policy _____

_____

_____

Import tariff _____

_____

_____

Dumping _____

_____

_____

Import quota _____

_____

_____

Export subsidies _____

_____

_____

Regional trade agreements _____

_____

_____

Free-trade areas _____

_____

_____

Customs unions _____

_____

_____

Safeguard provision _____

_____

_____

Escape clause _____

_____

_____

REVIEW QUESTIONS

Problem 1: The following questions test your knowledge of the WTO's rules.

1a. How would you know if a foreign firm was dumping its product in your domestic market? _____

_____

_____

1b. Suppose that several countries decided to reduce tariffs exclusively on each others' products but maintain their tariffs on other countries' products. Would this agreement violate the WTO's "most favored nation" principle? Why or why not? _____

_____

_____

1c. Why is "most favored nation status" called "normal trade relations" in the United States?

_____

_____

....

Memorize the appropriate article in GATT for each of the relevant key terms.
  Be patient. Each of the articles highlighted in this section will be featured at some point in the next several chapters.

TIPS

....

2 The Gains from Trade

ESSENTIAL CONCEPTS

A simple partial equilibrium framework is introduced to analyze the effect of Home's trade policy on its welfare. There are two types of actors in Home, consumers and producers. In Figure 8-1, Home's consumers are represented by a demand curve (D) and Home's producers are represented by a supply curve (S). When Home is in autarky, the price (P^A) and quantity (Q_0) in this market is determined by the intersection of supply and demand. Now suppose that the country could trade with the outside world at fixed world prices. If the price on the world market is below the price in Home in autarky, then Home's consumers will expand their demand and its producers will contract their supply. When Home's demand exceeds its domestic supply, the country must import the difference. Home's import demand curve is shown on the right-hand panel of Figure 8-1. Given a world price P^W, a country imports M_1, which is equal to $D_1 - S_1$.

Figure 8-1

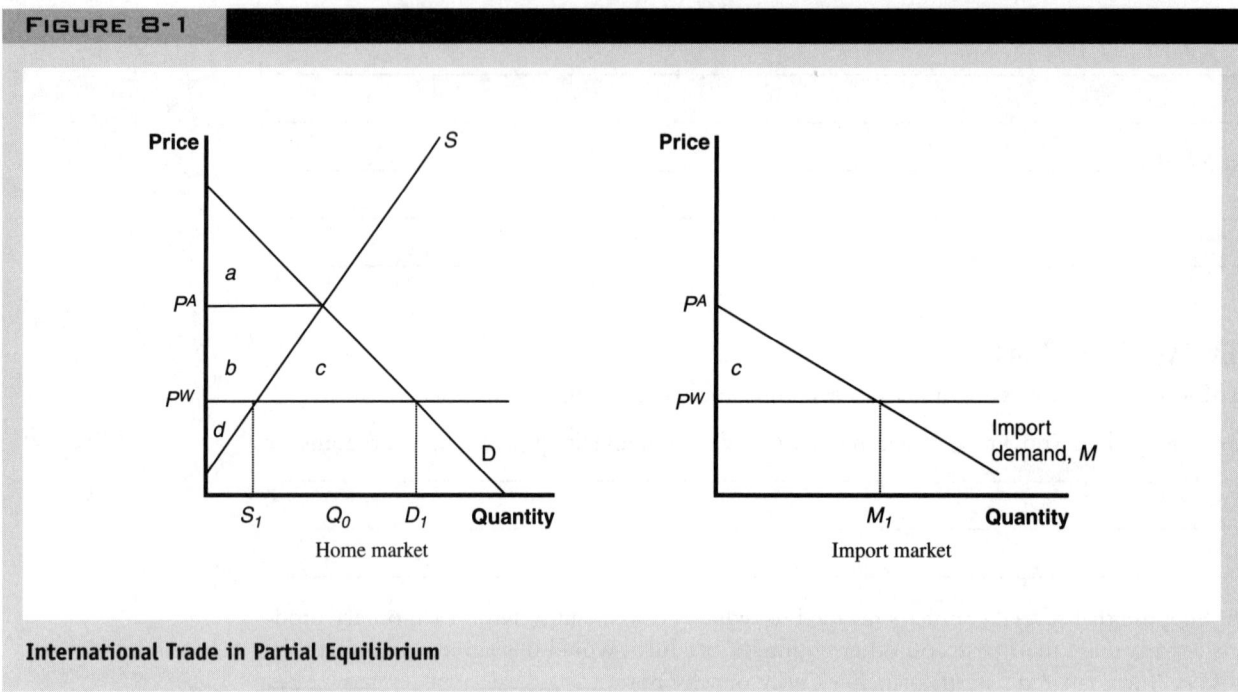

International Trade in Partial Equilibrium

To measure welfare in this framework, we rely on the concepts of *consumer surplus* and *producer surplus.* The surplus that accrues to a consumer who buys D_1 units of a good when the price is P^W is equal to the area under the demand curve up to D_1 (the total utility of consuming that much of the good), less the amount that the consumer had to pay, or price P^W multiplied by D_1 (the foregone utility of consuming other goods). In Figure 8-1, given a price of P^W, the consumer surplus is equal to the sum of the areas *a, b,* and *c.* Because international trade lowers the price of the import good, trade improves the well-being of consumers by the area $b + c$, as shown in the left-hand panel of Figure 8-1.

The producer surplus associated with selling S_1 units at a price P^W is the revenue earned $(P^W \cdot S_1)$ less the total payments to variable factors (the area under the supply curve up to S_1). In Figure 8-1, the producer surplus given a price of P^W is the area *d.* International trade lowers the price in an import industry relative to autarky and so harms producers whose revenues fall by more than their variable costs. In Figure 8-1, the loss imposed on producers by international trade is the area *b.*

International trade creates winners and losers in this model, but the gains to the winners exceed the losses to losers. In Figure 8-1, the gains from trade are measured by the area *c.* Notice that this welfare effect is measured by the area of a triangle. The area of a triangle is easy to calculate: It is one half of the product of the base and height of the triangle. Finally, notice that the gains from trade can also be measured by triangles in either diagram.

KEY TERMS

Use the space provided to record your notes on the following key terms.

Consumer surplus _____

_____

_____

Producer surplus _____

_____

_____

Import demand curve _____

_____

_____

Small country _____

_____

_____

REVIEW QUESTIONS

Problem 2: Anne is willing to buy one tomato if the price of tomatoes is $3 and two tomatoes if the price of tomatoes is $2. If the price of tomatoes is $2, what is Anne's consumer surplus?

_____

_____

Problem 3: Suppose tomatoes are grown using land (a specific factor) and labor (a mobile factor). If the revenue of tomato growers is $100 and the wage bill (amount paid to the mobile factor) is $60, what is the producer surplus in the tomato industry? _____

_____

Problem 4: Figure 8-2 shows the trading equilibrium for a small country with import demand *M* facing a fixed world price for a good.

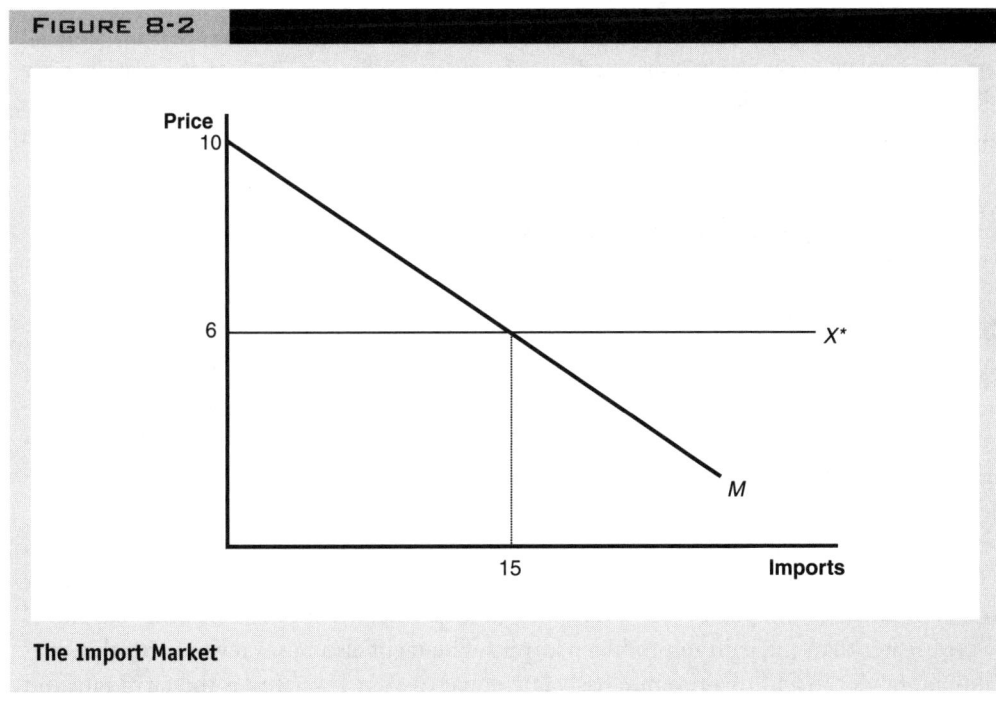

FIGURE 8-2

The Import Market

4a. What is the autarky price in this small country? _____

4b. What are the national welfare gains from trade for this economy compared with national welfare in autarky? _____

_____

_____

4c. The following Home Market diagram shows Home's domestic supply and demand for the good. Fill in the information from Figure 8-2 (prices and imports) and your answer to problem 4b (gains from trade) in this diagram.

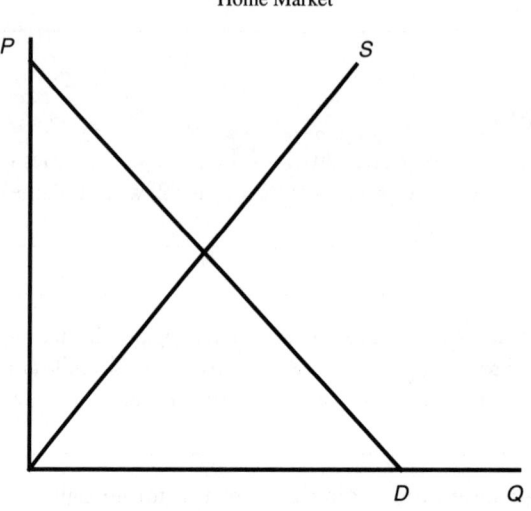

Home Market

....

TIPS   When a country goes from autarky to free trade, the price on the world market becomes the price in the importing country. Home's producers would not be able to sell any goods for a price higher than the world level.

The diagrams used in the book have linear supply and demand curves. This means that the measurement of deadweight losses always involves calculating the area of triangles. The area of a triangle is one half of the product of the triangle's base and its height.

....

3 Import Tariffs for a Small Country

ESSENTIAL CONCEPTS

A *small country* faces a horizontal export supply curve. It cannot affect the world price of its imports by changing its behavior. When Home puts a tariff of size t into place, the price facing home consumers and producers is equal to the fixed world price P^W plus the tariff t. As shown in Figure 8-3, consumers reduce their demand and producers increase their supply and imports fall.

The increase in the price in the home market lowers consumer surplus by the area $a + b + c + d$. At the same time, the increase in price in Home increases its producer surplus by the area a. Because the country is an importer, the loss of consumer surplus is always greater than the gain in producer surplus. The tariff also raises revenue for the government, however, and this revenue has value equal to $t \cdot M_1$, where t is the tariff rate and

FIGURE 8-3

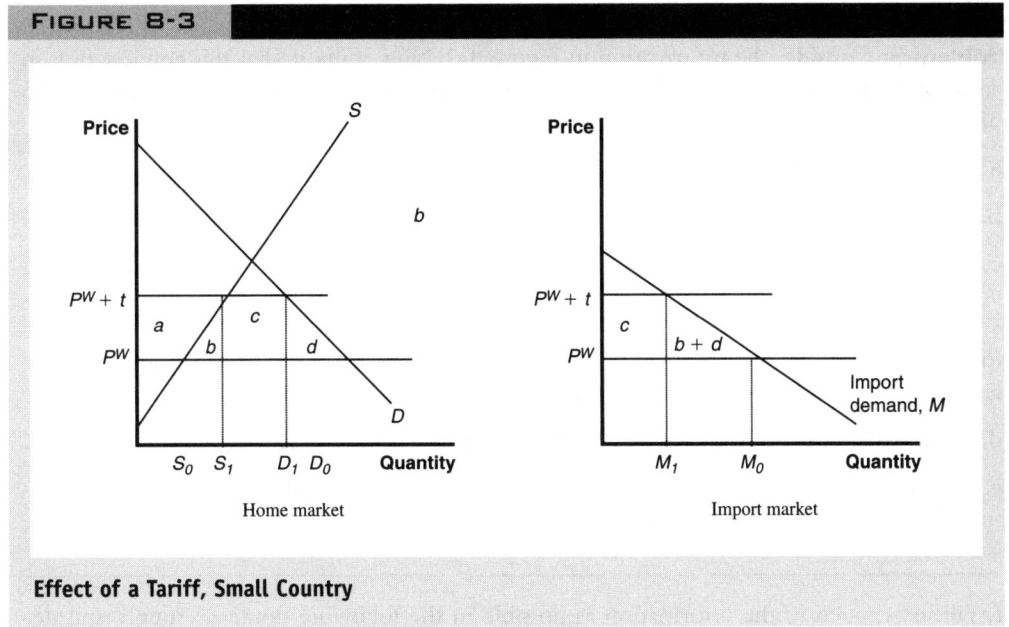

Effect of a Tariff, Small Country

M_1 is the amount of the good imported. In Figure 8-3 (both panels) this is the area c. On net, a tariff imposed by a small country must reduce the welfare of that country by the area $b + d$. These welfare losses are called the *deadweight loss* of the tariff and are equal to the sum of the *production loss* (area b) and *consumption loss* (area d). The deadweight loss appears in both the Home Market and Import Market diagrams and can be easily calculated using the formula for the area of a triangle.

KEY TERMS

Use the space provided to record your notes on the following key terms.

Deadweight loss _____

_____

_____

Production loss _____

_____

_____

Consumption loss _____

_____

_____

Dispute settlement system _____

_____

_____

Tariff war _____

_____

_____

REVIEW QUESTIONS

Problem 5: Consider the information in Figure 8-2. Now suppose that this country puts in a tariff of $2 per unit imported. Suppose that the country's imports fall from 15 units to 7.5 units.

5a. What is the effect of the tariff on the domestic price? _____

5b. What is the value of tariff revenue raised by this tariff? _____

5c. What is the effect of the tariff on national welfare (provide a number)? _____

_____

Now suppose that the tariff causes the revenue of domestic firms to rise by $9 and the payments to variable factors of production to rise by $4.

5d. What is the effect of the tariff on producer surplus? _____

5e. Given your answers to questions 5b through 5d, what is the effect of the tariff on consumer surplus? _____

_____

5f. Fill in as much of the information as possible in the following domestic supply and demand diagram.

Home Market

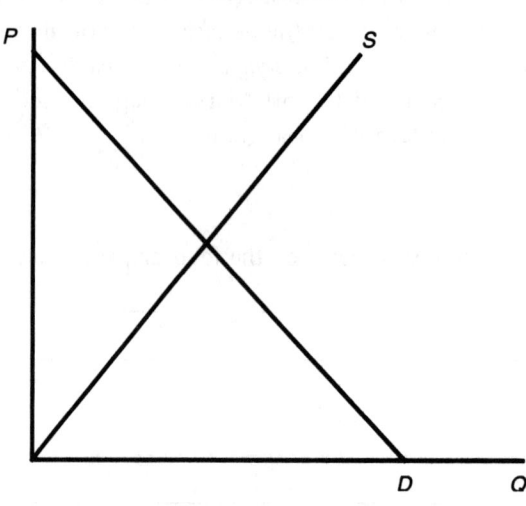

···

TIPS   You should be comfortable understanding the relationships between the information in the Home Market diagram and the Import Market diagram.

···

Problem 6: Home has a tariff of $2 on the import of a pair of shoes. Home is small, and the price of shoes on the world market is $15. Home had been producing 100 pairs of shoes and consuming 300 pairs of shoes. Now suppose that Home gets rid of its tariff entirely. As a result, consumption of shoes rises by 25 pairs and production of shoes falls by 25 pairs. Assume that Home's supply and demand curves are linear.

6a. What is the impact of the tariff removal on producer surplus? (Provide a number.)

_____

6b. What is the impact of the tariff removal on consumer surplus? (Provide a number.)

_____

6c. What is the impact of the tariff removal on government revenue? (Provide a number.)

_____

6d. Is the country better or worse off after the tariff is removed and by how much? _____

_____

6e. Use the following diagram to illustrate the information provided in the questions and answers to the other parts of the problem.

Home Market

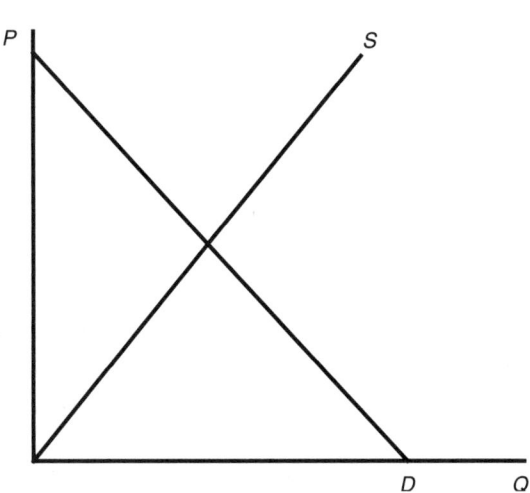

4 Import Tariff for a Large Country

ESSENTIAL CONCEPTS

If Home is a *large country*, it can alter world prices by changing its demand on the world market. To model a large country, we assume that the country faces an export supply curve that has a positive slope, as shown in the right-hand panel of Figure 8-4. By imposing a tariff, the government raises the price in Home, inducing producers to supply more and consumers to demand less so that imports contract for any given world price. This reduction in demand pushes down the world price in Import Market, shown in Figure 8-4 as the decrease in the world price P_0^W to P_1^W. Meanwhile, the domestic price rises from P_0^W to $P_1^W + t$.

The reduction in the world price is called the *terms-of-trade gain* for Home, and it represents an increase in Home's welfare. The gain occurs because Home has pushed some of the incidence of the tariff onto foreign producers. Total tariff revenue accruing to the government is shown in both panels of Figure 8-4 as the area $c + e$, of which the area e is paid by foreign producers. The remainder of the welfare analysis for Home is similar to the case of the small country. Because the price rises in Home (P_0^W to $P_1^W + t$), consumer surplus falls by the area $a + b + c + d$ and producer surplus rises by the area a. The total impact of the tariff on national welfare is then $e - (b + d)$. The key result is that if the government chooses its tariff carefully, then the terms-of-trade gain exceeds the dead-

FIGURE 8-4

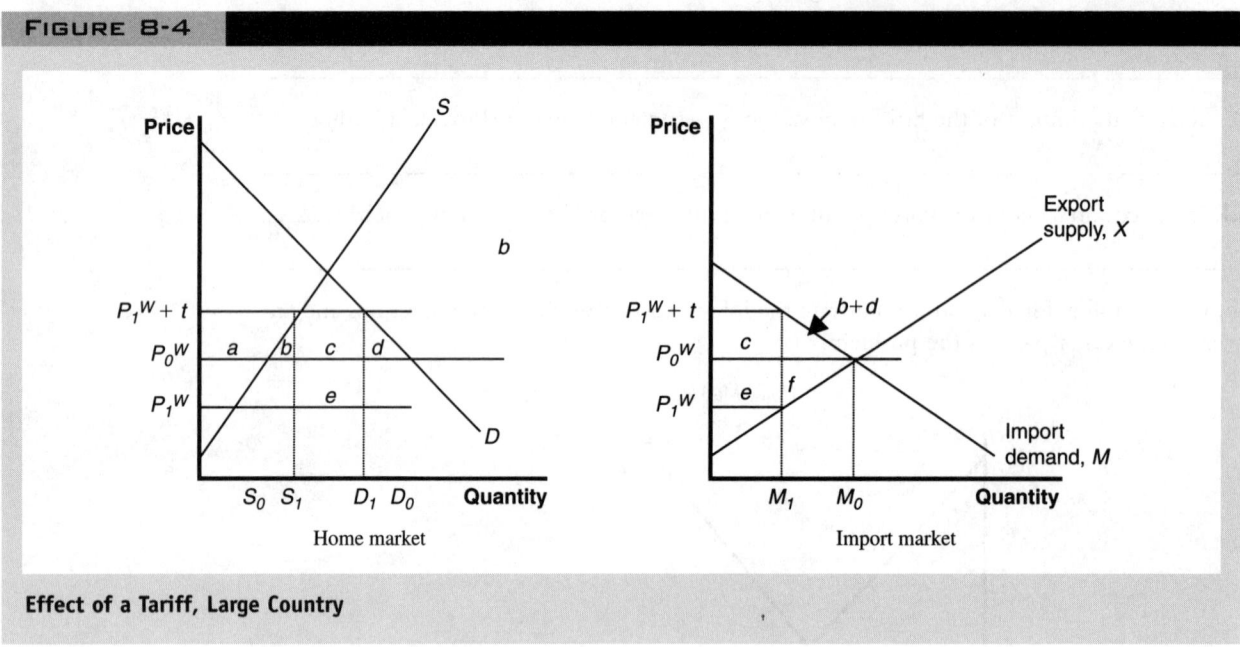

Effect of a Tariff, Large Country

weight loss and Home is better off with a tariff than it is with free trade. The tariff rate that maximizes the welfare gain for Home is called the *optimal tariff*.

Home's welfare gain comes at the expense of its trading partner, where producer surplus falls by more than consumer surplus rises in response to the lower world price. Total losses to the exporting country are shown as the area $e + f$ in the Import Market in Figure 8-4. By imposing a tariff, Home might precipitate a *trade war* by inducing its trading partner to impose *retaliatory* tariffs on Home products as punishment. Finally, because free trade maximizes global efficiency, a tariff necessarily leads to welfare losses through production and consumption losses, which are equal to $-(b + d + f)$.

KEY TERMS

Use the space provided to record your notes on the following key terms.

Large country _____

_____

_____

Terms of trade _____

_____

_____

Terms-of-trade gain

_____

_____

Optimal tariff

_____

_____

REVIEW QUESTIONS

Problem 7: Suppose Home is importing 100 units of a good at a world price of $10/unit. Home then puts in a tariff of $2 per unit. As a result of the tariff, the price paid in Home rises to $11 per unit and imports fall to 50 units.

7a. What impact has the tariff had on the world price? _____

_____

7b. What tariff revenue is raised by this tariff? _____

7c. Assuming that the country's import demand curve is linear, what is the deadweight loss in Home caused by this tariff? _____

7d. By how much did this tariff raise or lower Home's welfare?

_____

7e. By how much did this tariff raise of lower Foreign welfare?

_____

7f. What is the effect of the tariff on world welfare? _____

7g. Use the following domestic supply and demand diagram for the exporting country to illustrate the welfare impact of Home's tariff on consumer surplus, producer surplus, and national welfare. Where possible, provide numbers.

The exporter's domestic
market

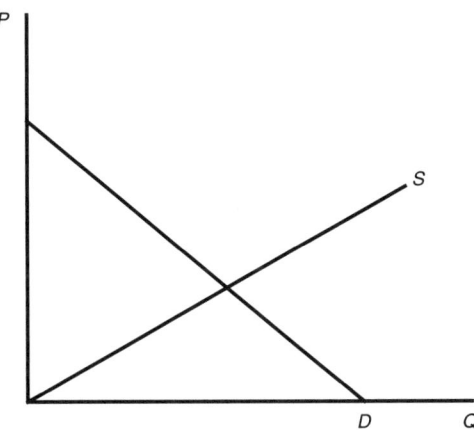

When Home imposes a tariff, its consumers and producers react to a price that exceeds the world price by the size of the tariff. When the tariff is imposed, the price in Home increases by *t*, causing consumers to demand less and producers to supply more. The demand for imports then falls, pushing down the price on the world market. The new equilibrium occurs when at the new world price plus the tariff, Home consumers and producers want to import the same quantity that Foreign producers and consumers want to sell at the new world price.

TIPS

Problem 8: The optimal tariff formula states that the tariff that raises national welfare the most is inversely related to the elasticity of the export supply curve. Provide an intuitive explanation for why this is so. _____

_____

_____

TIPS

A tariff is just a tax on imports. As we know from introductory economics, the incidence of a tax falls on both suppliers and consumers. If we think of the importing country as the consumer and the exporting country as the supplier, then it makes sense that the steeper the supply curve, the more the effect of a tax is borne by the exporting country.

5   Import Quotas

ESSENTIAL CONCEPTS

A quota is a limit on the number of imports allowed into a country. If Home imposes a quota, its government requires anyone importing the good to have a *quota license*. In the presence of a quota, the price in Home rises above the world price in order to make Home's excess demand (equal to domestic demand minus domestic supply) equal the amount of the quota. As in the case of the tariff, a higher domestic price reduces consumer surplus by more than it increases producer surplus. The fact that the price in Home exceeds the world price means that quota licenses have value as they give their owner the right to buy low at the world price and sell high at the domestic price. The total value of quota licenses is called the *quota rent*.

Who gets the quota rents? There are several possibilities. First, if the government auctions the quota licenses in a perfectly competitive market, then the quota rents accrue to the government. In this case, the welfare effect of a quota is *equivalent* to a tariff that restricts imports by the same amount. The diagrams for a quota would be drawn in exactly the same way that they would be for a tariff. Second, the quota rents could be given away. One potential problem with giving the quota licenses away is that people engage in *rent-seeking* behavior: They use real resources to lobby the government in order to obtain quota licenses. In fact, quota rents are often given to the governments of the exporting countries to distribute as they please. When quota rents are given to foreigners, the effect of the quota on national welfare is unambiguously negative in both the small- and large-country cases.

KEY TERMS

Use the space provided to record your notes on the following key terms.

Quota licenses _____

_____

_____

Quota rents _____

_____

_____

Equivalent import tariff _____

_____

_____

Rent seeking _____

_____

_____

Voluntary export restraint (VER) _____

_____

_____

Voluntary restraint agreement (VRA) _____

_____

_____

Multifiber arrangement (MFA) _____

_____

_____

REVIEW QUESTIONS

Problem 9: Consider two scenarios for a small country. In one case, the government imposes a tariff on the import of a good. In the second case, the government imposes a quota that restricts imports by the same amount as the tariff and distributes the quota licenses by selling them on a perfectly competitive market.

9a. Compare and contrast the welfare effects of these two policies given the fixed world price. _____

_____

_____

9b. Now suppose that the protected good's price falls on world markets after the tariff and quota are in place. If you were a producer in the protected market, would you rather be protected by the tariff or by the quota? Explain. _____

_____

_____

Problem 10: Consider a large country that is importing 100 units of a good at $10 a piece. The government of the importing country puts in a quota of 50 units, which is enforced by having the government of the exporting country distribute these licenses. As a result of this quota the Home price rises to $13 and the price on the world market drops to $8.

10a. What is the value of the quota rent? _____

10b. What is the effect on the export country's total welfare (provide a number)? _____

_____

_____

10c. What is the effect on the import country's total welfare (provide a number)? _____

_____

_____

10d. Illustrate the welfare effects on the importer and exporter countries in the following export–import diagram.

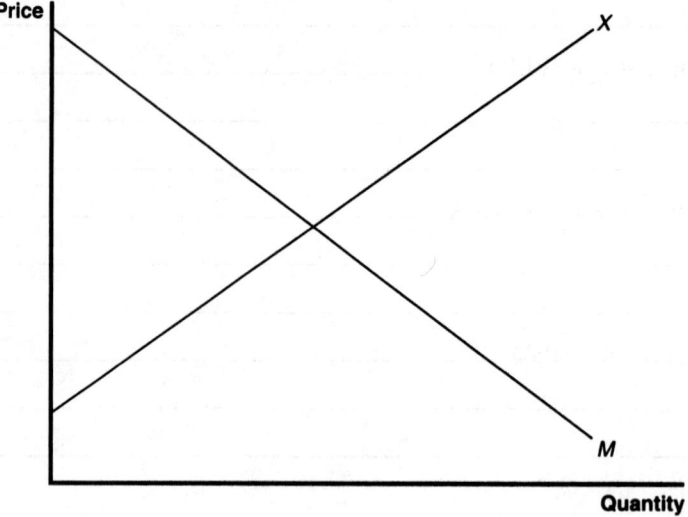

10e. If instead the importing country allowed the exporting country to sell the import licenses, what would be the welfare effect of the quota on the two countries? _____

_____

_____

_____

Problem 11: Why would a country give the quota rents to the exporting country? _____

_____

_____

. . . .

TIPS

The effect of a quota on national welfare depends on how the quota rents are distributed. Read problems on quotas carefully.

. . . .

9

Import Tariffs and Quotas under Imperfect Competition

Overview

Perfect competition is a useful abstraction that economists use as a starting point in their analyses. No market is perfectly competitive, however, so it is important to consider the affects of trade policies when markets are imperfectly competitive. This chapter considers two broad types of imperfect competition. The first type occurs when firms, either domestic or foreign, have *market power*. Firms with market power have some control over the prices that they receive for their output. The second type occurs when there are *market failures*, such as *imperfect capital markets* or the existence of *externalities*. Market failures often justify government intervention.

Trade policy can have very different welfare effects when firms have market power. One benefit of international trade is that imports limit the ability of domestic firms to exploit their market power. These pro-competitive effects of international trade remain even when the government implements a tariff, but they are largely eliminated when the government implements an import quota. The differential effect of the two policies arises because a tariff continues to allow imports to respond to price changes in the home market, whereas a quota does not.

When a country is served by a single foreign monopolist, a country's tariff policy interacts with the price-setting behavior of the foreign firm. Home is always large in the sense that its tariff policy alters the price received by the foreign firm, but terms-of-trade gains only arise when the demand curve has a particular shape. Finally, the nature of a government's tariff policy also matters in the welfare implications. An *antidumping* policy threatens foreign firms with tariffs if they set a price in the home market that is below some measure of "fair value." When foreign firms raise their price in the home market to avoid these tariffs, the home market's consumer surplus falls and no tariff revenue is collected.

Market failures that are distinct from the existence of the market power of firms also have important implications for trade policy. When capital markets are imperfect and it takes time for firms to learn how to produce efficiently, potentially prosperous industries may never come into being because firms have no way to cover short-term losses. When there are positive externalities across firms, such as *knowledge spillovers*, industries may only be viable if they reach a certain size. Market failures of these sorts justify *infant industry protection:* Temporary trade barriers give new industries time to become internationally competitive.

1 Tariffs and Quotas with Home Monopoly

ESSENTIAL CONCEPTS

To analyze the effect of trade policies when the Home industry is imperfectly competitive, we adjust the partial equilibrium model by assuming that Home has only one firm with an upward-sloping marginal cost curve. In autarky, the Home firm is a monopolist and so faces a downward-sloping marginal revenue curve. The firm maximizes its profits by choosing the quantity that sets marginal revenue equal to marginal cost. As a result, the price facing Home consumers is greater than the firm's marginal cost. We assume that Home is small in the sense that there is a fixed world price for the good. With free trade, the Home price becomes the fixed world price and so the monopolist becomes a price taker. Because the Home firm has no incentive to restrict output, competition from imports can lead to an increase in the amount that the Home firm is willing to sell!

Tariffs and import quotas have different effects on welfare because they affect the market power of the Home firm differently. With a tariff, the Home firm would lose all its sales if it raised its price above the world price plus the tariff. Hence, the Home firm continues to be a price taker. As long as the Home firm is a price taker, the welfare effect of a tariff is the same as in the case of many Home firms. With a quota, imports cannot respond to price increases by the Home firm. The quota reduces the demand facing the domestic firm, but the firm still faces a downward-sloping demand curve for its output and so has an incentive to restrict output to raise the price. Hence, the quota leads to a higher price and less consumption than does a tariff.

KEY TERMS

Use the space provided to record your notes on the following key terms.

Market power _____

_____

_____

Marginal revenue _____

_____

_____

REVIEW QUESTIONS

Problem 1: Consider an industry in which Home (a small country) has a single firm with an upward sloping marginal cost curve. The price on world markets is P^W.

1a. In the following diagram, show the quantity sold and price charged by the monopolist if international trade is not allowed.

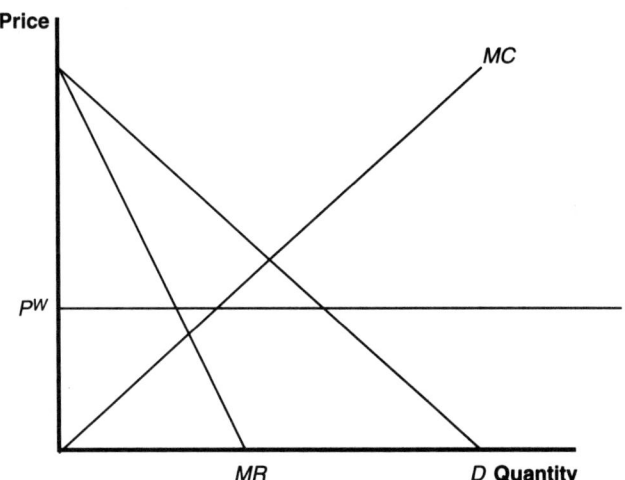

1b. What price is charged by Home's single firm if international trade is allowed? _____

_____

_____

1c. How does international trade affect the quantity sold by Home's single firm? Illustrate your answer in the previous diagram. _____

_____

1d. How does going from autarky to free trade affect the welfare of the monopolist? _____

_____

_____

1e. How does going from free trade to autarky affect consumers' welfare? _____

_____

_____

1f. How does going from autarky to free trade affect national welfare? _____

_____

1g. Suppose the world price were very low (below the intersection of *MR* and *MC*). In this case, how would the monopolist's output react to being exposed to free trade? _____

_____

_____

···

Although producer surplus and profit are different concepts, the producer surplus here continues to be the excess of revenue (price times quantity sold) over the payments to variable factors of production (the area under the marginal cost curve). The difference here is that we are no longer measuring producer surplus with a triangle but with a trapezoid.

TIPS

···

Problem 2: Could free trade increase consumer surplus relative to autarky even if it did not lead to any imports? Explain. _____

_____

_____

Problem 3: Consider an industry in which Home (a small country) has a single firm with an upward sloping marginal cost curve. The price on world markets is P^W. The country is originally engaged in free trade and it imposes a (nonprohibitive) tariff of size t.

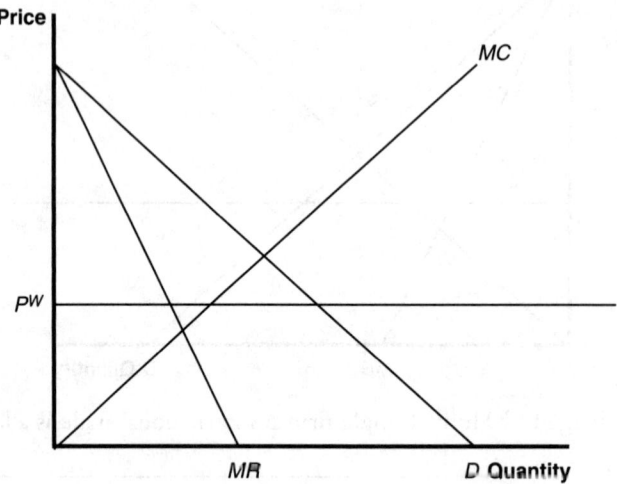

3a. Use the previous diagram to show the effects of this tariff on producer surplus, consumer surplus, and government revenue.

Now suppose instead that the government imposed a quota that yielded the same level of imports as the tariff t.

3b. Which policy (the quota or the tariff) has a larger effect on consumer surplus? Explain.

_____

_____

3c. Would the quota rent created by this quota be bigger than, smaller than, or exactly the same as the revenue generated by the tariff? Explain. _____

_____

···

TIPS

With a tariff the Home firm continues to be a price taker, whereas with a quota the firm has market power. The difference is that with a quota imports cannot respond to a higher price charged by the Home firm.

···

2 Infant Industry Protection

ESSENTIAL CONCEPTS

This section addresses different kinds of *market failure* that are sometime used to justify policies that restrict imports. A key assumption of the model considered in this section is that there is some form of increasing returns to scale over time. Domestic firms have high costs in the short run, but they could have low costs in the long run if they expand their output. Market failures can keep these kinds of increasing returns from being exploited. Two types of market failures, (1) imperfect lending markets and (2) positive *externalities,* are considered. To analyze the effect of imperfect capital markets, we suppose that there is a single firm that has high costs because it has little experience. This firm would make negative profits in the short run because of its high costs, but over time its costs would fall if it were to gain sufficient experience. The firm might be viable in the long run but still fail if it cannot get loans to cover its losses in the short run. A tariff would reduce the firm's losses in the short run (at the expense of lower consumer surplus) but would no longer be needed in the long run once the firm's costs fell to internationally competitive levels. To understand the role of externalities, consider the example of *knowledge spillovers.* Suppose that (1) firms learn from experience so that the knowledge created by one firm is increasing in its output; (2) knowledge from one firm is learned by another (i.e., it spills over); and (3) knowledge lowers a firm's costs. In this setting, firms do not produce enough knowledge and so industry-wide costs are high.

A tariff that expands industry output lowers industry cost, and so firms in the industry can then become competitive on world markets. A tariff that is intended to give firms "time to grow" is called *infant industry protection.* Under the right circumstances, the tariff will help the industry lower its costs so that it will no longer need to be supported by tariffs in the future. A government contemplating this type of policy needs to weigh the short-run cost to consumer surplus induced by a tariff against the long-run benefit of increased producer surplus. This type of argument can also be used to justify protecting existing firms that have fallen behind their international competitors. If a firm has good prospects but is currently struggling and cannot obtain loans from banks, then the government can protect the industry temporarily. An example of such an experience is discussed in the Harley-Davidson case study in the textbook.

KEY TERMS

Use the space provided to record your notes on the following key terms.

Infant industry _____

_____

_____

Externality _____

_____

_____

Market failure _____

_____

_____

Knowledge spillover _____

_____

_____

Problem 4: Suppose you are a government official in charge of tariff policy. A businessperson approaches your office and argues that she could establish a world-class cucumber operation if only a tariff were applied to cucumber imports for next 5 years.

4a. What costs would the proposed policy have on the country? _____

_____

4b. If the world price of cucumbers were P, what would have to be true about the cost of production in cucumbers now and in 5 years to make this a reasonable policy? _____

_____

_____

4c. If capital markets in the country were perfect, would that change your opinion about the validity of this proposal? _____

_____

_____

4d. What other policies could you suggest that would also serve to support an infant industry?

_____

_____

Problem 5: A foreign multinational opens an affiliate in Home. The multinational is the only firm in the industry, and it lobbies the government for infant industry protection.

5a. If the multinational's argument for protection were that capital markets were imperfect, would it be in Home's best interest to follow a policy of infant industry protection in this industry? Explain. _____

_____

_____

_____

5b. If the argument were that there are knowledge spillovers in this industry, would it be in Home's best interest to follow a policy of infant industry protection? Explain. _____

_____

_____

Problem 6: What kind of market failure would justify the protection of Harley-Davidson?

_____

_____

TIPS

For infant industry protection to make sense, a government must be able to identify a real market failure. How would the government know that the industry will eventually become competitive?

3 Tariff with Foreign Monopoly

ESSENTIAL CONCEPTS

When a foreign monopolist supplies the Home market, Home can influence the price charged for its imports. A monopolist chooses to supply the level of output that sets its marginal revenue equal to its marginal cost, and in turn this level of output determines the price in the market. A tariff on a foreign monopolist increases the marginal cost of serving the market and so influences both the level of output supplied by that monopolist and the implied price.

Home can increase its welfare by applying a tariff if the marginal revenue curve facing the monopolist is steeper than the demand curve (as is the case with linear demand). The reason for this is that the monopolist optimally chooses not to pass on all of the tariff increase to consumers, creating a terms-of-trade–like gain for the country. That is, the monopolist bears some of the cost of the tariff. If this gain outweighs the consumer surplus loss (remember there are no producers in Home!), then the country will be better off. The example of the tariff on Japanese trucks illustrates this effect. When the tariff on Japanese trucks was raised from 4% to 25%, the price of a truck to U.S. consumers rose by 12%.

REVIEW QUESTIONS

Problem 7: The demand in Home for a good produced by a foreign monopolist is given by the equation $P = 100 - Q$, where P is the price and Q is the quantity sold. The marginal revenue curve facing the foreign monopolist is then $MR = 100 - 2Q$. Suppose that the foreign monopolist has a constant marginal cost of $10 per unit.

7a. What price does the foreign monopolist charge if there is no tariff? _____

_____

_____

7b. Now suppose that Home puts a $10 per unit tariff on imports of the good. What price does the foreign monopolist charge? _____

_____

_____

7c. What is the impact of the tariff on Home's welfare? _____

_____

_____

_____

Problem 8: Consider the demand and marginal revenue curves in Figure 9-1. These curves are drawn so that the marginal revenue curve is "flatter" than the demand curve ("constant elasticity," for those who care).

8a. Use the following diagram to confirm that a tariff will raise domestic prices by more than the amount of the tariff.

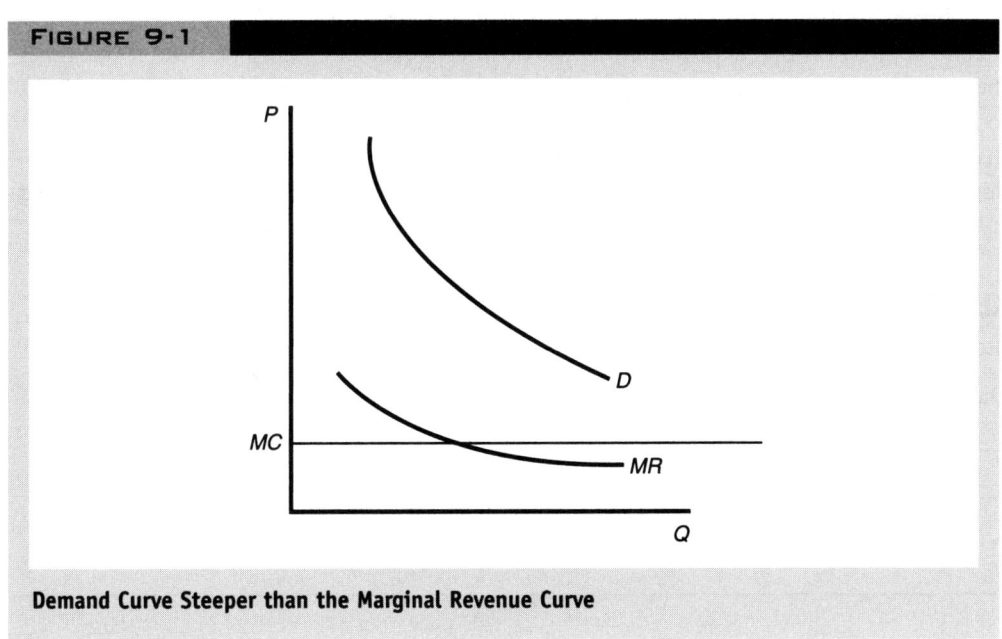

FIGURE 9-1

Demand Curve Steeper than the Marginal Revenue Curve

8b. In this case, can a tariff on the foreign monopolist raise national welfare? Explain. _____

_____

_____

··

TIPS

Home can always affect the price charged by the foreign firm, but whether there is a terms-of-trade gain from the tariff depends on the shape of the demand curve.

The equation for marginal revenue for a linear demand curve was derived in Chapter 6. Review that discussion.

··

4 Policy Response to Dumping

ESSENTIAL CONCEPTS

As discussed in detail in Chapter 6, the phenomenon of "dumping" naturally arises in models of imperfect competition. An imported product is being dumped (a) if its price is below the price that the exporter charges in its own local market or (b) if the exporter's local price is not available; then dumping is determined by comparing the import price with (1) a price charged for the product in a third market or (2) the exporter's average costs of production. Under the rules of the WTO, an importing country is entitled to apply an antidumping tariff when a foreign firm is dumping its product and this dumping has caused "material injury" to domestic firms.

Unlike other trade policies, such as the *safeguard tariff,* a foreign firm can influence the level of a tariff that it faces in a market by changing the price that it charges for its good. The antidumping duty (the tariff) that is actually applied will be equal to the difference between the price charged by the firm and its "fair value." By raising its price to the "fair value," the foreign firm can avoid a tariff on its product altogether. It is for this reason that antidumping policy creates a situation in which the home country loses from the mere existence of the policy. Prices are high because of the threat of the antidumping duty, but the antidumping duty is never applied so there is no tariff revenue.

The application that is presented in the chapter is crucial reading because it illustrates the excessive usage of antidumping policy. Evidence that antidumping policy often leads to a change in the behavior of foreign firms is the high percentage of antidumping cases that are withdrawn and settled. U.S. antidumping law actually permits U.S. firms to withdraw their case and agree with foreign firms on the level of prices and market shares. That is, the law encourages collusion between domestic and foreign firms in the U.S. market.

KEY TERMS

Use the space provided to record your notes on the following key terms.

Dumping _____

_____

_____

Antidumping duty _____

_____

_____

Countervailing duty _____

_____

_____

Material injury _____

_____

_____

Discriminating monopoly _____

_____

_____

Safeguard tariff _____

_____

_____

REVIEW QUESTIONS

Problem 9: Consider the following (fictional) claim of a government official. "Since we implemented our antidumping policy, we have not applied antidumping duties to any foreign products. Therefore, the policy could not have had any effect on foreign producers." Discuss.

_____

_____

_____

Problem 10: Why do firms make claims of dumping so often? _____

_____

_____

Problem 11: Under the antidumping procedure in the United States, can antidumping duties be applied if there is no domestic competitor? _____

_____

_____

There was a time when antidumping was justified by the fear of "predatory pricing." Modern treatments of dumping rarely mention this possibility because the way that antidumping laws are applied tends to reduce rather than increase competition.

TIPS

10

Export Subsidies in Agriculture and High-Technology Industries

Overview

Export and production subsidies provided by developed-country governments to local farmers are perhaps the single most contentious issue in the current WTO negotiations. The effects of these subsidies are analyzed using the perfectly competitive, partial equilibrium model first introduced in Chapter 7. The assumption of perfect competition in agriculture is reasonable given the relatively large number of farms. Both export and production subsidies aid the producers that receive them, but both types of subsidies inevitably reduce the national welfare of the country offering them. Of the two types of subsidies, the production subsidy raises producer surplus with the least amount of harm to national welfare because it does not lower consumer surplus. This result is an example of the *targeting principle:* Policies that have a direct impact on a government objective are more efficient than policies that have an indirect impact.

Export and production subsidies tend to lower the terms of trade of a large exporting country. The change in the terms of trade has an impact on foreign countries. Importing countries are made better off as the lower price increases their consumer surplus by more than it reduces their producer surplus. Other countries that export agricultural products are hurt, however, as their terms of trade deteriorate as well. In general, producers not receiving the subsidies are made worse off, and this helps explain why subsidies are a hot button issue in the current WTO negotiations.

Subsidies are also relatively common in high-technology industries where imperfect competition is the normal state of affairs. Because strategic behavior is common in imperfect competition, *game theory* is used to understand the *strategic* impact of government subsidies. Unlike the case of perfect competition, subsidies in imperfectly competitive industries are shown to have the potential to increase the welfare of the country that offers them. These welfare gains arise if the subsidy can cause profits that would otherwise be enjoyed by foreign producers to be *shifted* to domestic producers. The benefits of subsidies in these industries are not guaranteed, however, and depend on the details of the international competition in that industry. The well-publicized case of Boeing and Airbus' competition in the global market for large, wide-bodied aircraft is used to illustrate the issues involved.

1   WTO Goals on Agricultural Export Subsidies

ESSENTIAL CONCEPTS

Agriculture is one of the important issues at the current Doha negotiations of the WTO. Progress has been made in the negotiations to eliminate agricultural export subsidies, but production subsidies and tariffs on agricultural products continue to be sticking points. The agricultural subsidies and tariffs imposed by developed countries have a serious impact on the terms of trade of many developing countries, such as Brazil, because these countries have a comparative advantage in agriculture. On the flip side, developed countries want developing countries to open their markets in service industries where developed countries have a comparative advantage. One goal of the current negotiations is to improve the access of developing countries to developed countries' markets in manufacturing industries. Currently, the target is to allow developing countries to have tariff-free access to developed countries' markets in 97% of imported products. The key issues to absorb from this section are largely factual. Table 9.1 in the textbook summarizes the negotiating agenda.

KEY TERMS

Use the space provided to record your notes on the following key terms.

Common agricultural policy (CAP) _____

_____

_____

Indirect subsidies _____

_____

_____

Domestic farm supports _____

_____

_____

REVIEW QUESTIONS

Problem 1: Why would developed-country food aid to developing countries be an area of discussion in trade talks? _____

_____

_____

Problem 2: Could a tax credit on the purchase of fertilizer be an issue at the WTO? Explain.

_____

_____

TIPS

The focus of the GATT at its inception in 1947 was to lower trade barriers in manufacturing. Agriculture and services were largely ignored at the time. This is one reason for the importance of these areas in recent rounds of negotiations.

2 Agricultural Export Subsidies in a Small Home Country

ESSENTIAL CONCEPTS

The perfect competition, partial equilibrium model introduced in Chapter 7 is used to analyze the impact of an export subsidy. In the case of a small Home country, the world price is fixed at P^W. An export subsidy of size s raises the amount that producers earn by selling their product on world markets to $P^{W+}s$. Because producers would be unwilling to sell their product in Home for any less than what they can receive by exporting their output, the domestic price rises to $P^{W+}s$. The higher domestic price induces Home producers to expand their supply and Home consumers to contract their demand, leading to an increase in the volume of the country's exports. Because at any given world price, Home is willing to export more, the export supply curve is shifted to the right in the world market diagram.

Because Home is an exporter of the subsidized good, the higher price in Home expands producer surplus by more than it reduces consumer surplus. Home's national welfare falls, however, because the cost of the subsidy to the government is greater than the gain in producer surplus. Hence, the export subsidy creates deadweight loss equal to the sum of the production and consumption losses (producers are making too much and consumers are demanding too little). In the case of linear supply and demand, the deadweight loss can be calculated as the area of a triangle. The triangle has height equal to the size of the subsidy, and the base is the increase in exports.

KEY TERMS

Use the space provided to record your notes on the following key terms.

Consumption loss _____

_____

_____

Production loss _____

_____

_____

REVIEW QUESTIONS

Problem 3: Explain why a country that imposes an export subsidy often enacts an import tariff on the same product simultaneously. _____

_____

Problem 4: Figure 10-1 illustrates Home's export supply curve. Home is small and faces a world price of $10, at which it is willing to sell 100 units. Suppose that Home's government offers an export subsidy of $1 per unit export and exports rise to 120 units.

4a. What is the cost of the subsidy to the government? _____

_____

_____

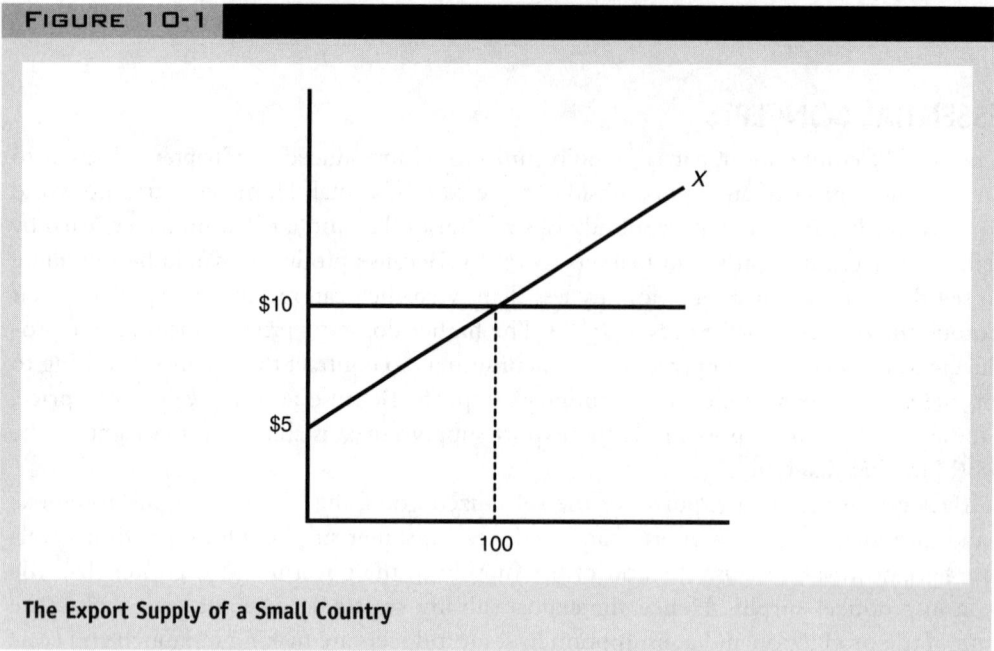

The Export Supply of a Small Country

4b. What is the effect of the subsidy on national welfare? _____

_____

_____

4c. Show the deadweight loss and cost of the subsidy in Figure 10-1.

Problem 5: A small home country imposes an export subsidy of size *s*. The effects of the subsidy are shown in Figure 10-2.

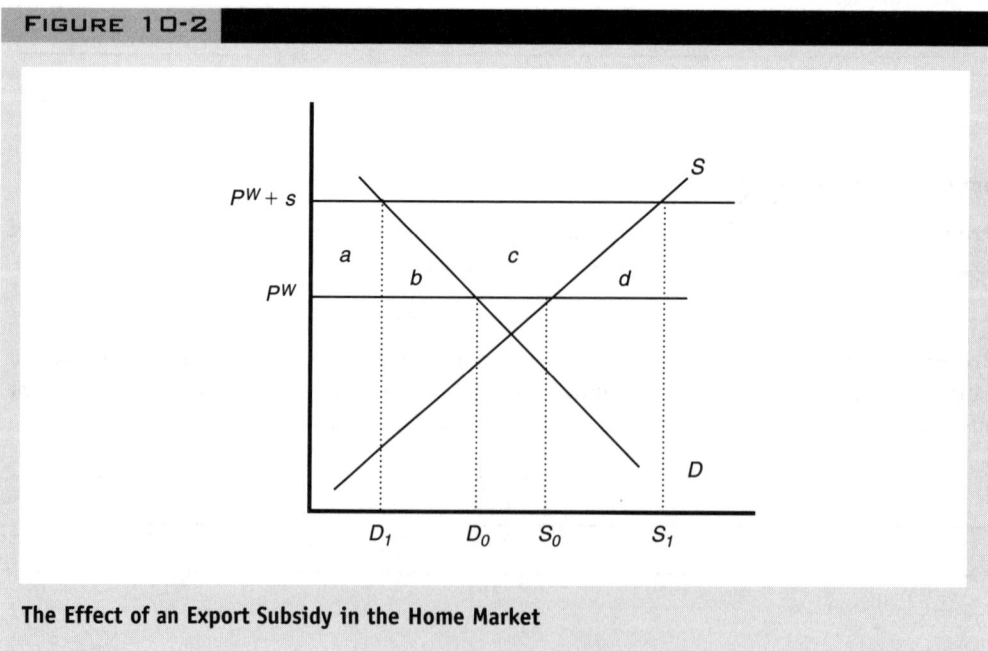

The Effect of an Export Subsidy in the Home Market

5a. What is the cost of the subsidy to the government? _____

5b. What is the effect of the subsidy on producer surplus? _____

5c. Using the information on prices and quantities, provide a formula for the size of the consumption loss. _____

Problem 6: Suppose Home is an importer of chocolate. The country is small and so the price of chocolate on world markets is fixed. Could the country use an export subsidy to turn the country into an exporter of chocolate? Explain. _____

_____

_____

....

There are gains from trade between countries, but this does not mean that exports should be subsidized. This is not obvious to many who have not taken a class in international trade.

TIPS

....

3 Agricultural Export Subsidies in a Large Home Country

ESSENTIAL CONCEPTS

In the perfect competition, partial equilibrium model, an export subsidy hurts a large exporter even more than it hurts a small exporter. An export subsidy induces Home to increase its supply on world markets. Because Home is large, it faces a downward-sloping import demand curve and the increased supply of the good on world market drives down the world price. Thus, an export subsidy gives rise to a *terms-of-trade loss* for the exporting country. This loss represents a transfer of welfare from the Home country's government to foreign consumers. Home's welfare falls by the sum of the deadweight loss and the terms–of–trade loss of the subsidy.

KEY TERMS

Use the space provided to record your notes on the following key term.

Terms of trade _____

_____

_____

REVIEW QUESTIONS

Problem 7: Home is a large exporter of bikes on international markets. The country exports 100 bikes for $100 apiece. The government imposes an export subsidy of $10 per bike. As a result, exports rise by 50 units and the world price of bikes falls to $95 per bike.

7a. What is the cost of the export subsidy to the government? _____

_____

7b. What is the effect of the subsidy on Home's welfare? (Provide a number.) _____

_____

_____

7c. What is the effect of the subsidy on Foreign's welfare? (Provide a number.)

_____

_____

7d. Show the effect of the export subsidy on the welfare of consumers and producers in the importing country Foreign on the following diagram.

Foreign market

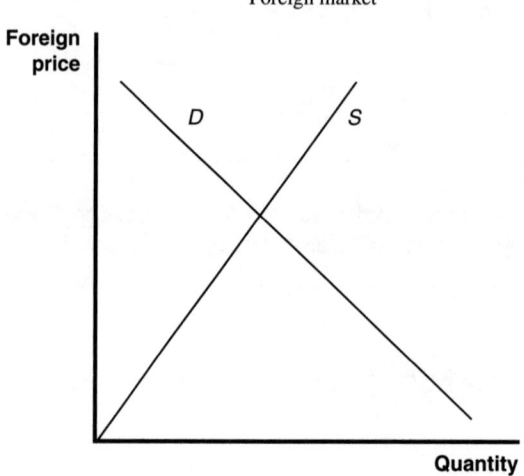

7e. Use the following world market diagram to illustrate the terms-of-trade effects and deadweight losses to each country.

World market

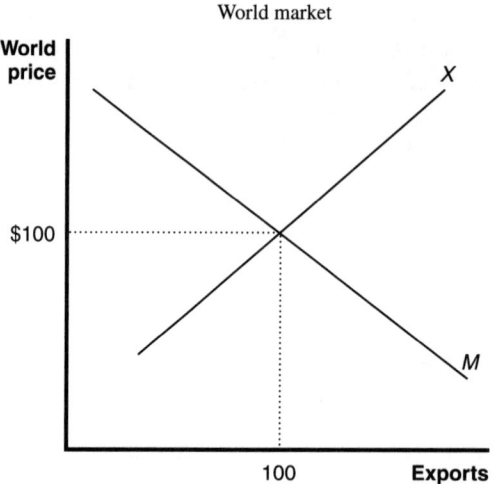

7f. Could Foreign accuse Home firms of "dumping" their product in their market?

_____

7g. What other WTO-sanctioned trade policy could be implemented by Foreign in this situation? _____

_____

It is important to notice that Home's terms-of-trade loss exceeds Foreign's national welfare gain. This motivates the argument that if increasing Foreign's welfare is the main objective of a policy, a direct cash payment to Foreign is more efficient.

Export subsidies create price gaps between exporting and importing countries that could result in the importing country charging the exporting country with dumping.

Problem 8: Suppose that Home imposes an export *tax* so that to export one unit of a good, an exporter would have to pay T. Home is large on world markets.

8a. Using the following diagram, illustrate the effect of the export tax on the volume of exports, the price on world markets, and the price in the home market.

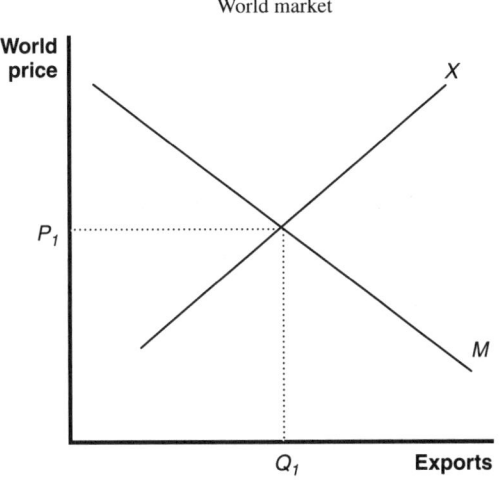

World market

8b. What is the effect of the export tax on Home's producer surplus, consumer surplus, and government revenue? _____

_____

_____

8c. Compare and contrast the effect of an export tax on national welfare with that of an export subsidy. _____

_____

_____

....

An export tax is just a negative export subsidy. As such, its welfare effects are exactly opposite those of an export subsidy. Whereas an export subsidy inevitably causes a loss of national welfare, an export tax (like an import tariff) can raise domestic welfare.

TIPS

....

4 Agricultural Production Subsidies

ESSENTIAL CONCEPTS

Export subsidies lower a country's welfare but raise the surplus enjoyed by its producers. If the primary goal of the policy is to increase producer surplus, then a *production subsidy* will accomplish this goal at a lower cost than an export subsidy. To see this, consider a small home country. A production subsidy raises the price paid to producers to the world price plus the subsidy, but it has no impact on the price paid by consumers. Because the price paid by consumers does not change, there is no loss in consumer surplus when a production subsidy is paid. Hence, a production subsidy raises producer surplus in a manner similar to that of an export subsidy, but there is no consumption distortion associated with the production subsidy. Because a production subsidy achieves the same objective as an export subsidy while causing less damage, it is the preferred policy. The *targeting prin-*

ciple holds that it is best to use the policy instrument that achieves the objective most directly.

Both types of subsidies will result in terms-of-trade effects if the exporter is a large country. For this reason, a production subsidy also falls under Article XVI of the GATT. However, because domestic consumption does not fall in the case of the production subsidy, the effect of the subsidy on exports is smaller than it would be if an export subsidy were used to raise producer surplus by the same amount. Hence, the terms-of-trade loss caused by a production subsidy is smaller than the loss caused by an export subsidy.

KEY TERMS

Use the space provided to record your notes on the following key terms.

Production subsidy _____

_____

_____

Targeting principle _____

_____

_____

REVIEW QUESTIONS

Problem 9: Consider the information in Figure 10-3. A subsidy of size $s = \$5$ has altered the production of a small home country.

_____

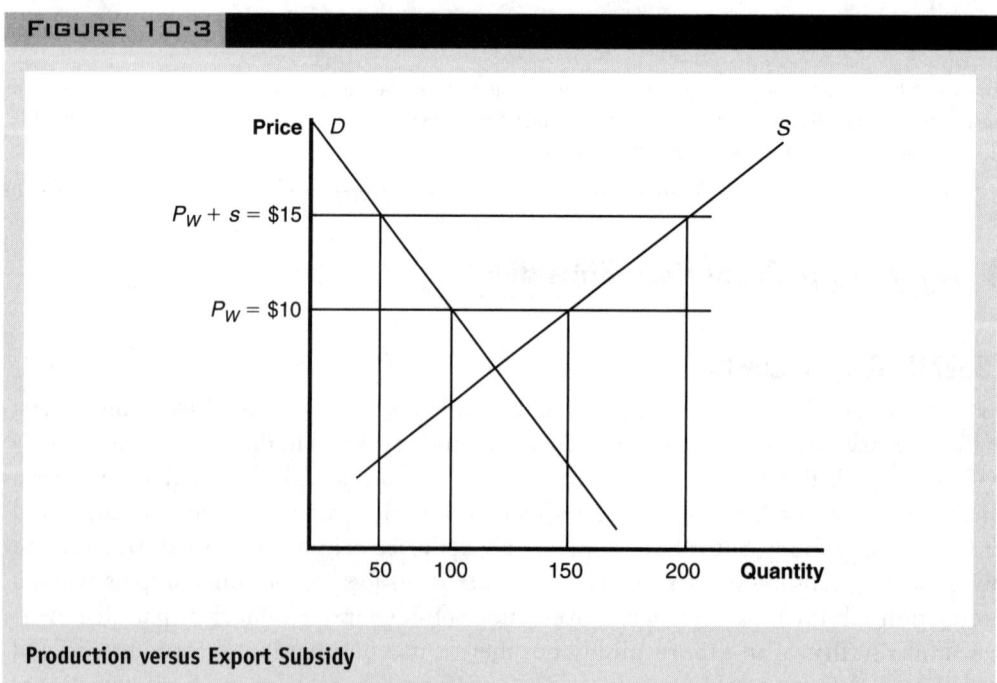

FIGURE 10-3

Production versus Export Subsidy

9a. Is the budgetary cost to the government to induce producers to make 200 units higher for a production or export subsidy? _____

_____

9b. What is the size of the production loss (provide a number) of either a production subsidy or an export subsidy? _____

_____

9c. What is the size of the consumption loss for the two types of subsidies? _____

_____

9d. How large is the additional national welfare loss if an export subsidy is chosen rather than a production subsidy? _____

_____

9e. If Home were a large country, which type of subsidy would have the biggest impact on Foreign's producers? _____

_____

_____

9f. If Home were a large country, what would be the effect of a production subsidy on consumer surplus in Home? Explain. _____

_____

_____

_____

Any policy that has an impact on world prices has an effect on foreign welfare.

TIPS

Problem 10: Suppose Home, a small country, is importing a good and the government wishes to raise the producer surplus by offering a production subsidy. Could the subsidy induce the country to become an exporter of the good? _____

_____

_____

Problem 10 illustrates just how distortionary subsidies can be. An import tariff could never induce a country to become an exporter in this framework.

TIPS

5 High-Technology Export Subsidies

ESSENTIAL CONCEPTS

Our analysis of the model with perfect competition led to the very strong implication that subsidies, whether they are subsidies to exports or to production, lowered the subsidizing country's welfare. Yet, such subsides are common. There are two possible explanations. First, these subsidies may worsen national welfare but are implemented by governments that favor producers over consumers, perhaps for political reasons. Second, there is something important missing in the model and these subsidies are actually in the national interest. It is this second possibility that is explored in the final section of this chapter.

One possible motive for subsidies is to increase the volume of an activity that provides positive *externalities* to others. Such externalities are thought to be important in high-technology industries. Because this argument is familiar to the earlier discussion on infant industry protection in Chapter 9, this possibility is not discussed in any detail here.

Another possible motive for subsidies occurs when there is *imperfect competition* in an industry. When an industry is imperfectly competitive, two issues arise. On one hand, firms in these industries behave strategically and their actions are best understood using *game theory*. On the other hand, firms in imperfectly competitive industries may earn profits. Under these conditions, it is possible that government subsides can change the nature of competition between firms in such a way that profits earned by foreign firms are shifted to domestic firms. Such a shift of profits can improve the national welfare of the country offering the subsidy.

The classic critique of this argument is that for such "strategic trade policy" to be desirable the conditions in an industry have to meet a number of criteria, and these conditions are not easily assessed by the government. When these criteria are not met, the subsidy could reduce national welfare in much the same way that it would reduce welfare in the perfectly competitive model. Whatever the effect of the subsidy on the welfare of the country imposing the subsidy, the subsidy always has an impact on the welfare of the other country.

Because game theory will be used more than once in this book and because not all introductory economics classes deal with game theory, it is worth some review. In the games considered in this book, there will always be two players who have to decide which of two actions they will take. Each action taken by one player yields a payoff to the player, but the size of this payoff depends on the action taken by the other player. It is this fact that gives rise to the need for a player to have a "strategy:" If the other player chooses action A, I will choose action B. A Nash equilibrium to a game occurs when each player is choosing the action that gives the highest payoff to that player given the action chosen by the other player.

Consider the following example. The two players are Hank and Mick, who have been arrested by the police for two crimes. The police have hard evidence that each is guilty of a minor crime and believe that they have committed a more serious crime. They are being separately questioned by the police, and each can take two actions: They may (1) *confess* to the serious crime or (2) keep *quiet*. If both Hank and Mick choose to keep quiet, they will both be convicted of the minor crime and will serve 2 years in jail. If both Hank and Mick confess, they will each serve 4 years. If only one of the two confesses, then the one that confesses will serve only 1 year in jail and the other will serve 6 years in jail. Hank and Mick want to serve as little jail time as possible.

This game is known as the "prisoner's dilemma," and it is used as an example at several junctures in the book. The key point made by this example is that two players (in this book, generally governments conducting policy) would be better off if they could cooperate, but each player has an incentive to deviate from cooperative behavior. As a result, the strategic behavior of the players results in their being made worse off. To see this, let us analyze the game. The first step is to organize the information so that the relationship between the payoffs to each player and the actions of each player is clear. This is done in the following payoff matrix.

		Mick	
		Confess	Quiet
Hank	Confess	−4 −4	−6 −1
	Quiet	−1 −6	−2 −2

In this payoff matrix, each row corresponds to the action taken by Hank and each column corresponds to an action taken by Mick. In each box, the number in the lower left-hand corner corresponds to the payoff to Hank and the upper right-hand corner corresponds to the payoff to Mick given the permutation of actions chosen by the two players. For instance, if Mick confesses and Hank does not, Hank will get a payoff of −6 and Mick will get a payoff of −1. (Jail time is bad, so the numbers are negatives!)

The *Nash equilibrium* to the game occurs when each player is choosing the action that yields the highest payoff to that player *given the action chosen by the other player.* Suppose Mick was to confess; then the best action for Hank to take would be to confess as well, because −4 is greater than −6. If Mick were to stay quiet, Hank's best action would be to confess, because a payoff of −1 is better than a payoff of −2. Given the symmetry of Mick's payoffs to Hank's payoffs, the Nash equilibrium of this game is that both Hank and Mick confess because only then will each player be choosing the best action given the action of the other.

Although the prisoner's dilemma example has a single equilibrium, other games with different payoffs can have more than one. This is the case in the Boeing-Airbus game presented in the textbook. To see how sensitive the equilibrium is to the payoffs, suppose that in the Mick and Hank example both players can avoid any jail time if neither confesses while all the other payoffs remain the same. In this case, the game has two equilibria: one in which both confess and one in which both stay quiet. Without any additional information, we cannot predict which equilibrium will be observed.

KEY TERMS

Use the space provided to record your notes on the following key terms.

Duopoly _____

_____

_____

Game theory _____

_____

_____

Nash equilibrium _____

_____

_____

First mover advantage _____

_____

_____

Externality _____

_____

_____

Payoff matrix _____

_____

_____

REVIEW QUESTIONS

Problem 11: Consider the Airbus–Boeing model outlined in the textbook.

11a. Is there any welfare loss analogous to the deadweight loss in this model? _____

_____

_____

11b. What would happen to welfare in the two countries if the United States were to retaliate against European Union subsidies by offering a subsidy of its own? _____

_____

_____

11c. Given your answer to 11b, explain the motivation for the United States and the European Union to sign their 1992 trade agreement on large aircraft. _____

_____

_____

TIPS
The argument made in this section fits the details of the Airbus-Boeing relationship quite well, but few other industries fit the description this well.

As well as conditions in the large-body aircraft fit the model, the subsequent distress that Airbus has experienced suggests that one should be careful using the model to interpret the situation in the industry.

11

International Agreements:
Trade, Labor, and the Environment

Overview

International agreements impose restrictions on the policies of their signatories. Countries allow their own policy options to be restricted by an agreement because the agreement also restricts the policies of the other participating countries. For instance, countries that belong to the WTO are expected to adhere to a set of obligations, such as the most favored nation principle. This chapter discusses international agreements that influence polices in areas that are relevant to international trade, including trade policy, labor standards, and environmental regulation.

The World Trade Organization is the result of a *multilateral trade agreement* that is designed to overcome a particular *prisoner's dilemma* between countries. Countries have an incentive to protect domestic industries, but tariffs and quotas have a negative impact on their trading partners. If everyone has an incentive to protect, then the outcome can result in collectively small gains from trade. Each party would be better off with free trade but, given the protection offered by other countries, sees it in its best interest to offer protection as well.

A *regional trade agreement* (RTA) requires its adherents to allow free trade to its signatories while maintaining tariffs on countries outside the agreement. These agreements can create trade between participating countries, but they can also divert trade from countries outside the agreement. Regional trade agreements often include *side agreements* on *labor standards*. These standards involve regulations on labor issues such as occupational safety and child labor. Developing countries accept these labor standards in order to be allowed into regional trade agreements with developed countries. Policymakers in developing countries and many trade economists worry that these agreements might be *disguised protectionism,* inspired at least in part by a desire to increase the cost of production in low-wage countries.

The final type of international agreement discussed in the chapter is *multilateral environmental agreements,* which deal specifically with environmental policy. Many issues arise within the context of the WTO, which allows countries to maintain their own environmental regulations as long as these regulations are equally applied to foreign and domestic firms. A larger, perhaps more contentious, issue is whether international trade tends to harm the environment. This concern has theoretical justification, particularly in the case of *common property.* International trade can exacerbate the *tragedy of the commons,* leading to more rapid depletion of natural resources, and can give rise to a different form of the prisoner's dilemma. Once again, the existence of a prisoner's dilemma suggests the need for more extensive international agreements.

1 International Trade Agreements

ESSENTIAL CONCEPTS

Multilateral trade agreements and regional trade agreements are designed to reduce trade barriers between countries. Multilateral agreements involve a wide range of countries, whereas RTAs are often limited in scope to as few as two countries. With more than 140 member countries, the WTO is the crowning example of a multilateral trade agreement. The WTO owes its existence to the desire among its members to overcome a prisoner's dilemma. To illustrate the nature of the prisoner's dilemma, consider a world with two countries, Home and Foreign. Home exports good A and imports good B, and Foreign imports good A and exports good B. By imposing the optimal tariff on good B, Home can increase its welfare at Foreign's expense because its terms-of-trade gain exceeds its deadweight loss. Foreign's welfare falls by the sum of its terms-of-trade loss and its deadweight loss. Foreign can increase its welfare at Home's expense by applying a tariff on good A. When both countries apply a tariff, the terms-of-trade gains in their import goods are exactly canceled out by the terms-of-trade losses in the export goods, so all that is left is deadweight loss in both industries. The outcome is the Nash equilibrium to the prisoner's dilemma game. The WTO is designed to overcome the prisoner's dilemma by (1) imposing rules on the application of trade policies, (2) providing a forum for countries to negotiate lower tariffs on each other's goods, and (3) providing a dispute settlement mechanism.

An alternative to multilateral trade agreements is *regional trade agreements.* RTAs occur when several countries eliminate trade barriers between signatories to the agreement but maintain tariffs against countries outside the agreement. These agreements are inherently discriminatory because countries outside the agreement do not get the same treatment. This exception to the MFN principle is allowed in Article XIV of the GATT. Because these agreements are inherently discriminatory, their detractors often refer to them as *preferential trade agreements.*

RTAs come in two forms: *free-trade areas* and *customs unions.* Although both types of agreements involve free trade between members, customs unions require member countries to share a single tariff code on countries outside the agreement, whereas free-trade areas allow countries to have different tariff codes. Countries impose *rules of origin* to avoid the importation of goods into the lower-tariff country in a free-trade area followed by trans-shipment to the higher-tariff country.

Although RTAs lower trade barriers between countries, they may or may not increase welfare. RTAs have two types of effects on trading patterns. *Trade creation* occurs when a member country imports a product from another member country that it formerly produced for itself. *Trade diversion* occurs when a country switches its import supplier from a country outside the agreement to a country inside the agreement. Trade diversion can lead to a welfare loss for the importing country because it no longer collects tariff revenues. From a global point of view, trade diversion causes a less efficient use of the world's resources as production is reallocated away from a low-cost producer to a high-cost producer.

KEY TERMS

Use the space provided to record your notes on the following key terms.

Multilateral agreement _____

_____

_____

Terms-of-trade gain _____

_____

_____

Prisoner's dilemma _____

_____

_____

Regional trade agreements _____

_____

_____

Preferential trade agreements _____

_____

_____

Free-trade area _____

_____

_____

Customs union _____

_____

_____

Rules of origin _____

_____

_____

Trade creation _____

_____

_____

Trade diversion _____

_____

_____

REVIEW QUESTIONS

Problem 1: The prisoner's dilemma set out in the textbook featured a world with two large countries. Would this logic hold if there were only one large country and many small countries? Explain. _____

_____

_____

Problem 2: Suppose that many small countries were to form a customs union. What impact might the customs union have on the prisoner's dilemma? _____

_____

_____

TIPS

The assumption that the two countries are identical in the formulation of the prisoner's dilemma is important. If one country gains more from following its optimal tariff than the other, it becomes less clear that country would benefit from international trade agreements.

Problem 3: Suppose that Home joins a free-trade area. Is it possible that Home simultaneously imports a homogeneous good from outside the free-trade area and exports the same good to a member of the free-trade area? Explain.

_____

_____

_____

Problem 4: Use the diagram for Home's market to show an example of trade creation in a RTA.

Home Market

Problem 5: Home's market could be served by its own producers, who have constant marginal cost of C_H; by country B, whose producers have marginal cost C_B; or by country A, whose producers have marginal cost C_A. Home has the largest marginal cost and country A has the smallest marginal cost. Home initially applies the most favored nation tariff t to both A and B.

5a. If Home forms a regional trade agreement with country A, could this agreement lead to trade diversion? If so, under what circumstances? _____

_____

_____

5b. If Home forms a regional trade agreement with country B, could this agreement lead to trade creation? If so, under what circumstances? _____

_____

_____

Now suppose that Home does not produce the good at all. The marginal costs for countries A and B and Home's demand are shown in Figure 11-1.

5c. Illustrate the case of trade diversion in Figure 11-1 by drawing the effect of the tariff on the cost of the country outside the regional free-trade arrangement.

FIGURE 11-1

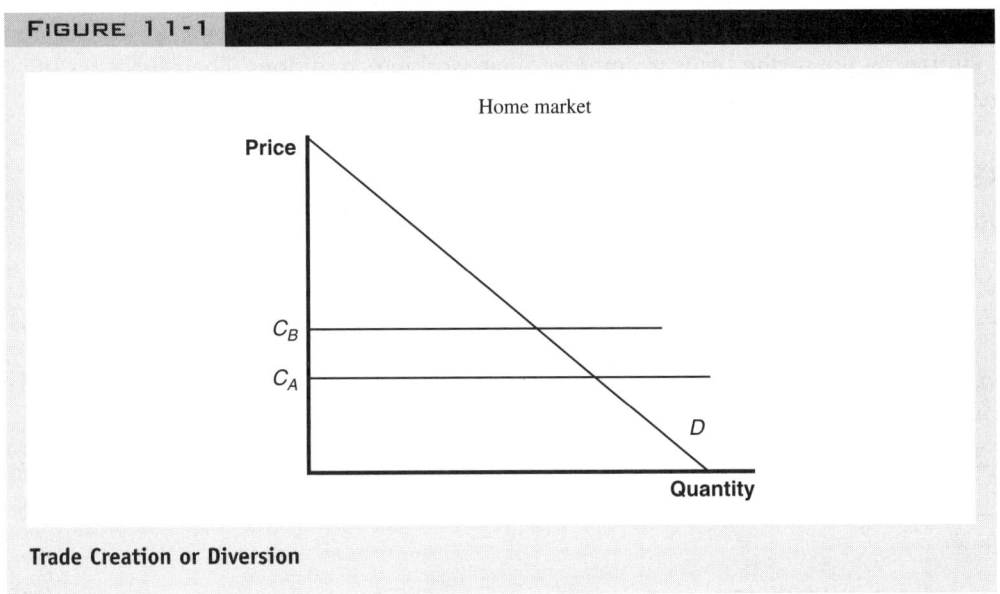

Home market

Trade Creation or Diversion

5d. In your diagram answer to question 5c, is there any welfare benefit from the RTA? Explain. _____

_____

_____

It is possible that even in a particular industry a regional trade diversion could improve a country's welfare if it leads to a substantial increase in imports. Experiment with different drawings of Figure 11-1 so that an RTA results in different magnitudes of changes in consumer surplus relative to loss tariff revenue.

2 International Agreements on Labor Issues

ESSENTIAL CONCEPTS

RTAs are often accompanied by *side agreements* that are not directly related to trade policies. When the levels of economic development differ substantially across countries within the RTA, these side agreements are often over *labor standards,* which cover areas such as occupational health and safety, child labor, and minimum wages. Consumers and policymakers favor labor standards out of concern for working conditions abroad. Labor unions often push for labor standards as part of trade agreements out of concern that poor labor standards abroad create more competition for U.S. workers.

Economists and policy makers in developing countries are skeptical about the motive for and benefits of attaching labor standards to trade agreements. Many see the emphasis on labor standards as a form of *disguised protectionism* because the regulations may result in much higher costs of production in the affected countries. Of particular concern is pressure to require developing country firms to pay a *living wage*. Although a living wage is not well defined, it can be construed to mean a wage that is higher than the norm in developing countries. Economic theory suggests that wages that are well above the market wage would either increase unemployment in developing countries or would force people into the unregulated informal sectors.

Finally, some evidence is presented that nongovernmental organizations (NGOs) have been effective at reducing some of the most egregious forms of abuse in developing countries by pressuring firms to improve their working conditions. Their successes suggest that bad publicity can be an effective tool for changing firms' behavior.

KEY TERMS

Use the space provided to record your notes on the following key terms.

Labor standards _____

_____

_____

Living wage _____

_____

_____

REVIEW QUESTIONS

Problem 6: According to a survey by the National Bureau of Economic Research, consumers were willing to pay a premium for items made under good working conditions. How could a NGO use this sentiment to improve working conditions in developing countries?

_____

_____

Problem 7: Explain why economists are wary of trade agreements with developing countries that include labor standards? _____

_____

_____

Problem 8: Suppose there are two sectors in an economy: the formal sector, which is subject to government regulations, and the informal sector, which is not subject to government regulations. Each sector has a specific factor associated with it, and labor is mobile between the two sectors. Prices of the goods produced by the two sectors are fixed on world markets. Suppose the government imposed a "living wage" on the formal sector that was above the market wage.

8a. What would happen to employment in the formal sector? Explain. _____

_____

_____

_____

8b. What would happen to the wage paid in the informal sector? Explain. _____

_____

_____

_____

3 International Agreements on the Environment

ESSENTIAL CONCEPTS

Many environmentalists are suspicious of international trade in general and the WTO in particular. Policies toward the environment can run afoul of WTO rules when they have consequences for international trade. For instance, the U.S. Marine Mammal Protection Act requires that tuna fishers use nets that do not inadvertently catch dolphins. When imports of tuna from Mexico were banned by the United States in 1991, the GATT (the WTO did not yet exist) ruled that the ban violated GATT rules on nondiscrimination. In looking at WTO rules, however, it is not obvious that they are stacked against the environment. *Article XX* of the GATT allows countries to adopt any environmental laws they please, provided that these laws are applied uniformly to domestic and foreign producers. The problem arises when a country regulates the *production process method* rather than the product itself. Past WTO rulings have not allowed countries to ban imports on the basis of their production process method, ruling that such a ban is essentially an effort to force one country's regulations onto another. The WTO has had no problem, however, with products being labeled in such a way to report the production process method so that concerned consumers can avoid products made in an environmentally unfriendly way.

Does international trade by its very nature accelerate the degradation of the environment? This is an open question, and plenty of examples can be found to support either side of the argument. For instance, in the United States the most fuel-efficient cars tend to be built by foreign manufacturers, so limiting these imports would worsen fuel efficiency in the United States. Those who are concerned that international trade has a negative impact on the environment can find plenty of theoretical support for their argument. This is particularly true in areas in which natural resources are *common property*. Common property tends to be overused, a phenomenon commonly referred to as the *tragedy of the commons*. International trade can exacerbate the tragedy of the commons by directing global demand toward the resource of a particular country or region, so that there is even more overuse of natural resources under free trade. Examples abound. For instance, the overharvesting of tropical wood is certainly encouraged by a large global market. Global pollutants, such as carbon dioxide emissions, present a problem similar to the tragedy of the commons: Weak regulation can give a country a production advantage while all countries suffer the consequences of the pollution. As another example of a prisoner's dilemma, this situation calls for multilateral agreements.

KEY TERMS

Use the space provided to record your notes on the following key terms.

Multilateral environmental agreements _____

_____

_____

Tragedy of the commons _____

_____

_____

Common property _____

_____

Kyoto protocol _____

_____

_____

REVIEW QUESTIONS

Problem 9: Home requires the use of at least 40% recycled paper in cardboard boxes and bans imports of Foreign boxes because they use no recycled paper.

9a. If Foreign complains to the WTO, how is the WTO likely to rule? _____

_____

_____

9b. If Home were to require cardboard boxes manufacturers to label the recycled paper content of their boxes, would this violate WTO rules? _____

_____

_____

Problem 10: Suppose that rich countries have stronger feelings toward the environment than poor countries, goods differ in the amount of pollution they create, and pollution regulations impose higher costs on "dirtier" industries. How might a reduction in tariffs brought about by the WTO affect pollution? _____

_____

_____

_____

Problem 11: The "sneed" industry produces a product that everyone needs as well as a great deal of pollution. Suppose that many identical countries have sneed firms. The pollution can be controlled using alternative production techniques, but this raises the marginal cost of production.

11a. If the pollution created by the sneed industry is primarily local, is an international agreement necessary? _____

_____

_____

Now suppose that the pollution created by the sneed industry is global.

11b. If all countries require the sneed industry to use the low pollution production technique, what happens to the price of sneeds on world markets? _____

_____

_____

11c. Suppose that your country is the only one not to sign on to an international agreement requiring the use of low pollution production techniques. What happens to producer surplus in your sneed industry once the agreement is put into place? _____

_____

_____

_____

11d. Given your answer to 11c, explain why might it be hard to get all countries to sign on to an international agreement on sneed production techniques? _____

_____

_____

Problem 10 gets at the "pollution haven hypothesis." The hypothesis is that tariff reduction is likely to lead to a migration of the production of dirty industries to poor countries with poor environmental regulations.

Problem 11 makes the point that when there are many countries there is an incentive for individual countries to free ride on the beneficial actions of others.

TIPS

Answers to Study Guide Problems

Trade in the Global Economy

1. In the example given in the book, the United States has a large trade deficit with China. But this does not mean that the goods are built entirely in China. In fact, China imports a lot of inputs from other countries, which in turn are part of the value of the good. In a sense, then, these imports contain value added from many countries.

2. Small countries that have many nearby trading partners have higher ratios of trade to GDP. Because the internal market is so large in a country like the United States, its international trade is a relatively small portion of its total output.

3. Hong Kong and Malaysia import a lot of goods, add a little value to these goods, and then re-export them to the rest of the world. The trade volumes are "gross" in the sense that they include value added from abroad, but GDP is "net" in the sense that it includes only local value added.

4. There have been two "golden eras" of globalization interrupted by a very long period when countries were more inward looking. The extent of outward orientation of an economy (the degree of globalization) depends in large part on government policies. A big increase in trade barriers can stop globalization.

5. False. There are substantial volumes of migration between countries at similar levels of development. It is important to remember that restrictions on immigration have a strong impact on who can move where.

6. A country may produce the same good in many different countries if the cost of shipping the good is high or if there are high tariffs. Either trade barrier makes local production desirable.

7. Vertical FDI is more likely to lead to an expansion of trade. Production of a good is moved overseas with the intention of lowering the cost of production. For instance, a U.S. multinational may produce washing machines in Mexico for the U.S. market. Horizontal FDI is more likely to lead to a contraction of trade because firms are substituting local production for exports from the country in which the multinational originates.

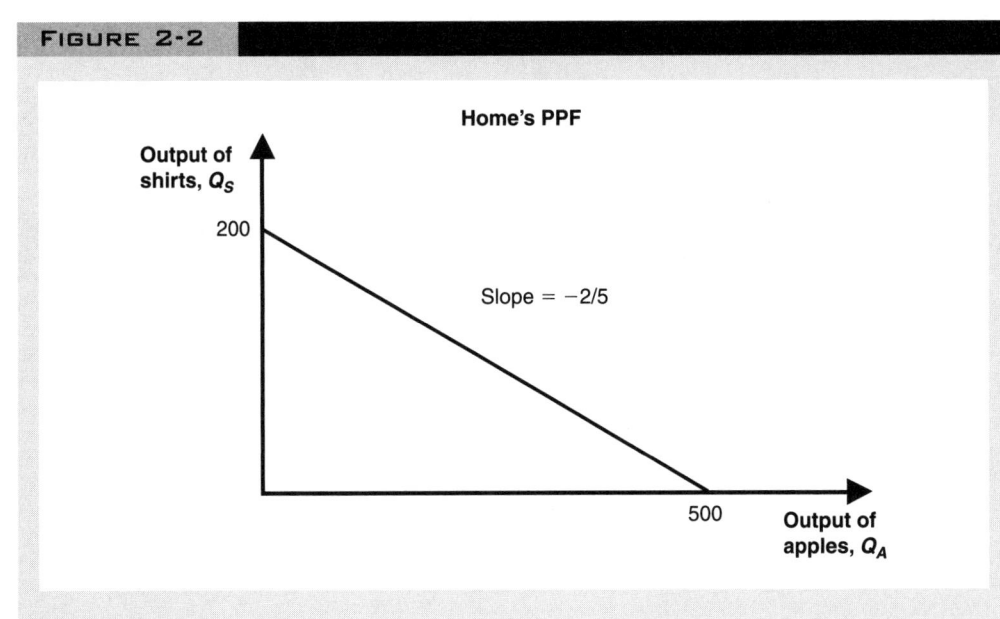

2

Trade and Technology: The Ricardian Model

1a. There is more than one way to arrive at this answer. The first is to reproduce the method used in the textbook: Calculate how many shirts can be produced if all 100 workers make shirts (100 workers · 2 shirts per worker), plot that on the Y axis, make the same calculation for the X axis (100 workers · 5 apples per worker), and then draw a line between them. The slope is then the rise (200) over the run (−500).

A more complicated (but illuminating) alternative is to formulate an equation for the PPF. Suppose that L_A is the number of workers making apples and L_S is the number of workers making shirts. If all workers are employed (which we assume!), then $100 = L_A + L_S$. The technology means that the amount of apples produced is $Q_A = 5 \cdot L_A$ and the amount of shirts produced is $Q_S = 2 \cdot L_S$. Combining this information we have

$$100 = \frac{Q_S}{2} + \frac{Q_A}{5} \Rightarrow Q_S = 200 - \frac{2}{5}Q_A.$$

This is the equation that is graphed in Figure 2-2.

FIGURE 2-2

Home's PPF

1b. We have assumed that the technology features no *diminishing returns*. No matter how many apples or shirts are being made, one worker can produces two shirts, or five apples. Thus, if one more worker is taken out of making shirts, the output of shirts always falls by 2 and the amount of apples always goes up by 5.

1c. The opportunity cost of apples is 2/5 shirts. This is the absolute value of the slope of the PPF drawn in problem 1a but only because apples are on the X axis and shirts are on the Y axis. To produce one more apple, 1/5 of a worker is required because $MPL_A = 5$. The 1/5 of a worker could produce 2/5 of a shirt (1/5 workers · 2 shirts per worker).

1d. The opportunity cost of shirts is 5/2 apples. This is *not* the slope of the PPF drawn in problem 1 because apples are on the X axis and shirts are on the Y axis. To produce one more shirt, 1/2 of a worker is required because $MPL_S = 2$. The 1/2 of a worker could produce 5/2 of a shirt (1/2 workers · 5 apples per worker).

1e. This is illustrated in Figure 2-3.

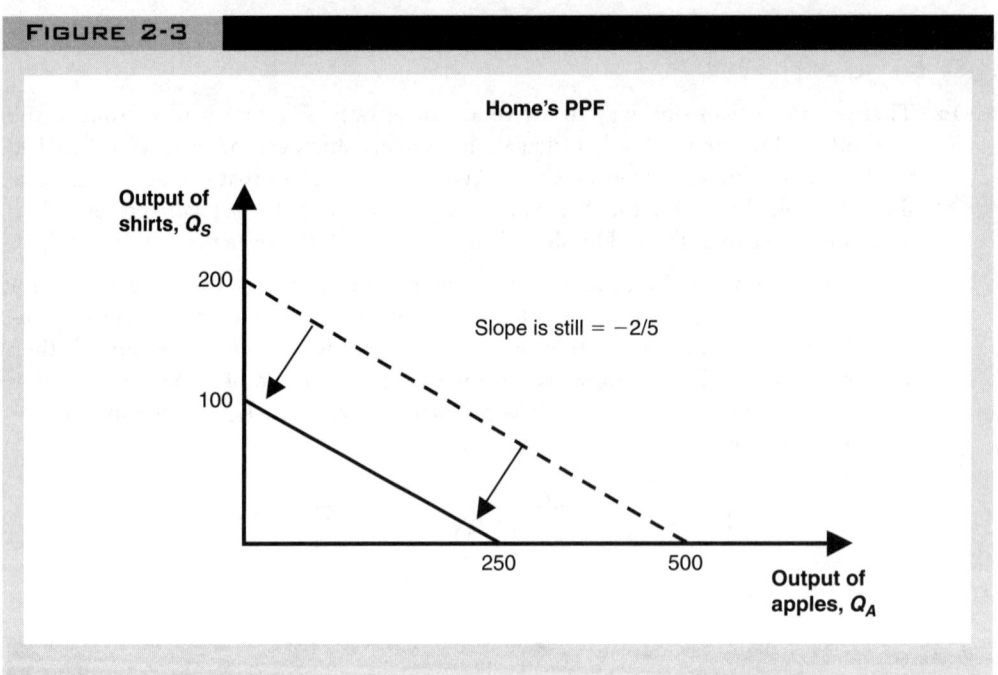

FIGURE 2-3

Home's PPF

Output of shirts, Q_S

Slope is still = −2/5

Output of apples, Q_A

1f. Changing a country's size just changes the X and Y intercepts, but it does not change the slope of the PPF and so does not affect the opportunity of cost of one good in terms of the other.

1g. In exactly the same way as it did in problem 1e, the PPF shifts inward so that the intercepts are half of what they had been before. See Figure 2-3.

1h. See Figure 2-4.

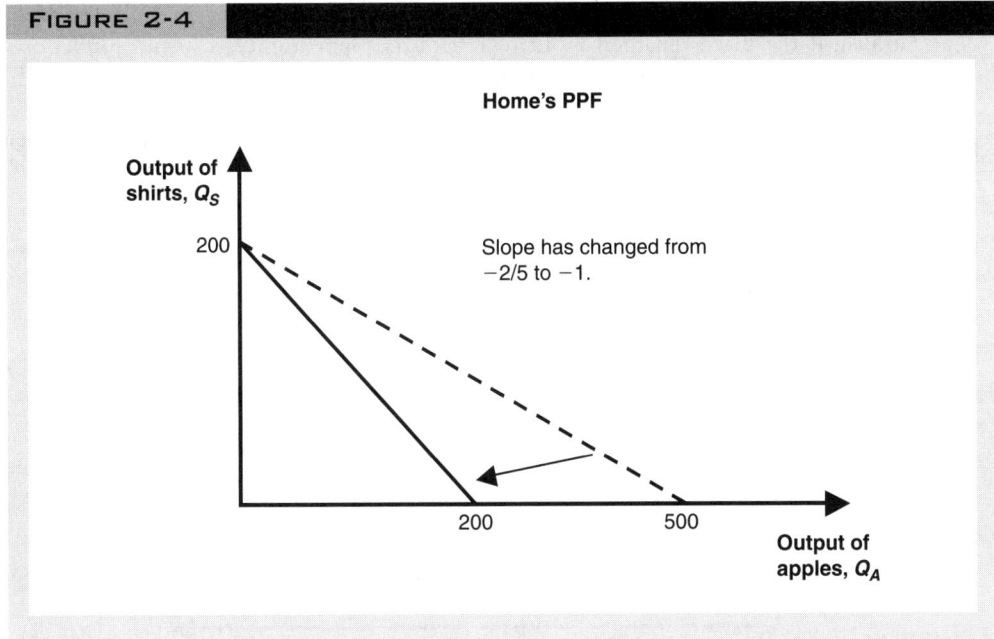

FIGURE 2-4

Home's PPF

Output of shirts, Q_S

200

Slope has changed from $-2/5$ to -1.

200   500

Output of apples, Q_A

1i. This change alters the opportunity cost of apples in terms of shirts because it has changed Home's "technology" in only one of the two goods. Now to make one apple, 1/2 of a worker is needed. Moving a worker out of the shirt industry reduces shirt production by 1/2 worker · 2 shirts per worker = 1 shirt.

2a. Firms are willing to supply any mixture of goods on the PPF (see Figure 2-2). A firm that makes shirts is willing to hire a worker if the cost of doing so is no greater than the value of sales generated by hiring that worker. A shirt-making firm will then hire a worker if the wage is no more than

$$MPL_S \cdot P_S = 2 \, \frac{\text{shirts}}{\text{worker}} \cdot \frac{\$5}{\text{shirt}} = \frac{\$10}{\text{worker}}.$$

An apple-making firm will hire a worker if the wage is no more than

$$MPL_A \cdot P_A = 5 \, \frac{\text{apples}}{\text{worker}} \cdot \frac{\$2}{\text{apple}} = \frac{\$10}{\text{worker}}.$$

A worker creates $10 worth of output making either good. Perfect competition and the fact that workers are free to move between industries mean that the wage must equal $10. Because firms make zero profits whatever level of output they produce (at the prices given), they are willing to make as much as consumers want of either good as long as the PPF allows it.

2b. The country will produce 500 apples. Plugging the information into the equations in the previous answer, it should be clear that one worker will create $20 of sales making apples and only $10 of sales making shirts. The wage of workers will then be bid up to $20 and so make it impossible for a shirt-making firm to break even. All workers then make apples, and the maximum number of apples they can make is 500.

3a. The budget constraint is

$$D_S = \frac{\$100}{\$1/2} - \frac{\$1/5}{\$1/2} \cdot D_A = 200 - 2/5 \cdot D_A.$$

This equation is graphed in Figure 2-5. If you did problem 1, this graph should look familiar. If the prices charged by firms reflect the opportunity costs in production, then the consumer's budget constraint is the same as the PPF in the Ricardian model.

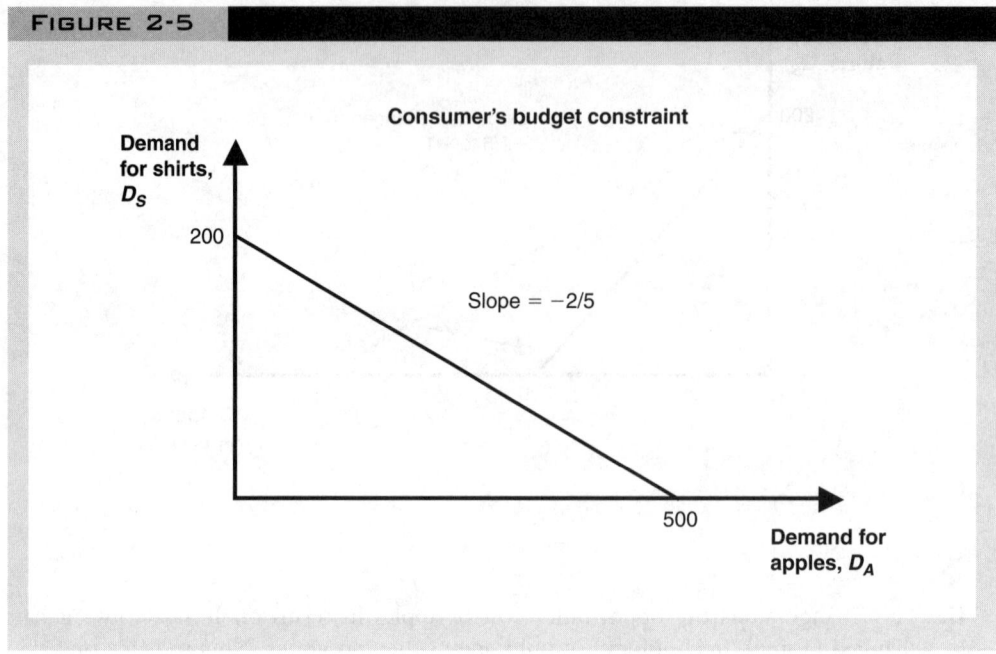

FIGURE 2-5

3b. There would be no change in the graph. Plugging the information into the budget constraint equation gives you exactly the same equation as for the last question. Equivalently, if the consumer were to spend all her income on shirts, she could buy $200/($1 per shirt) = 200 shirts. If the consumer were to spend all her income on apples she could buy $200/($0.40 per apple) = 500 apples. A straight line drawn between these two points on the graph will have a slope of $-2/5$ (see Figure 2-5).

3c. See Figure 2-6. The opportunity cost of an apple for the consumer has gone up even though the dollar price of an apple stays the same! Now, it costs the consumer 4/5 of a shirt to purchase one additional apple.

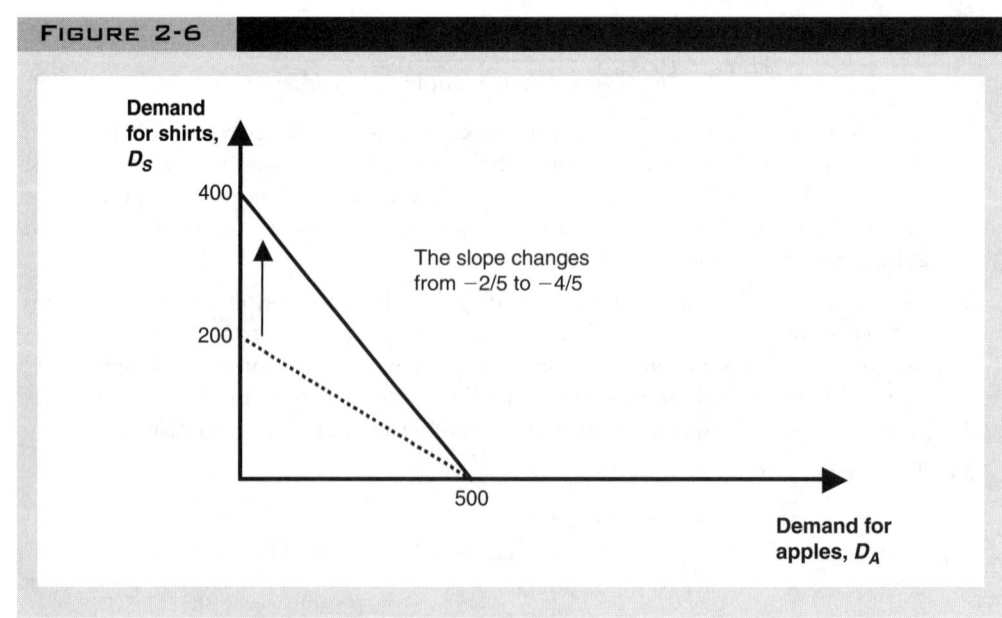

FIGURE 2-6

3d. See Figure 2-7. The opportunity cost of an apple has fallen by half. To obtain one more apple one needs only give up 1/5 of a shirt rather than 2/5 of a shirt.

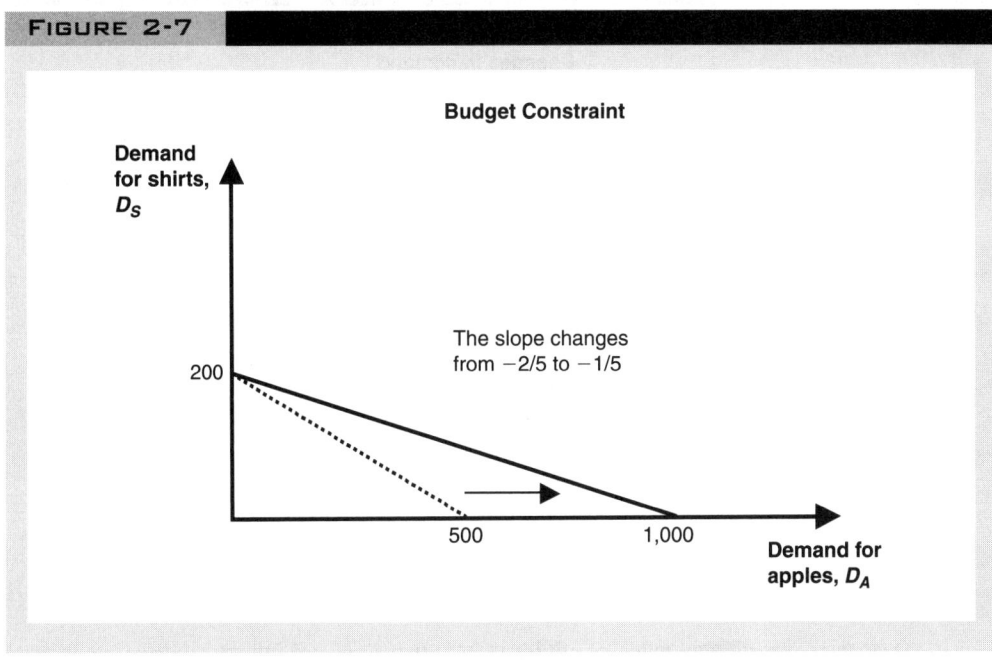

FIGURE 2-7

Budget Constraint

Demand for shirts, D_S

The slope changes from $-2/5$ to $-1/5$

200

500   1,000

Demand for apples, D_A

4a. Because consumers like more of both goods, when given a choice between A, B, and C, the consumer would always choose C.

4b. If given a choice between A and B, there is no way of knowing which will be chosen because the consumer gets the same amount of satisfaction out of both A and B.

4c. See Figure 2-8.

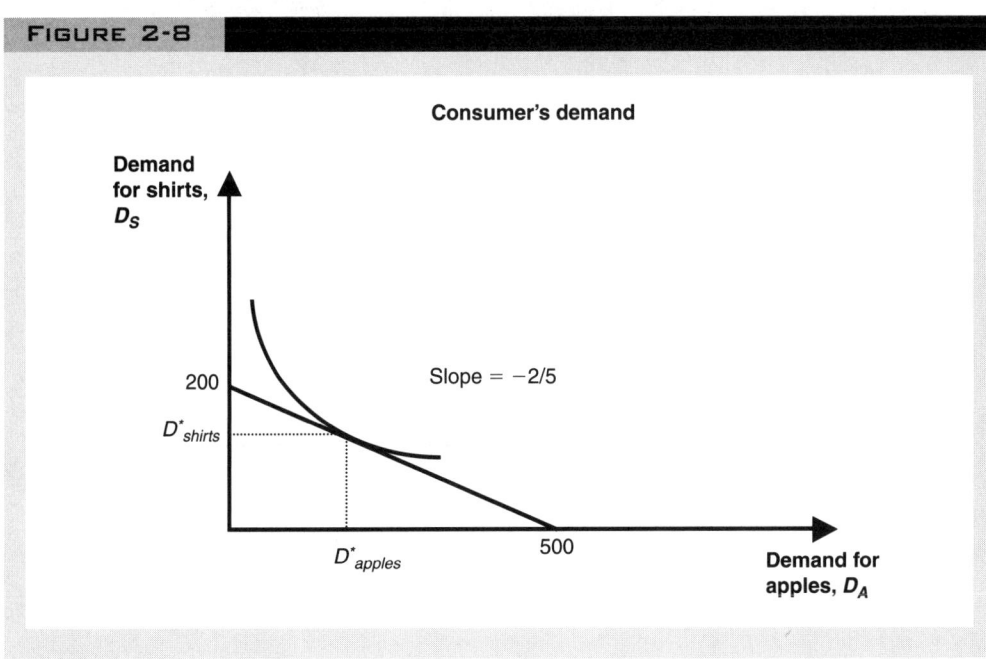

FIGURE 2-8

Consumer's demand

Demand for shirts, D_S

200

D^*_{shirts}

Slope $= -2/5$

D^*_{apples} 500

Demand for apples, D_A

4d. See Figure 2-9.

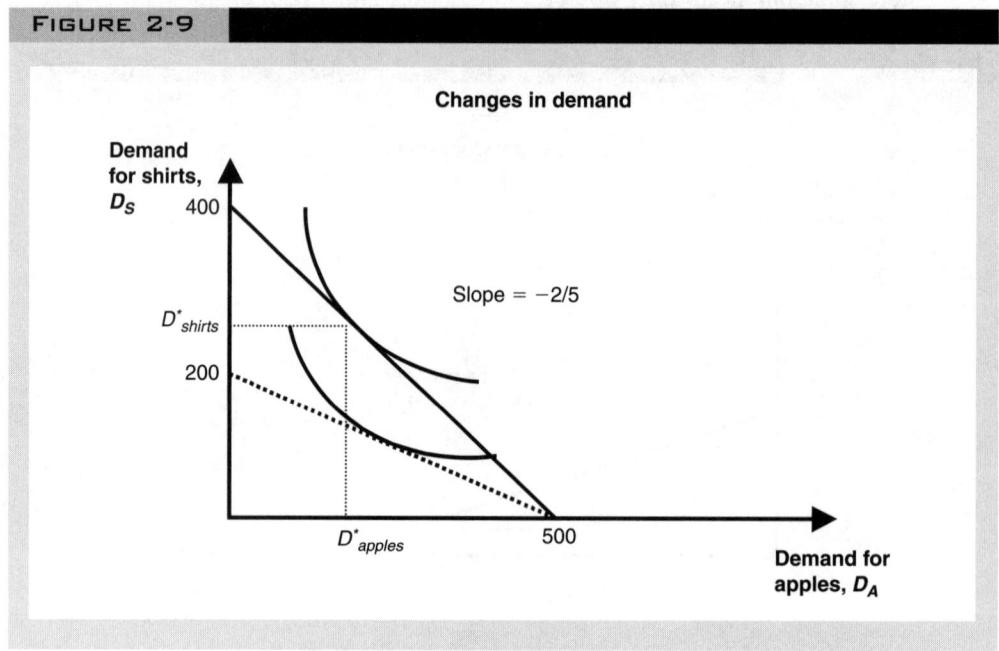

FIGURE 2-9

Changes in demand

5a. As long as the relative price of apples is 2/5, firms are willing to produce anywhere along the PPF. Whatever firms produce, workers' wages will equal the value of the sales of those firms because of perfect competition (and the fact that they are the only factor). Given this income and relative prices, workers' budget constraint is the same as the PPF. Whatever bundle they choose (where the indifference curve is tangent to the budget constraint), firms will supply. An example of an equilibrium is shown in Figure 2-10.

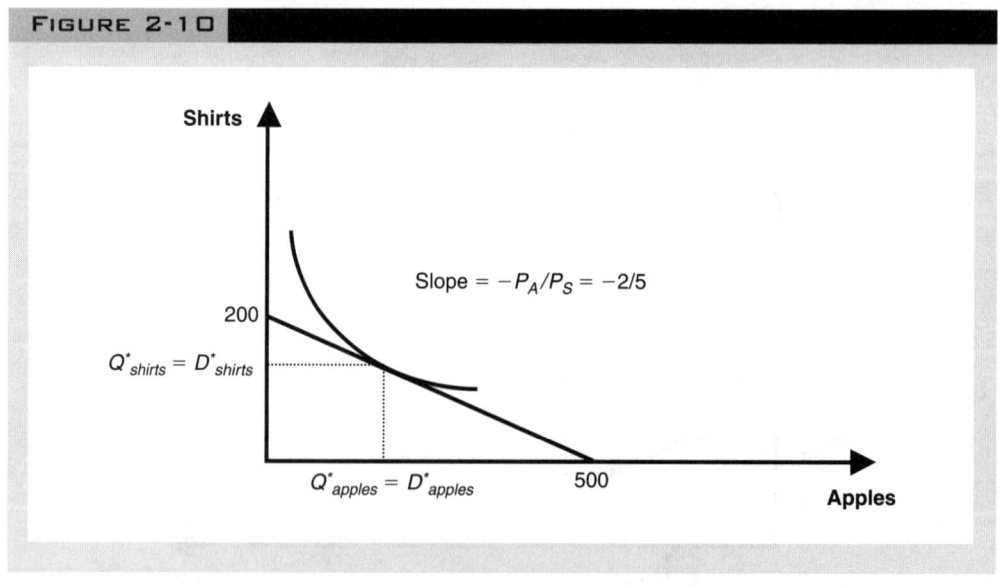

FIGURE 2-10

5b. In Figure 2-11, the quantity of apples demanded and supplied rises and the quantity of shirts demanded and supplied falls as the technology for producing apples improves. Note, however, that given the outward shift in the budget constraint, the consumer is free to consume more of both goods. The consumer purchases fewer shirts because apples have become relatively cheaper. Notice that the indifference curves will *not* cross.

FIGURE 2-11

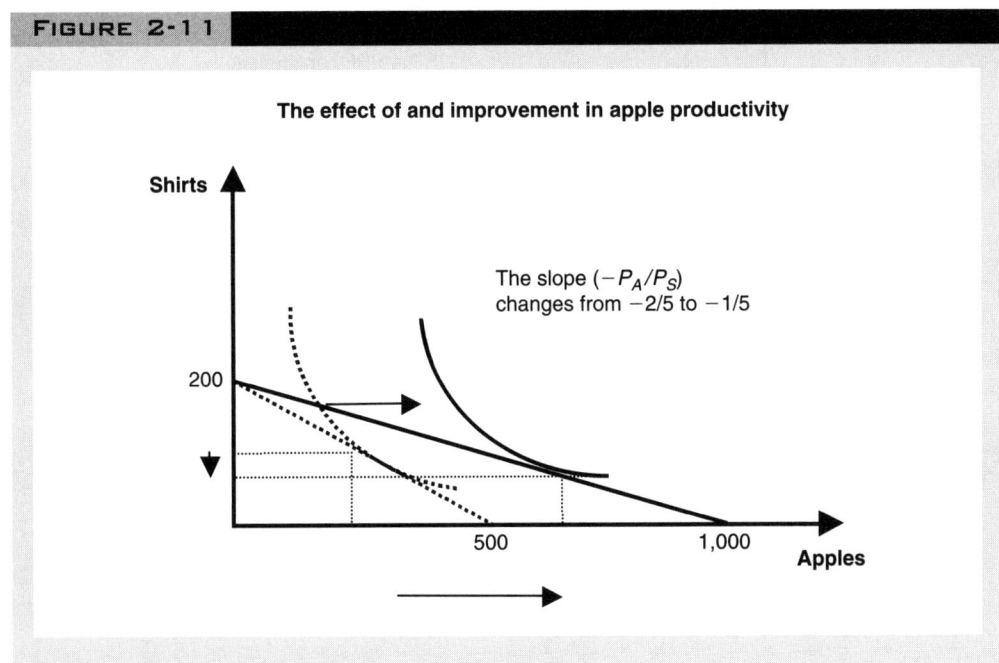

The effect of and improvement in apple productivity

5c. The higher relative price of apples on world markets induces apple firms to expand, driving up the wage and driving shirt producers out of business. Hence, the economy produces only apples. The income of workers is then 500 apples, which are worth P_A, so that their budget constraint is

$$P_A 500 = P_A D_A + P_S D_S.$$

After some algebra, the country's budget constraint (or consumption possibilities frontier) becomes

$$D_S = \frac{P_A}{P_S} 500 - \frac{P_A}{P_S} D_A = 500 - D_A,$$

which is graphed in the Figure 2-12.

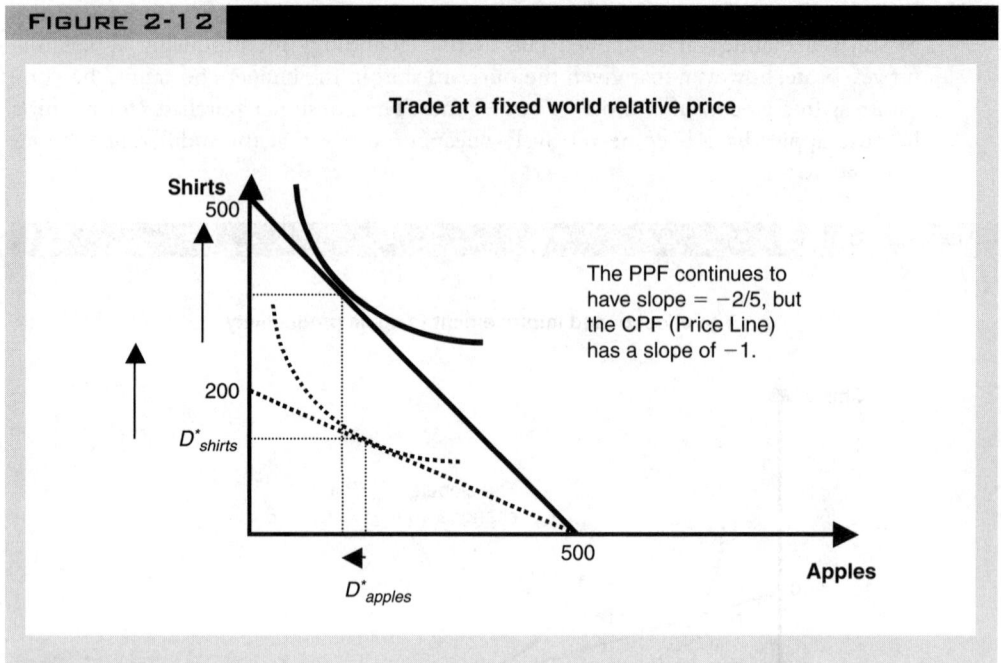

FIGURE 2-12

Trade at a fixed world relative price

The PPF continues to have slope = −2/5, but the CPF (Price Line) has a slope of −1.

6a. For Foreign to have a comparative advantage in apples, the opportunity cost in production for apples in Foreign must be less than one. Hence, a marginal product of labor in shirts in Foreign can be any number less than 6. If it were less than 4, then Home would also have an absolute advantage in shirts.

6b. There are no gains from trade if the opportunity cost of producing each good is the same in both countries. Because the opportunity cost of apples is one shirt in Home, any numbers for which the marginal product of labor was the same in both goods would create a situation in which there was no comparative advantage and so no gains from trade. For the wage to be twice as high in Foreign, Foreign labor must be twice as productive (in both goods in this case), so MPL for apples and shirts in Foreign must be 8.

7. The good in which a country has a comparative advantage will have a lower relative price than in the other country, and the opposite will be true of the good in which it has a comparative disadvantage. Firms in the industry of comparative advantage tend to expand into the foreign market, where the relative price is higher. A trade equilibrium then involves new relative prices in at least one country, and at least one country will specialize.

8a. The price of apples in terms of shirts P_A / P_S must lie between the autarky (no-trade equilibrium) relative prices in Foreign and Home, respectively. For if $P_A / P_S > 1$, then both countries would produce exclusively apples, and if $P_A / P_S < 3/4$, both countries would produce exclusively shirts. Hence, for both goods to be produced it must be the case that $3/4 \leq \dfrac{P_A}{P_S} \leq 1$.

8b. Foreign has a comparative advantage in apples because the opportunity cost of producing apples is lower than in Home. Hence, Foreign will export apples and import shirts. Because the question assumes that the world relative price is halfway between the no-trade equilibrium prices in each country, it must be true that $P_A / P_S = 7/8$ (halfway between 8/8 and 6/8). Because the price of apples in a trading equilibrium is higher than in the no-trade equilibrium, producers in Foreign specialize in apples. Given world prices, if the consumers in Foreign traded all their apples for shirts, they could afford 700 of them $(7/8 \cdot 800)$. The tangency of the indifference curve with the consumption possibilities frontier gives the actual amount demanded. The country exports $800 - D^*_{apples}$ units of apples and imports D^*_{shirts}. Foreign is illustrated in panel (a) of Figure 2-13, and Home is shown in panel (b).

FIGURE 2-13

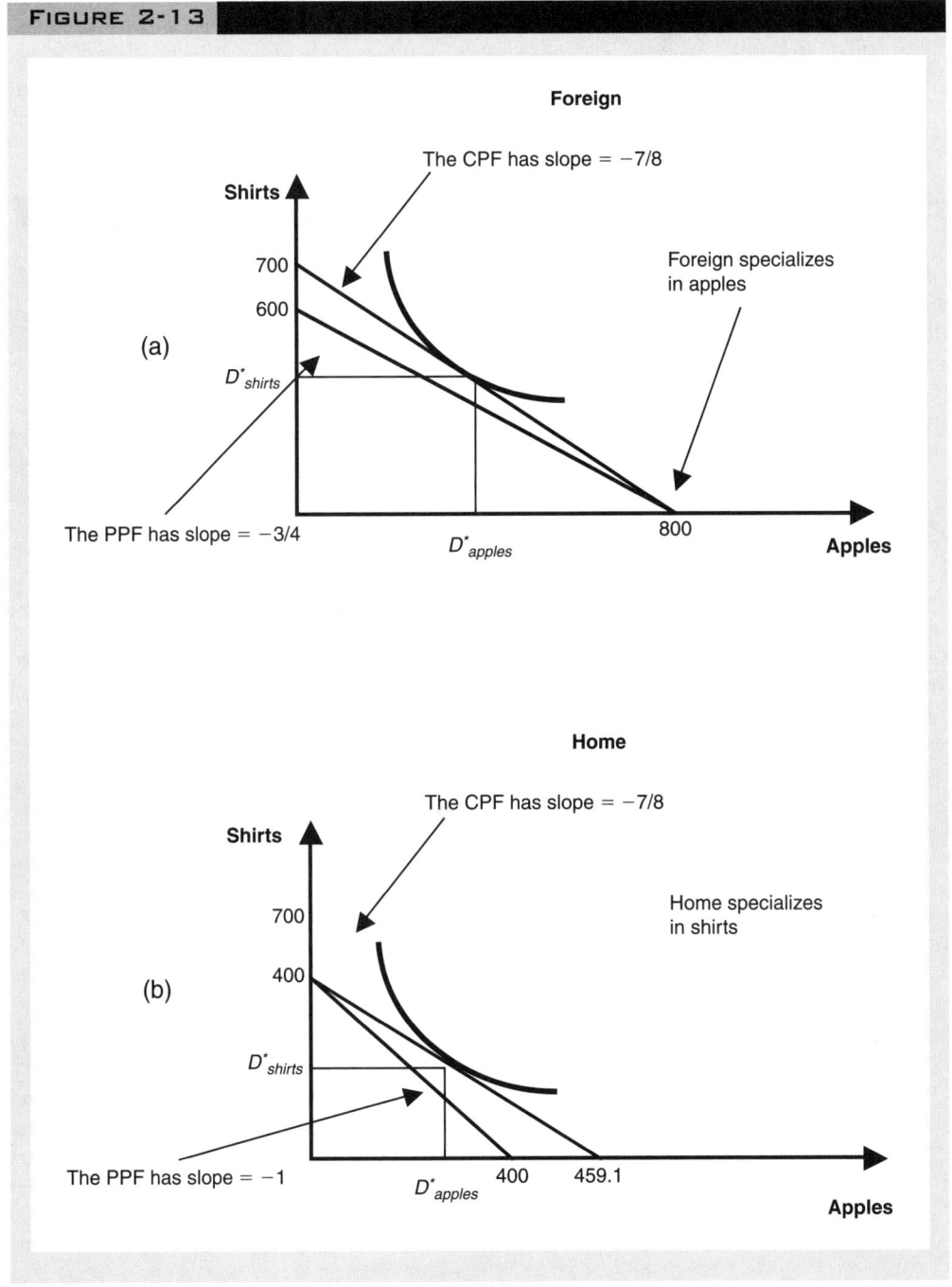

9a. The first step is to identify which good Home exports. Because the opportunity cost of shirts is lower in Home than in Foreign, Home will export shirts. Producers in Home are willing to make up to 400 units of shirts as long as the relative price of shirts is 1 and at this relative price consumers buy 225 shirts ($400 - 175 = 225$). This means that if Home is fully specialized in shirts and consumers buy 225 of them, there are 175 shirts available to export. This explains the flat portion of the export supply function shown in Figure 2-14. To get any more shirts available for export, Home consumers have to cut back their demand, which they will do if the relative price of shirts rises. The supply curve is getting steeper because consumers become less willing to substitute shirts for apples. Note also that Home can never export more than 400 shirts because this is the maximum amount of shirts that Home is capable of making!

FIGURE 2-14

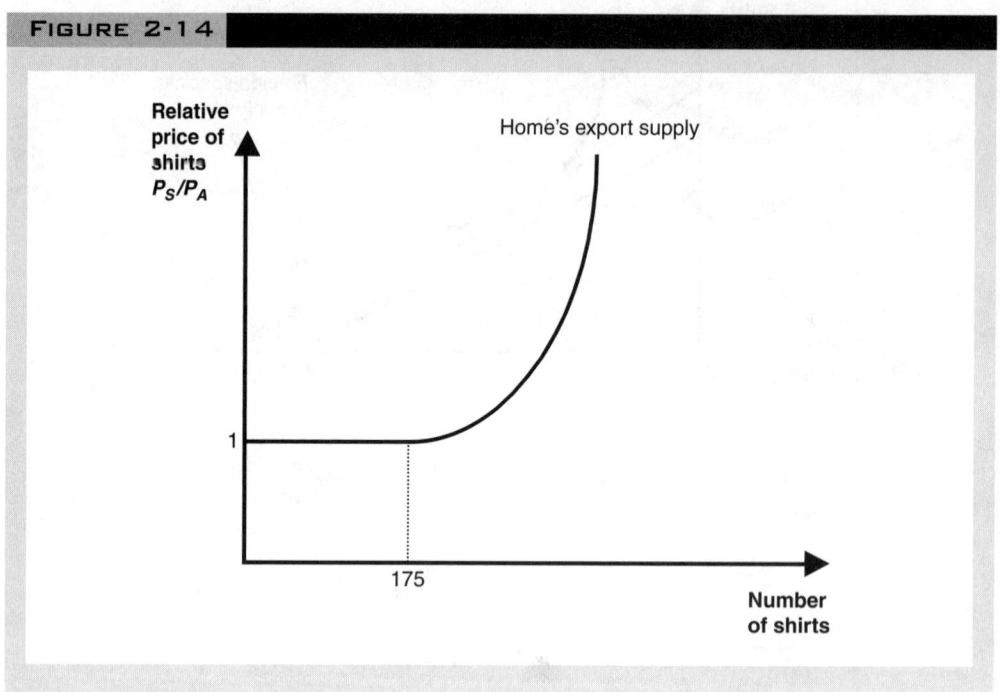

9b. Home export supply and foreign import demand is shown in Figure 2-15. If the world relative price of shirts in Foreign is 4/3, the foreign producers are willing to produce both goods. In this situation, Foreign shirt firms will produce some of the domestic consumption of 300 and import the rest on the flat portion of Foreign's import demand. If the world relative price of shirts falls below 4/3, then there is no production of shirts in Foreign and Foreign consumers start to buy more of the now cheaper good. Hence Foreign's imports begin to rise. This explains the downward-sloping part of Foreign's import demand.

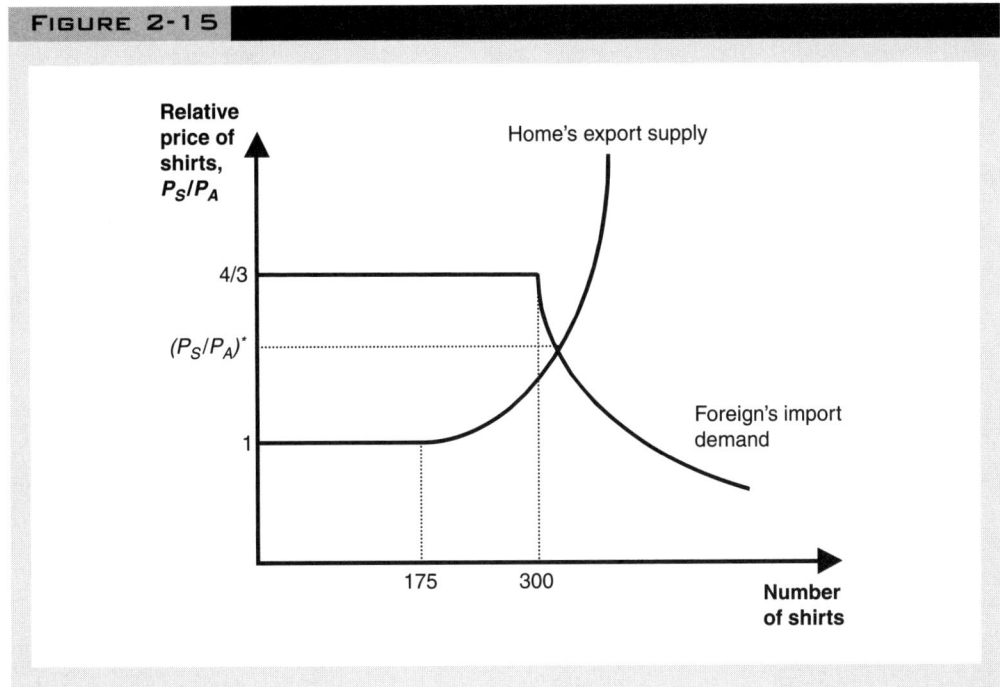

9c. Doubling the size of Home's economy doubles both its ability to produce and its desire to consume. Hence, as shown in Figure 2-16, when Home is completely specialized in producing shirts but the relative price of shirts is still 1, its consumers will produce 800 shirts, of which it will consume 450 shirts, leaving 350 for export. The shift in the export supply curve will reduce Home's *terms of trade,* that is, the value of what it exports in terms of the price of what it imports. The case shown here has Home not fully specialized in its export good; that is, it continues to produce some, but not all, of its import good. The reduction in Home's terms of trade could have been less extreme.

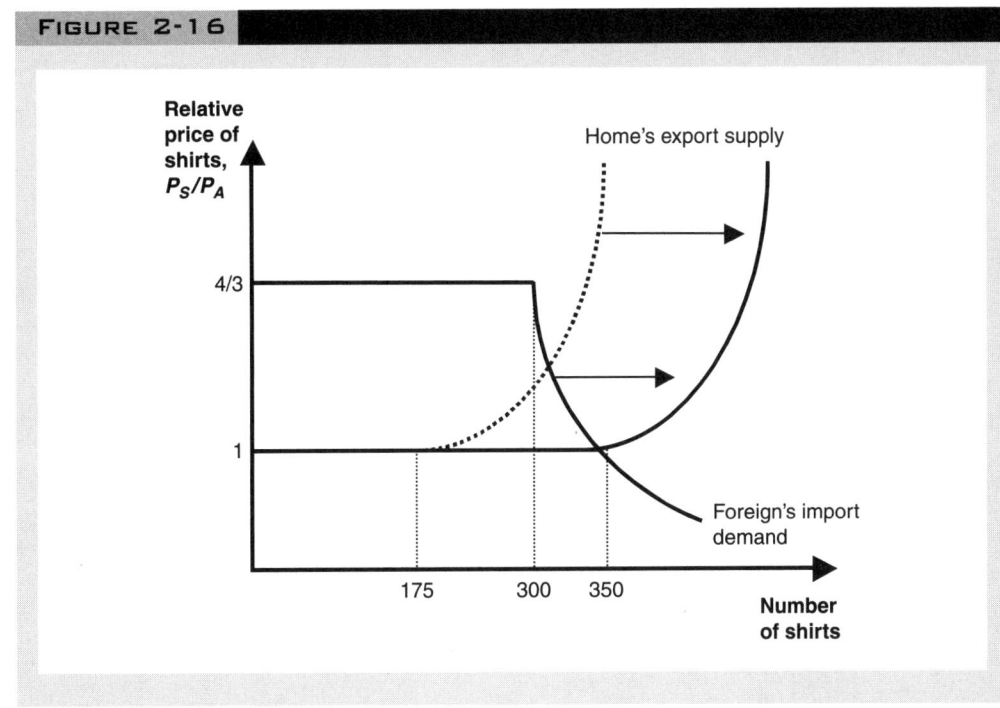

3

Who Gains and Who Loses from Trade?

1a. If the use of both inputs is doubled, then the volume of output is doubled as well. This is an example of a "constant returns to scale" technology.

1b. If the use of only one input is increased, then output will rise but at a decreasing rate. If labor is increased by a factor of 2, then output will increase by a factor of $\sqrt{2}$. Note that it is the same constant returns to scale technology, but there are diminishing returns if only one factor is increased.

1c. Suppose that there are 100 units of capital, so that $Q_M = 10\sqrt{L_M}$. A reduction of employment by 1 lowers output by $\Delta Q_M = 10\left(\sqrt{L_M} - \sqrt{L_M - 1}\right)$. Plugging in the numbers and using a calculator to solve it, reducing employment by one unit lowers output more when $L_M = 10$ than when $L_M = 100$. This highlights the implications of diminishing marginal product of labor.

2a. The opportunity cost of M in terms of A is given by the absolute value of the slope of the PPF. This is higher at point 2 than point 1. Figure 3-1 shows an example of an "increasing opportunity cost PPF."

2b. When all labor is put into Agriculture, the marginal product of labor in Agriculture (MPL_A) is very low (little land per laborer) and the marginal product of labor in Manufacturing (MPL_M) is high (lots of unused machines). Hence, as labor is moved out of Agriculture into Manufacturing, initially there is only a very small drop in Agricultural production and a very large increase in Manufacturing output: The opportunity cost of M in terms of A is low. As more labor is moved, the MPL_A is getting larger and MPL_M is getting smaller. Hence, output of agriculture starts falling at a faster rate and output of manufacturing expands at a slower rate: The opportunity cost of M in terms of A is high.

2c. A profit-maximizing firm will choose a labor force that makes the value of the marginal product of labor equal to the wage. In this example, the value of the marginal product is $20 per worker, so in equilibrium it had better be the case that the wage is $20.

2d. Because $P_M MPL_M = W = P_A MPL_A$ in equilibrium, $MPL_A > MPL_M$ because $P_M > P_A$.

2e. The value of the marginal product of labor is $40, and workers are being paid only $25. This means that revenues could be expanded by more than costs if another worker is hired. Hence, you are employing too few workers.

2f. If P_M / P_A falls (e.g., suppose that P_M drops while P_A is fixed), then workers will be induced to move out of manufacturing into agriculture. As more workers enter agriculture, the land/labor ratio falls. Hence, the marginal product of labor in agriculture falls. This can be seen directly in Figure 3-3. The fall in the price of a unit of manufacturing goods reduces the value of the marginal product of labor in manufacturing from the dotted curve to the solid curve. This reduction in labor demand lowers the nominal wage and so induces the agricultural industry to expand (a movement along the demand curve for labor in agriculture). Because the amount of land is fixed, the land/labor ratio falls and the marginal product of labor in agriculture falls as well.

FIGURE 3-3

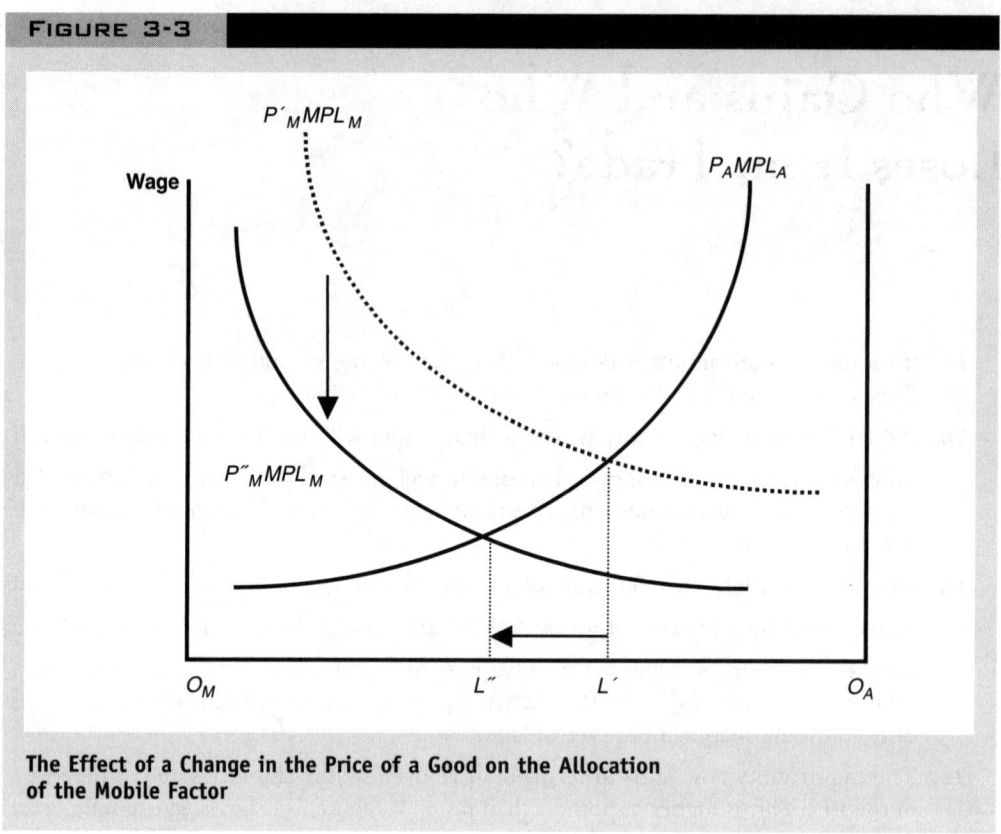

The Effect of a Change in the Price of a Good on the Allocation of the Mobile Factor

3a. See Figure 3-4 on the next page.

FIGURE 3-4

FIGURE 3-4

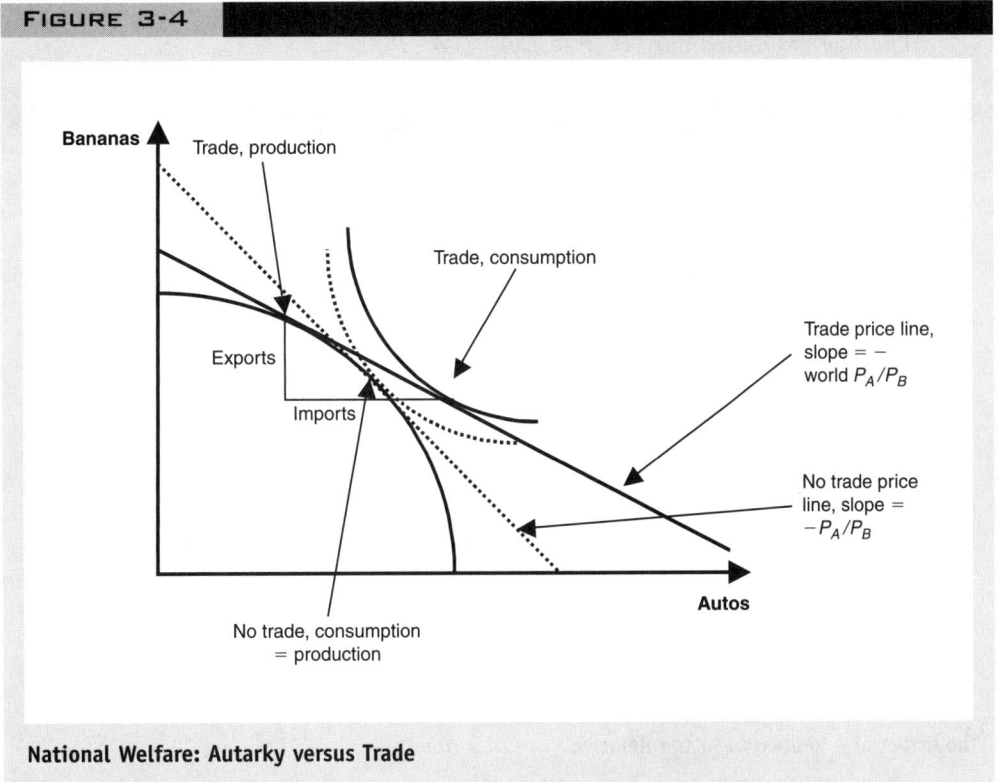

National Welfare: Autarky versus Trade

3b. The country is better off because the opportunity cost of producing a good in autarky is different than the opportunity cost of the good on international markets. By reorganizing production in the country and changing consumption patterns, the country can then expand the production of the good in which its opportunity cost in production is less than the opportunity cost on international markets, thereby obtaining more of both goods.

3c. Recall that the price of autos in terms of bananas is higher in Foreign than in Home in a no-trade equilibrium. In a trading equilibrium, the relative price of a good must lie between the autarky relative prices of the two countries because if it were not the two countries would like to export the same good. Hence, Foreign adjusts to international trade by cutting back production of autos, expanding production of bananas, and exporting bananas to Home in return for autos. Notice that the law of comparative advantage must hold: A country exports the good in which its autarky relative price is lower and imports the other good.

3d. In a free-trade equilibrium, the two countries face exactly the same relative prices. Producers adjust their production until the ratio of the value of the marginal product of labor is the same in both industries. Hence, the ratio of the marginal product of labor in autos to the marginal product of labor in bananas is the same in both countries. This in turn is equal to the slope of the PPF at the point where production occurs: The opportunity cost of producing autos in terms of bananas must be the same in the two countries.

4a. See Figure 3-5. Note that the diagram already expressed all variables in terms of the price of bananas. So a reduction in the relative price of autos (P_A / P_B) involves the shift in the value of the marginal product of autos when expressed in terms of bananas. This shift induces labor to move from auto production to banana production.

The amount of labor that moves across industries is captured by the distance L_1L_2. The wage expressed in terms of bananas (W / P_B) falls.

FIGURE 3-5

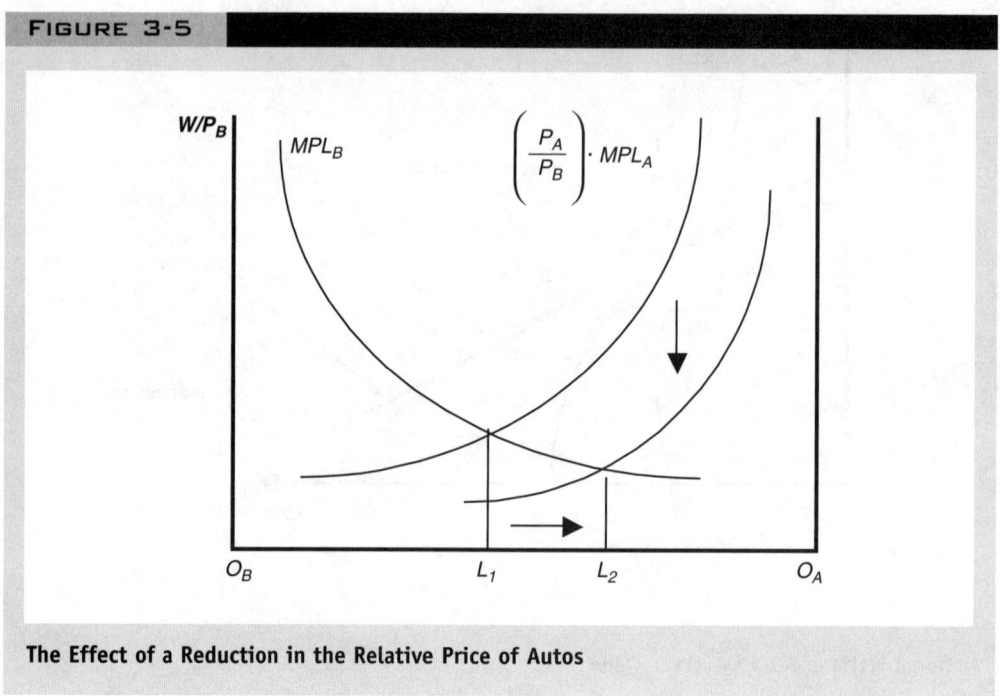

The Effect of a Reduction in the Relative Price of Autos

4b. Because $P_AMPL_A = W$, it follows that $MPL_A = W / P_A$. MPL_A rises because the amount of labor employed making A declines. Because MPL_A rises, it follows that W / P_A rises. Workers can afford more autos.

4c. Because $P_BMPL_B = W$, it follows that $MPL_B = W / P_B$. Because MPL_B falls (see Figure 3-5), it follows that W / P_B falls. Workers cannot afford as many bananas.

4d. The effect of trade on the well-being of workers is ambiguous if the workers spend their income on both goods.

5a. If labor were truly mobile between industries, then it would move into the higher paid industry until the wages were equalized.

5b. Workers may have skills that they have learned in their industry that cannot be transferred to other industries. Their wages fall when they are displaced because they lack the skills that are valuable to another industry. In some sense, these skills can be thought of as being specific to an industry. This idea helps explain why TAA includes providing retraining to workers displaced by trade.

6a. Because labor is unable to move, the marginal product of labor in computers must stay the same. Hence, the wage must rise by the same amount as the price of computers. This means that the real wage of computer workers in terms of computers is the same. Because the price of tulips has not changed, the real wage of computer workers in terms of tulips has risen.

6b. Because labor is unable to move, the marginal product of labor in tulips must remain the same, so the real wage of tulips in terms of tulips has stayed the same. Because computer prices have risen, however, the real wage of tulip workers in terms of computers has fallen.

7a. See Figure 3-6. (Autarky information is displayed in dotted lines, and trade information is displayed in solid lines.) Home has the higher autarky relative price of autos and so is the exporter of bananas. Home's supply of bananas increases and its supply of autos decreases, whereas the opposite is true in Foreign. Home's consumption of bananas is less than its supply of bananas, and its consumption of autos is greater than its supply of autos. The opposite is true in Foreign.

FIGURE 3-6

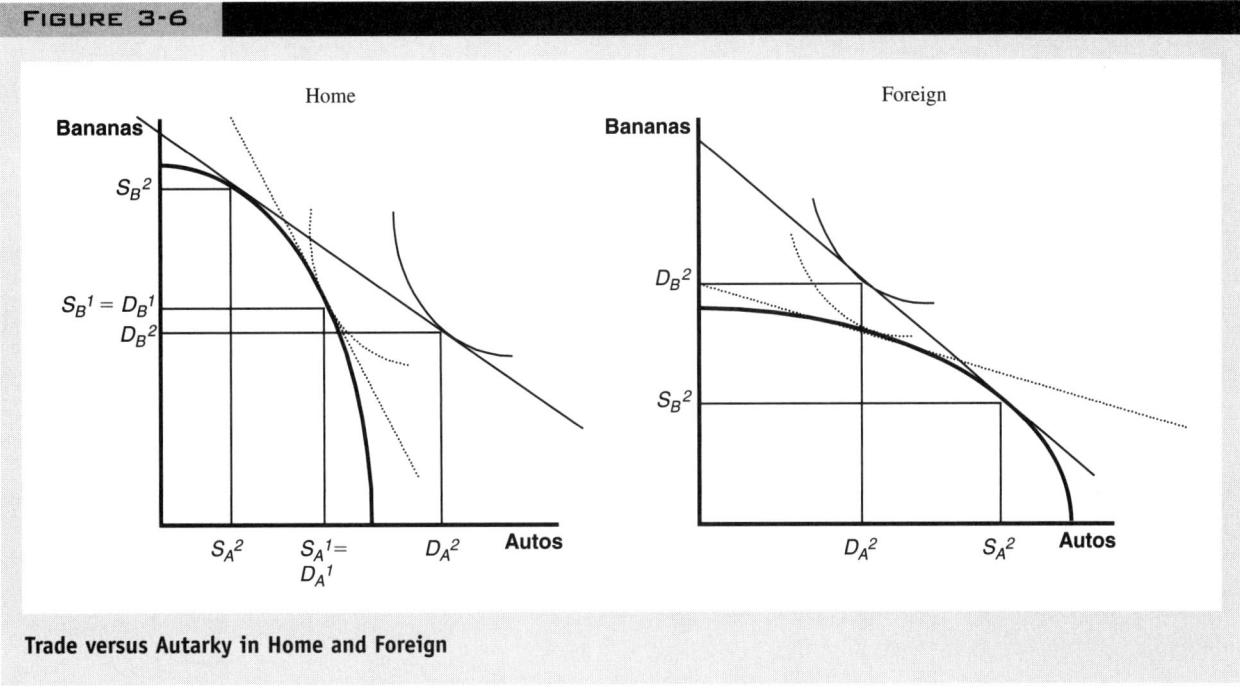

Trade versus Autarky in Home and Foreign

7b. The real rental of capital falls in Home. As labor is pulled out of auto production, the marginal product of capital (MP_K) falls. Because

$$MP_K = \frac{R_K}{P_A},$$

the income of a unit of capital has fallen relative to the price of autos. Now notice that

$$\frac{R_K}{P_B} = \frac{P_A}{P_B} \cdot \frac{R_K}{P_A}.$$

Because P_A / P_B goes down when the country trades, and because R_K / P_A falls as well, the nominal earnings of a unit of capital will buy less of both goods!

7c. Note that the relative price of autos goes up for Foreign, and so the argument for 7b applies here but in reverse. The real rental of capital rises in Foreign.

7d. The demand for land in Home rises as the country increases its production of bananas. The marginal product of capital rises as labor is moved from auto production into banana production. The value of the marginal product of land is the demand curve for land.

7e. Because global resources are used more efficiently, both countries can consume more than they did when they were not trading. Because the country gains-from-trade means that winners win more than losers lose, the winners could compensate the losers and everyone could be made better off.

4

Trade and Resources:
The Heckscher-Ohlin Model

1a. The answer is displayed in Figure 4-5. Shoes have a higher labor/capital ratio than computers when the wage/rental ratio is high and have a relatively low labor/capital ratio when the wage/rental ratio is low. Hence, one cannot call either good labor or capital intensive. The Heckscher-Ohlin model explicitly rules out this possibility!

FIGURE 4-5

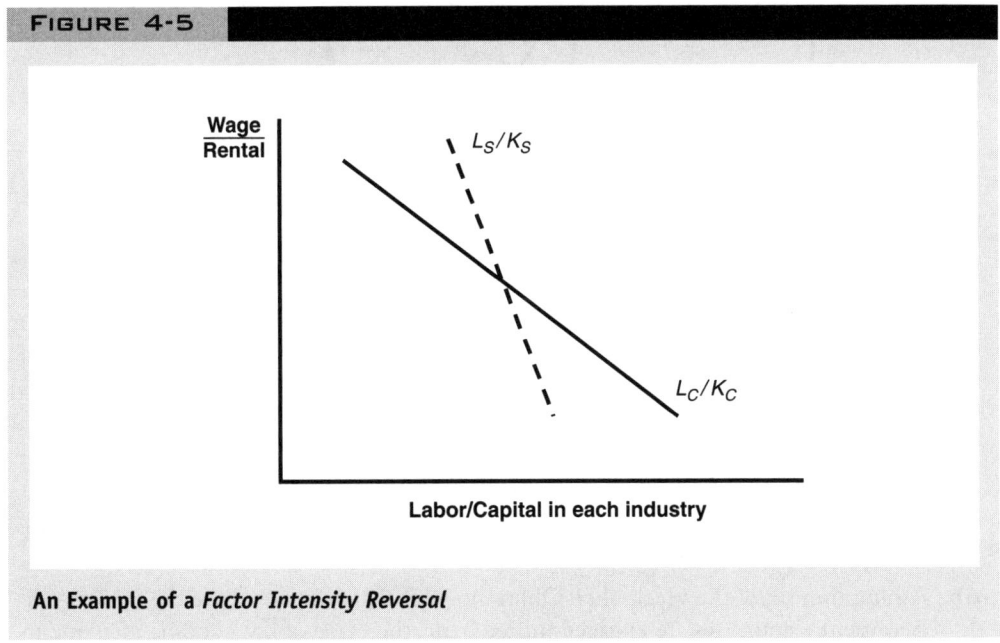

An Example of a *Factor Intensity Reversal*

1b. Factor abundance is measured as the ratio of the endowments of the factors. The capital/labor ratio in Home is 2, and it is 2.5 in Foreign. Foreign is capital-abundant relative to Home even though it has less capital than Home.

2a. Because consumers' tastes are the same in every country, the differences in relative prices in the two countries must stem from differences in the shape of the production possibility frontiers. A situation in which Home has a higher relative price of computers in a no-trade equilibrium is shown in the Figure 4-6. The curves relevant to Home are represented by solid lines, and curves relevant to Foreign are in dotted lines. Home's PPF is bowed out toward shoes, and Foreign's PPF is bowed out toward computers. Because tastes are the same in both countries, it is the difference in the shape of the PPFs that give rise to the difference in the no-trade equilibrium prices.

Why is Home's PPF bowed out toward shoes and Foreign's PPF bowed out toward computers? As capital is added to an economy, the PPF tends to bow out toward the capital-intensive good (computers in this example). As labor is added to an economy, the PPF bows out in favor of the labor-intensive good (shoes in this example). Thus, Foreign must have a higher capital/labor ratio than Home, so it is relatively capital-abundant.

FIGURE 4-6

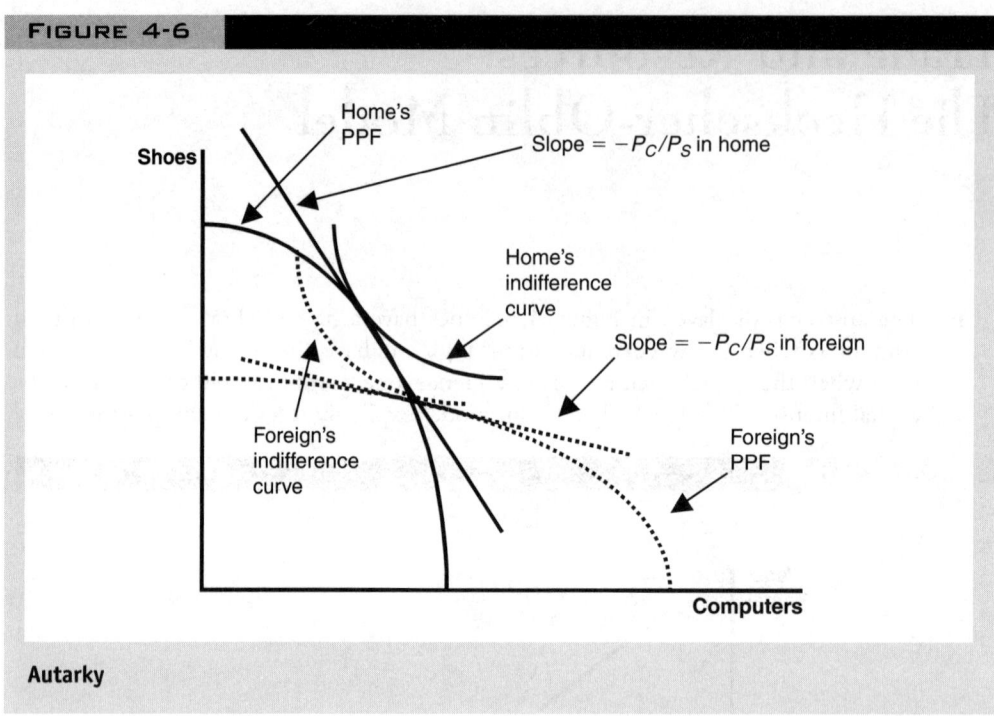

Autarky

2b. Foreign is producing a higher ratio of computers to shoes in a no-trade equilibrium than Home. The tastes are the same in the two countries, and the relative price of computers is lower in Foreign than in Home. This means that Foreign consumers must be consuming relatively more computers than shoes compared with Home consumers. Because the country must supply its own goods (there is no trade), Foreign must be producing a higher ratio of computers to shoes than Home.

3a. Because Home is labor abundant relative to Foreign and shirts are labor intensive relative to airplanes, the *Heckscher-Ohlin theorem* establishes that Home will export shirts.

3b. Assumption six of the Heckscher-Ohlin model is that countries have the same tastes. Because the countries are engaged in free trade, the price of the goods is the same in both countries. Hence, consumers in Foreign consume goods in the same ratio as those in Home.

3c. An increase in the endowment of capital will tend to further skew its PPF toward the capital-intensive good, airplanes. This means that for any relative price of airplanes, Foreign will supply more airplanes and fewer shirts, as shown in the left-hand side of the Figure 4-7. As a result, Foreign's export supply curve for airplanes shifts to the right, causing the relative price of airplanes to fall.

FIGURE 4-7

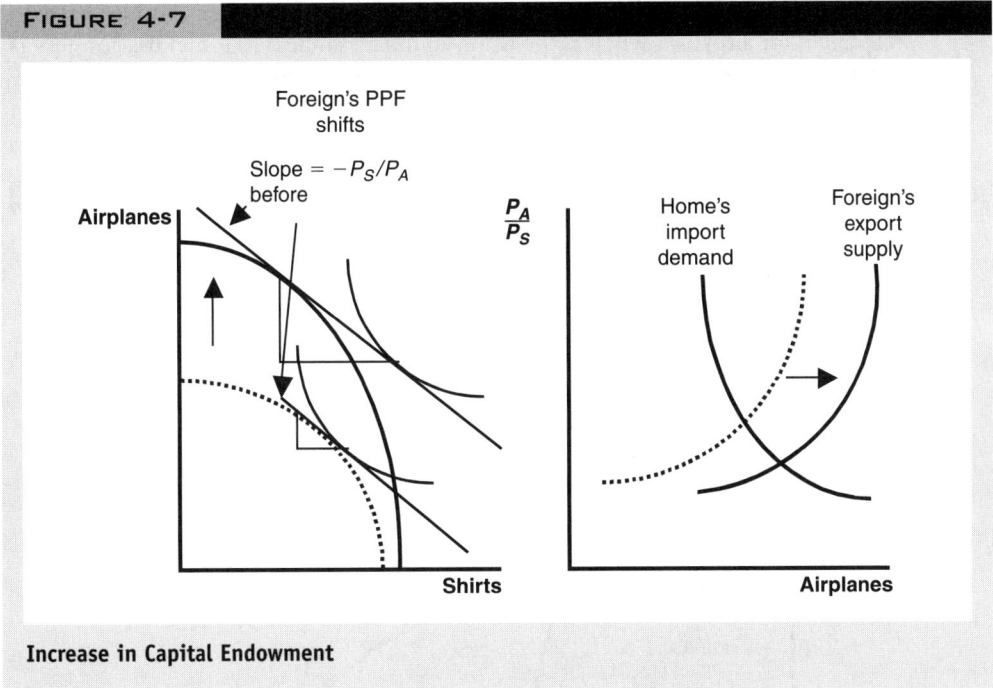

Increase in Capital Endowment

3d. As established in the last problem, an increase in Foreign's endowment of capital reduces the relative price of airplanes and so increases the relative price of shirts. This is a terms-of-trade improvement for Home, the exporter of shirts. Therefore, Home can get to a higher indifference curve. (See Figure 4-8.) Note that shirt output increases and airplane output falls as a result.

FIGURE 4-8

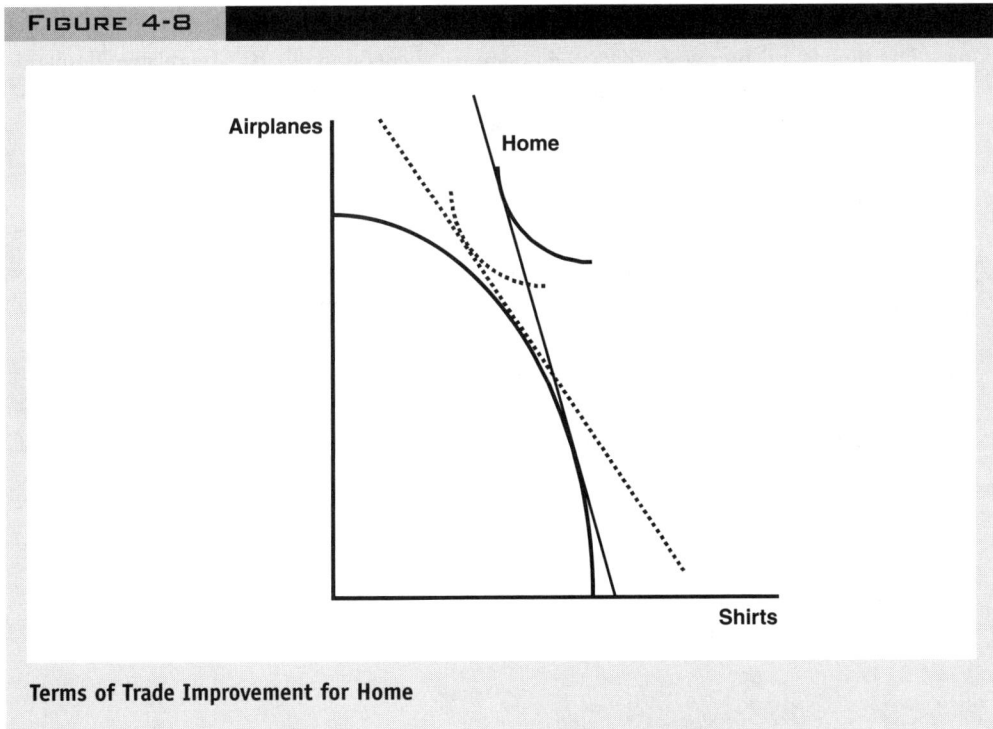

Terms of Trade Improvement for Home

4. Suppose that the capital-abundant country (Foreign) has consumers who have strong preferences for airplanes, whereas the labor-abundant country (Home) has consumers with strong preferences for shirts. Then it is possible that the trade pattern is exactly the opposite of that predicted by the Heckscher-Ohlin theorem, as can be seen in Figure 4-9.

FIGURE 4-9

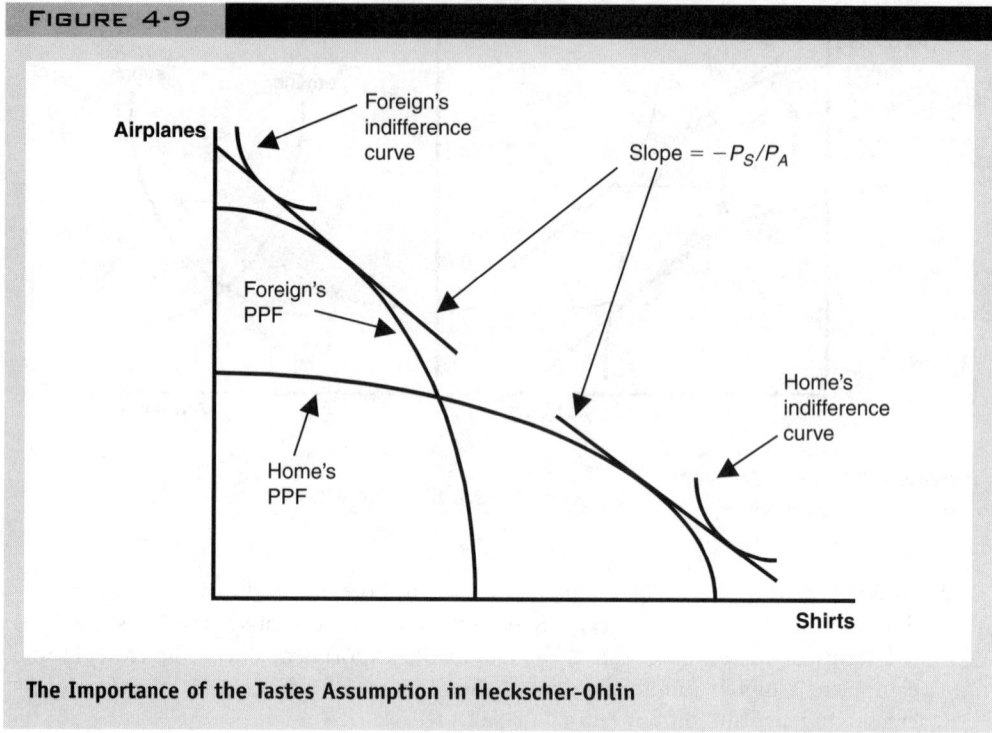

The Importance of the Tastes Assumption in Heckscher-Ohlin

5. There could be (1) factor intensity reversals, (2) technologies that differ across countries, and (3) tastes that differ across countries.

6a. The highest relative wage that could occur in this country is 10. The relative demand for the whole economy cannot exceed the relative demand for the shoe industry because it is a weighted average of the relative demands in the two industries.

6b. As resources are moved out of computers and into shoes, the relative demand curve for the economy shifts up. The weights in the weighted average now favor shoes over computers.

6c. An upward shift in the relative demand curve causes the relative wage to rise. Because the industry relative demand curves do not shift, this means that L / K must fall in each industry.

7a. The capital/labor ratio used by Ubetchan producers in both industries would rise. Engaging in free trade would lower the relative price of autos and thereby induce the auto industry to contract and the hat industry to expand. As factors are moved out of autos and into hats, the relative demand for capital would decrease, because autos are relatively more capital intensive than hats. This is shown as the leftward shift in the relative demand curve in Figure 4-10. The reduction in the relative demand for capital lowers the rental/wage ratio, which induces firms in the both the auto and shoe industry to substitute capital for labor. Note that the relative supply of factors in the economy, given by K^* / L^* in Figure 4-10, does not change.

FIGURE 4-10

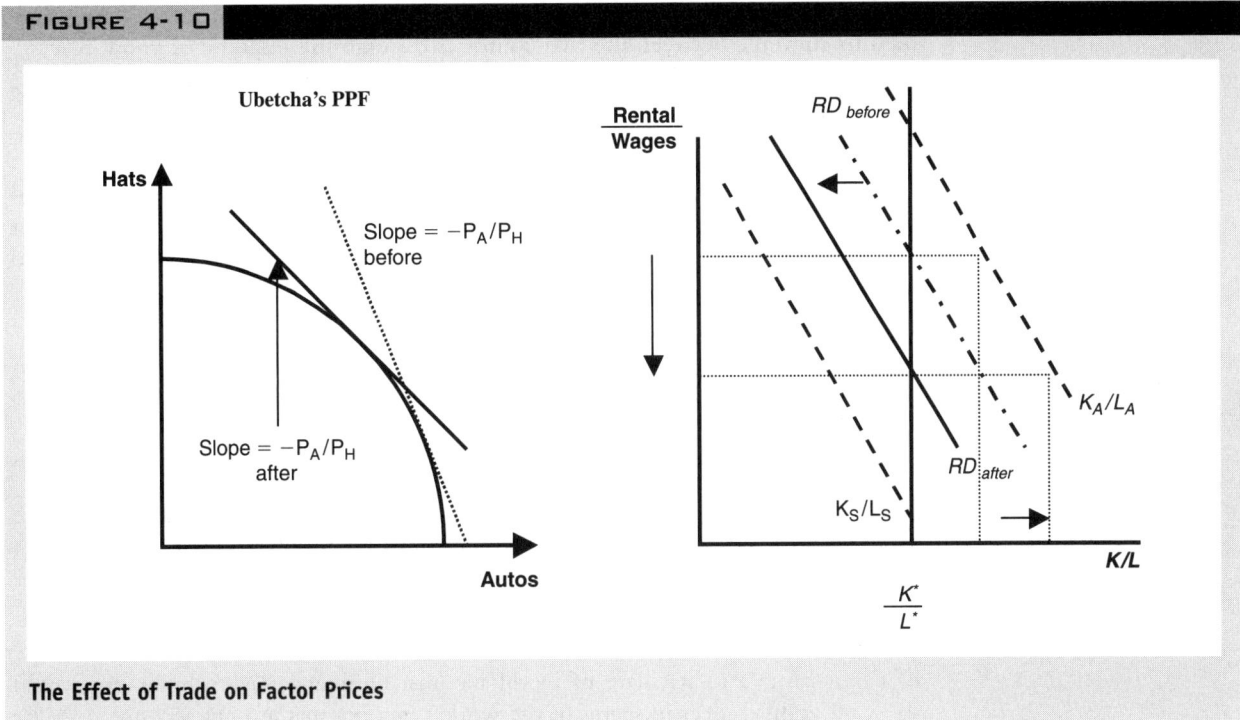

The Effect of Trade on Factor Prices

7b. Because the capital/labor ratio used by producers rises, the marginal product of capital should fall, as each machine has fewer workers using it.

7c. A political group that represented the economic interests of capital owners would lobby against free trade. By the Stolper-Samuelson theorem, the decrease in the relative price of the capital-intensive good induced by free trade would lower the real rental and raise the real wage.

8a. By the Heckscher-Ohlin theorem, the United States has a comparative advantage in skill-intensive goods, so free trade raises the price of skill-intensive goods. By the Stolper-Samuelson theorem, trade raises the real income of skilled workers while lowering the real income of unskilled workers. Hence, the Heckscher-Ohlin model is consistent with the survey results.

8b. One would expect exactly the opposite response in a skill-scarce country compared with the response in the skill-abundant country. Trade causes the relative price of goods to move in the opposite direction for this type of country.

9a. Because the two countries are absolutely identical, they should have exactly the same relative price of goods and factors in a no trade equilibrium. Hence, there is no motive for migration.

9b. Moving capital from Foreign to Home will skew Foreign's PPF (it shrinks but in a skewed way) toward doughnuts and Home's PPF outward toward sofas. The relative price of sofas will fall in Home and rise in Foreign. Applying the Stolper-Samuelson theorem, the real earnings of labor will rise in Home and fall in Foreign. Because they were starting at the same level (before the capital moved), Home must now have a higher real wage than Foreign.

9c. Labor would want to move from Foreign to Home.

9d. The migration of labor from Foreign to Home would tend to skew Home's PPF toward doughnuts and Foreign's PPF toward sofas. This has the opposite impact on the relative price of doughnuts and so has the opposite impact on real wages. Real wages tend to converge between the two countries through the response of goods prices.

9e. Yes, migration causes the relative price of doughnuts to fall (and sofas to rise). By the Stolper-Samuelson theorem, this implies an increase in the real rental to capital.

10. According to the Heckscher-Ohlin model, international trade increases the real income (through the Stolper-Samuelson theorem) of the abundant factor and reduces the real income of the scarce factor. In developing countries, labor is the abundant factor and so should gain from trade. If Bob were educated and fast thinking, he could say, "Oh yeah, what about the Leontief paradox?" Then you'd be pretty much sunk.

11. If Leontief had found that a bundle of U.S. exports contained a higher ratio of capital to labor than imports, then he would have concluded that the U.S. trade pattern was consistent with Heckscher-Ohlin. There would be no paradox.

12a. Because the country has a larger share of world GDP than it has of labor, it should be a net importer of labor services.

12b. If workers in Home are paid better than in the rest of the world, then they may be more productive than workers elsewhere. In this case, it could be that if effective labor were measured, Home in fact has a share of world effective labor that is greater than its share of GDP.

12c. Yes. A country's relative abundance or scarcity is its share of the world's stock of a type of factor relative to its share of world income. Differences in technologies would show up as differences in shares of the world's income that are not accounted for by differences in factor ownership. A really productive country will appear to be scarce in a larger set of factors and a less productive country will appear to be abundant in a larger set of factors.

5

Movement of Labor and Capital between Countries

1a. The expansion of land increases the marginal product of labor in agriculture for every level of possible employment. Because the prices of goods are fixed on world markets, this change raises the value of the marginal product of labor in agriculture from $P_A MPL_A$ to $P_A MPL'_A$ as illustrated in Figure 5-2. At the old level of employment (measured by the distance $L^* O_A$ in the figure) $P_A MPL'_A > W$, so agricultural firms hire additional labor until the labor employed in A is given by $L' O_A$. This drives up the wage and leads to a movement along the curve $P_M MPL_M$ until $P_M MPL_M = P_A MPL'_A = W'$.

FIGURE 5-2

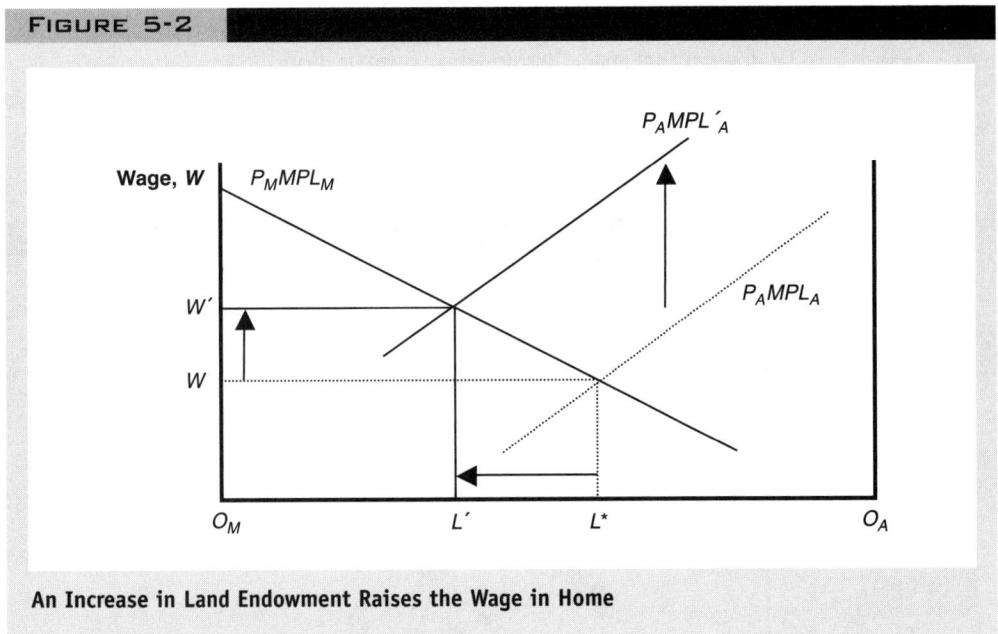

An Increase in Land Endowment Raises the Wage in Home

1b. Immigration leads to an increase in Home's labor endowment and so increases the size of the base of the diagram as illustrated in Figure 5-3. Note that the apparent shift in the $P_A MPL_A$ is not the result of any actual change in the value of the marginal product of labor in agriculture for a given level of employment. It is due to a shift in the origin O_A to the right, reflecting the increase in the labor endowment. The increase in the labor endowment is measured by the distance from O_A to O'_A. The wage will drop as a result of the increase in the endowment of labor. If there are no *moving costs*, then labor will move into Home until its wage level is equal to the world wage level.

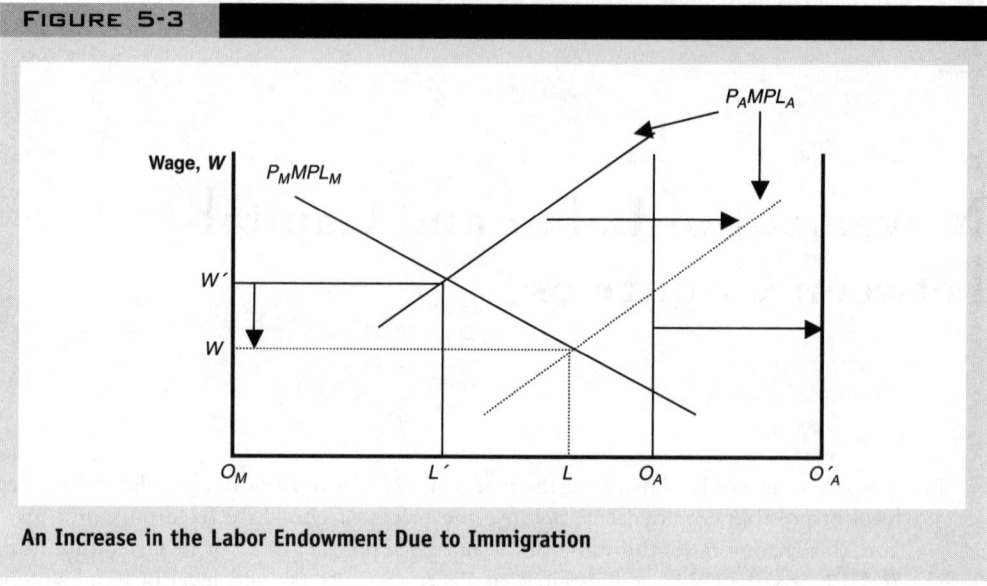

FIGURE 5-3

An Increase in the Labor Endowment Due to Immigration

1c. As shown in the answer to 1b, the increase in the endowment of labor reduces the wage. This induces both agriculture and manufacturing to add workers. Hence, the marginal product of capital and the marginal product of land both increase (the capital/labor ratio and the land/labor ratio rise). Because the prices of goods are fixed, this means that the real income of a unit of capital (R_K) and (R_T) both increase. Capitalists and landowners are made better off by immigration.

1d. The PPF shifts outward when more of the mobile factor is available, as shown in Figure 5-4. Because there are more workers employed in both industries after the inflow of workers, the level of output of each good must rise.

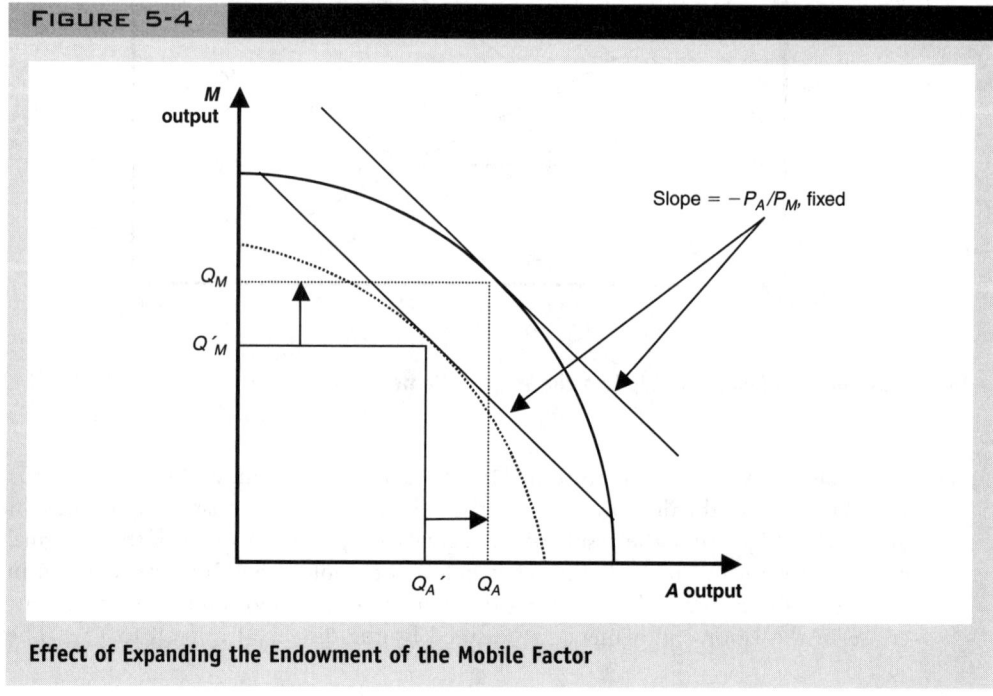

FIGURE 5-4

Effect of Expanding the Endowment of the Mobile Factor

2a. Airplanes are capital intensive relative to shirts because the capital/labor ratio is 5/3, which is greater than the capital/labor ratio in shirts, which is 1.

2b. To answer this question, we use the box diagram shown in Figure 5-5. The height of the diagram is the size of the country's endowment of capital, and the length of the base is the original size of the labor endowment. In the diagram, the slope of the line from O_S through point a is equal to 1, which is the capital/labor ratio in shirts, and the slope of the line from a to O_A is equal to 5/3, which is the capital/labor ratio in airplanes. Initially, the amount of capital employed in airplane manufacturing is given by the length of the line from K to O_A and the amount of labor used in making airplanes is given by the length of the line L to O_A. When laborers leave, the box becomes narrower and so we relabel the airplane origin $O_A{}'$ to reflect this fact. The slope of the line from b to O_A continues to be 5/3. The new intersection at b shows clearly that even though there is less labor available in the country, the amount of labor and capital employed in airplane manufacture has increased!

FIGURE 5-5

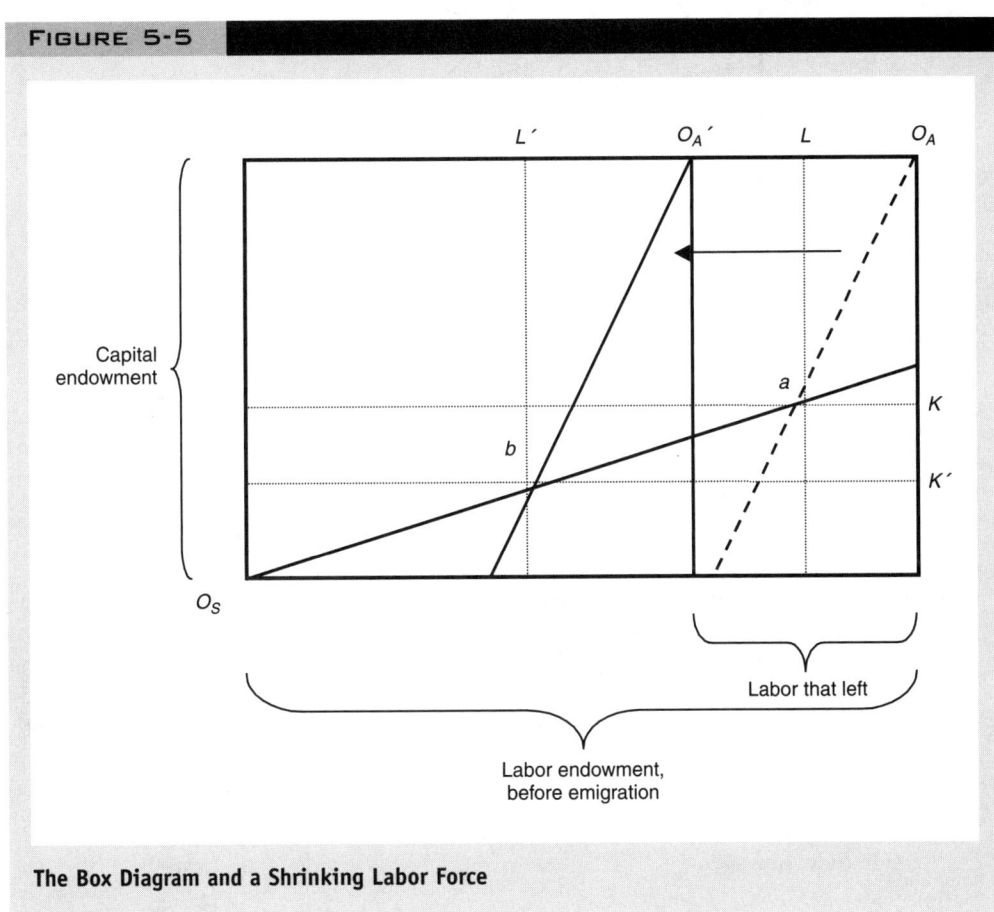

The Box Diagram and a Shrinking Labor Force

2c. Let Q_A be the output of airplanes and Q_S be the output of shirts. Let $\overline{K}$ be the country's endowment of capital, and let $\overline{L}$ be the country's endowment of labor. Using the production information in the question we have

$$\overline{K} = 5 \cdot Q_A + 2 \cdot Q_S$$

and

$$\overline{L} = 3 \cdot Q_A + 2 \cdot Q_S.$$

Doing a little algebra, we find that

$$Q_A = \frac{\overline{K} - \overline{L}}{2} \text{ and } Q_S = \frac{5\overline{L} - 3\overline{K}}{4}.$$

2d. The answer is shown in Figure 5-6. The shift in the PPF is consistent with the Rybczynski theorem in reverse: At fixed relative prices, a decrease in the endowment of labor leads to a reduction in the production of the labor-intensive good and an expansion in the production of the capital-intensive good.

FIGURE 5-6

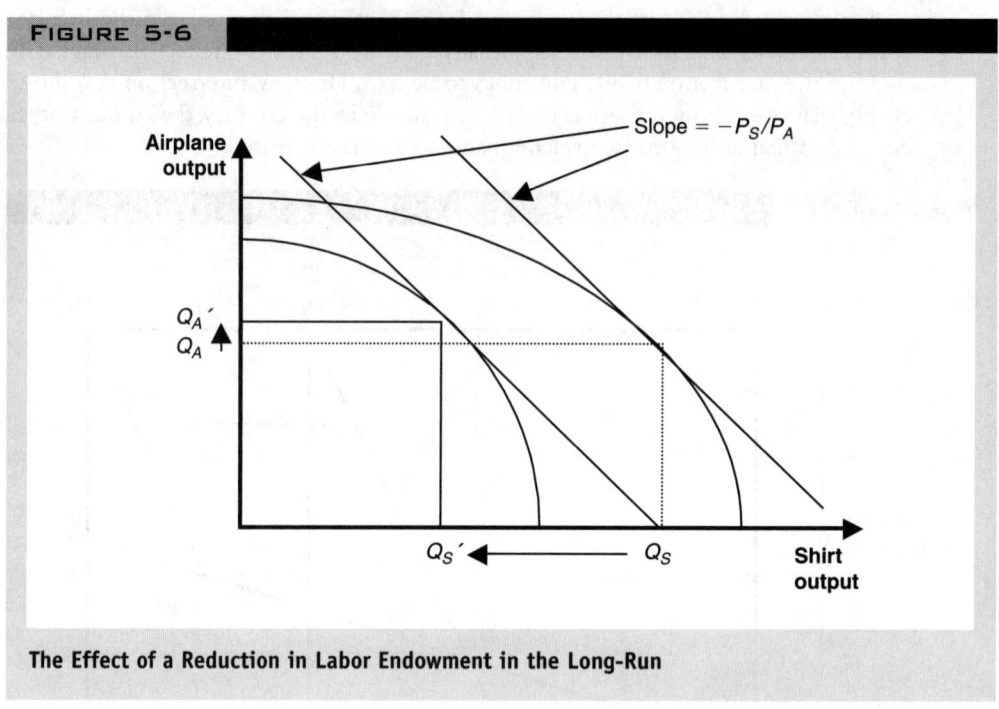

The Effect of a Reduction in Labor Endowment in the Long-Run

3a. The entry of computer workers into the country raises the marginal product of capital in the computer industry for any level of capital used in that industry, as shown in Figure 5-7. This induces capital to move into the computer sector, as shown by the shift from K to K'. Because the rental must rise, it must be that the marginal product of capital increases in both industries. This means that marginal product of both computer workers and shirt workers must fall (falling ratio of specific factor to mobile factor in each industry). Hence, both types of workers are hurt.

The fall in real income across computer and shirt workers will not be of the same magnitude, however.

FIGURE 5-7

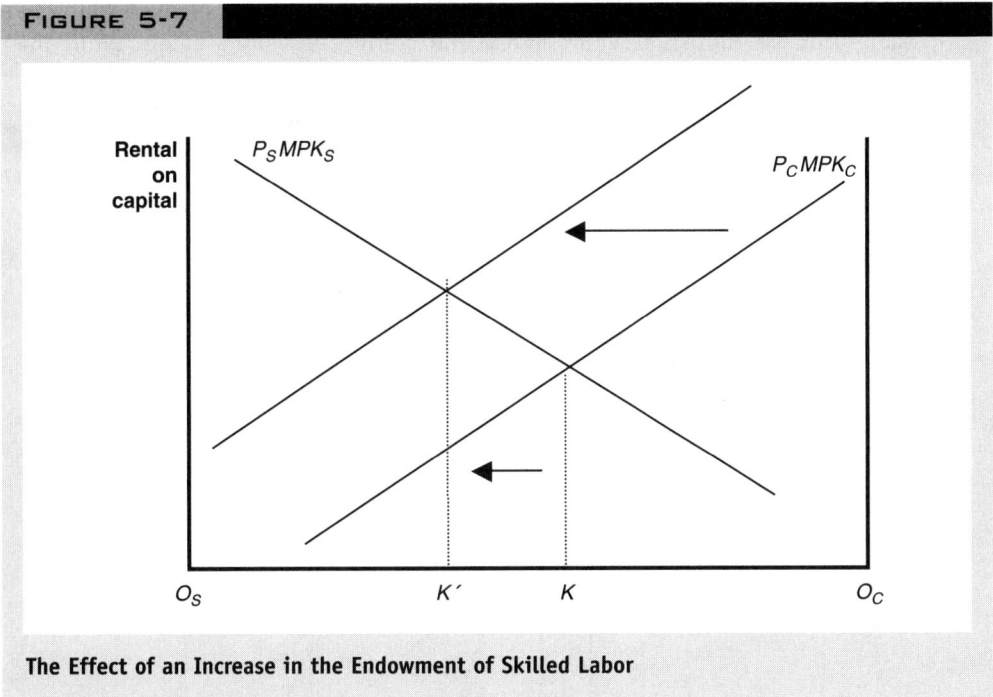

The Effect of an Increase in the Endowment of Skilled Labor

3b. In the long run the factor price insensitivity result must hold: There is no effect on the real wage of either computer or shirt workers. This is because workers can retrain and switch industries in the long run.

3c. In the short run the real rental must rise. Figure 5-7 demonstrates that the rental must rise, and because goods prices are fixed, an increase in the nominal rental is also an increase in the real. In the long run, the factor price insensitivity result must hold so there is no long-run impact on the real rental rate. Output of the labor-intensive good will expand and the capital-to-labor ratios in each industry will return to their normal level.

4a. True. It is estimated that there are 12 million illegal immigrants into the United States, but the number of legal immigrants is much higher. As a portion of the U.S. population, immigrants are most represented among the least and the most educated.

4b. False. Many immigrants into the United States are unskilled. However, a very substantial portion of the most highly skilled workers in the United States are immigrants. There is a U-shaped relationship between immigrants' share of the population and level of educational attainment.

4c. True. Low-skill apparel industry output expanded and high-skill industries contracted relative to other American cities.

5a. The problem involves the specific-factors model. Because Home has more labor than Foreign and everything else is the same, the marginal product of labor in Home must be lower than the marginal product of labor in Foreign in both industries. Hence, wages will be lower in Home. If the marginal product of labor is lower in Home than in Foreign in both industries, it must be true that the marginal product of capital is higher in Home than in Foreign. Hence, the rental rate in Home must be higher as well. This creates the motive for capital to leave Foreign, where the rental on capital is low, and enter Home, where the rental on capital is high.

5b. The increase in capital expands Home's PPF in favor of M as in Figure 5-8. Because labor is drawn out of agriculture into manufacturing, the output of agriculture must fall.

FIGURE 5-8

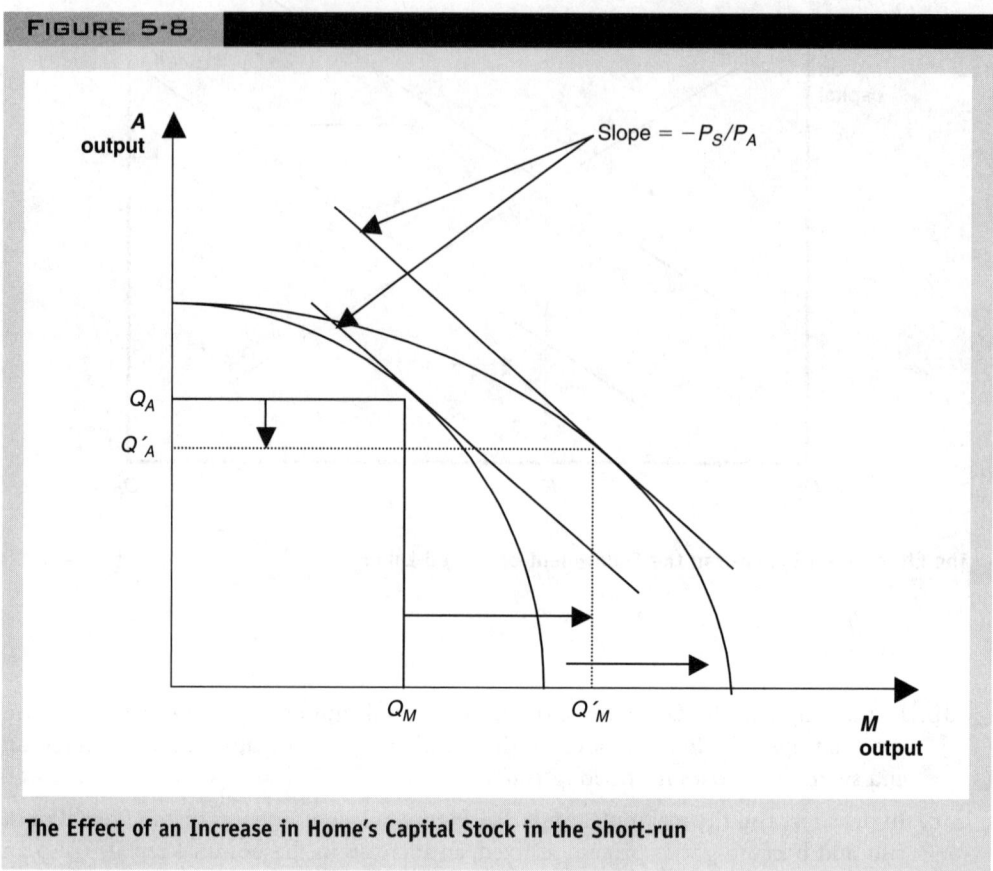

The Effect of an Increase in Home's Capital Stock in the Short-run

5c. The effect of FDI into Home is to raise the real wage. As shown in Figure 5-9, an increase in the capital endowment due to the inflow of capital shifts up the marginal product of labor in manufacturing for every level of manufacturing employment. The new capital increases the demand for labor in manufacturing and so drives up the wage. Because the prices of goods are fixed, this nominal increase in the wage is also a real increase. Because labor is drawn out of agriculture, the land/labor ratio rises so that the marginal product of land falls. Hence the earnings of the owner of a unit of land fall. Note that the capital/labor ratio must rise. To see this, note that the marginal product of labor in manufacturing has risen. For the marginal product of labor to rise in manufacturing, the capital-to-labor ratio must have increased. Hence the marginal product of capital falls, making the earnings of a unit of capital decline in real terms.

FIGURE 5-9

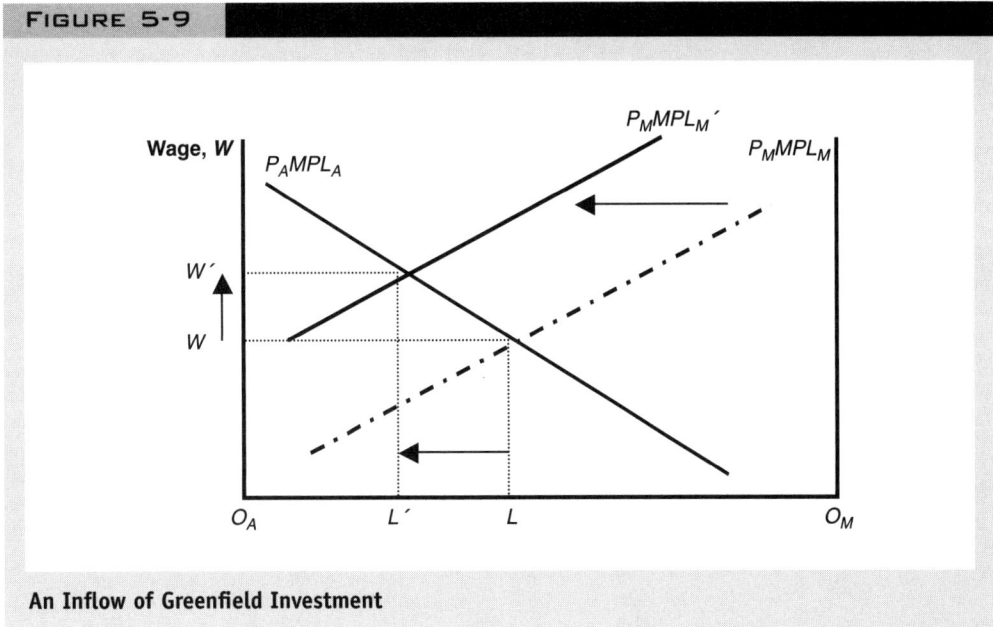

An Inflow of Greenfield Investment

5d. The effect of the outward flow of capital in Foreign is to lower labor demand by shifting down the marginal product of labor in manufacturing. Hence, the nominal and real wage falls in Foreign.

6a. The output of shirts rises! Why is this? Because capital is completely mobile between industries, we can simply apply the Rybczynski theorem. A reduction in the country's stock of capital reduces the output of the good that is intensive in that factor (airplanes) and increases the production of the other good (shirts).

6b. In the long run, the fall in the capital stock has no impact on the real wage because the reallocation of capital and labor between industries leaves the original capital/labor ratios in each industry unchanged. Because marginal products do not change in the long run, the real returns to factors stay the same. This is the factor price insensitivity result.

7a. The value of output is the area under the value of marginal product of labor curve. Given the straight line, this can be calculated as $25 \cdot 50 + (1/2) \cdot (30 \cdot 25) \cdot (150 - 100) = 1375$.

7b. The increase in output was 1375, but of this $25 \cdot 50 = 1250$ is paid to foreigners who have entered the country. Hence, the total gain to the country is 125.

7c. Home-specific factors gain from access to lower cost labor. They receive the 125 calculated in the previous problem plus the direct effect of paying the same workers less to the tune of $5 \cdot 100 = 500$, so the total gain to specific factors is 625.

8. There are big upfront moving costs to immigration. It may take years for immigrants to earn enough additional income to pay off these moving costs. Older workers expect to work for fewer years than younger workers and so may not be able to pay off these moving costs.

Increasing Returns to Scale and Imperfect Competition

1a. See the following table.

Quantity Sold	Price	Revenue	Marginal Revenue
1	7	7	7
2	6	12	5
3	5	15	3
4	4	16	1
5	3	15	−1
6	2	12	−3
7	1	7	−5

1b. The firm should make 3 units. The marginal revenue associated with selling the third unit is $3, which is greater than the marginal cost of $2.5, so selling the third unit increases revenue by more than it increases costs. For the fourth unit, the marginal revenue is $1, so the increase in sales revenue is less than the increase in cost.

1c. The firm's profit is (price − marginal cost) · quantity sold. If the firm makes 3 units, profit is ($5 − $2.5) · 3 = $7.5. Notice that the firm's profits fall to $6 if it sells one more unit.

2. The optimal price and quantity and the associated profits are shown in Figure 6-1.

FIGURE 6-1

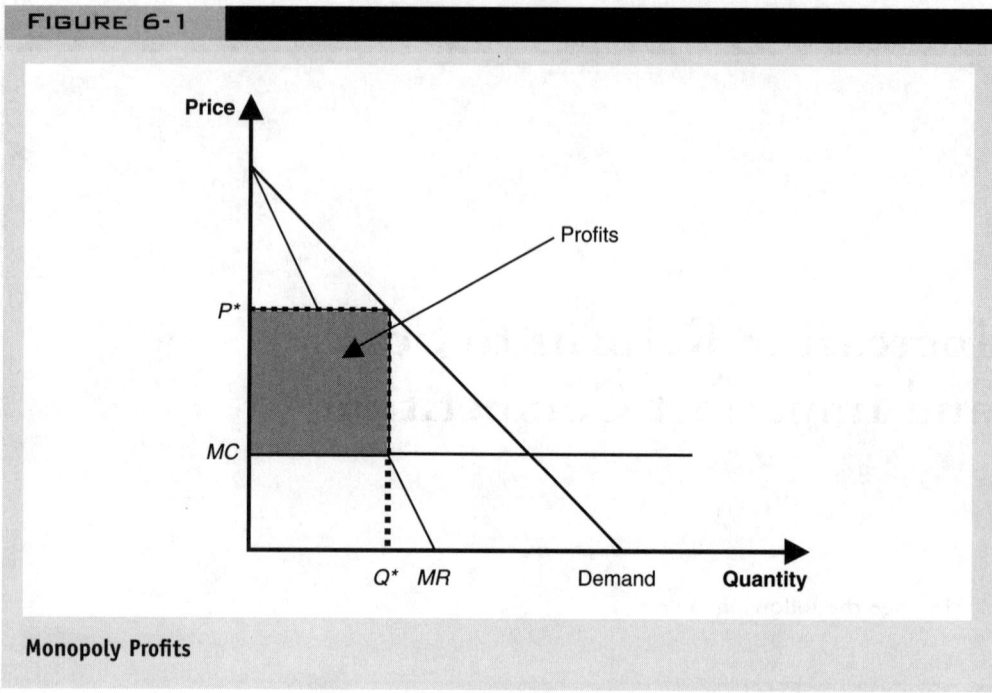

Monopoly Profits

3.   The demand curve, $D / 2$, shows how industry demand is split across two firms that charge identical prices for their own differentiated product. The demand curve d shows how much demand there will be for a firm's product if it should deviate from the typical industry behavior and charge a different price. If it lowers its price, it steals some customers from its competitor's variety, but if both firms lowered their price, then no firm steals customers from its competitors.

4.   The firm's average total cost is $(\$2 \cdot Q + \$100)/Q$. When $Q = 10$, $AC = \$12$. A firm selling 10 units must be getting a price of $12 to break even.

5a. The effect of increasing the number of products in the market is shown in Figure 6-2. The solid curve in D / N is demand per firm when each firm charges the same price before the increase in the number of products, and the dotted line labeled D / N' is the curve after the increase in products. The solid line labeled d is demand before the increase, and the broken curve labeled d' is demand after the increase.

FIGURE 6-2

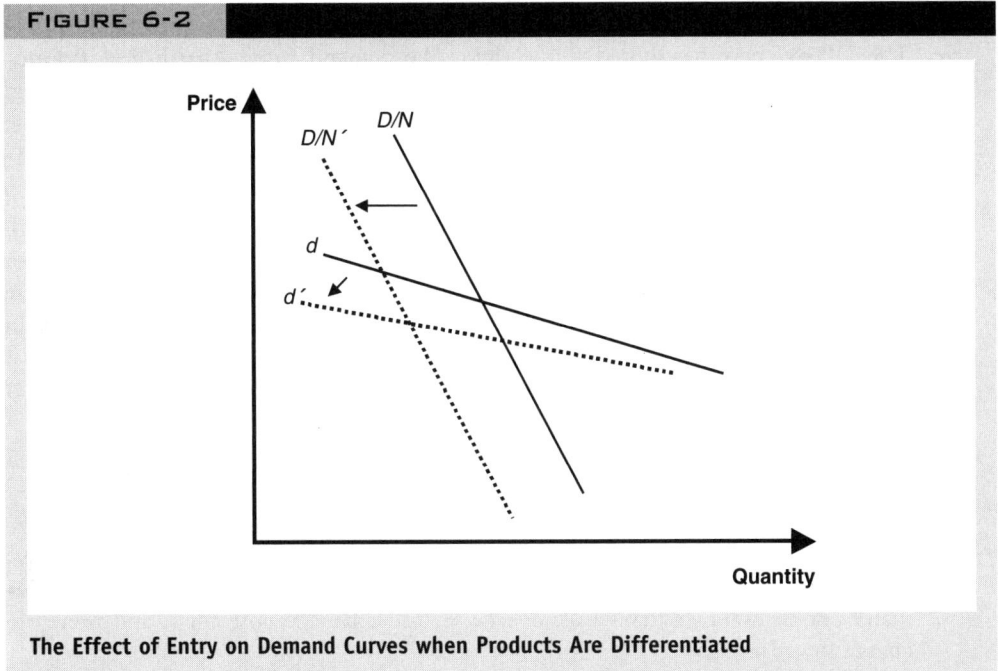

The Effect of Entry on Demand Curves when Products Are Differentiated

5b. The shift in the D/N curve is simple: The same amount of demand is split over a larger number of firms. The shift in the d curve is more complicated. The curve shifts down because the more products in the market, the less demand there is for any given product. It also becomes flatter because with increased product choice consumers become more sensitive to price differences across products.

6a. See the left-hand panel of Figure 6-3.

FIGURE 6-3

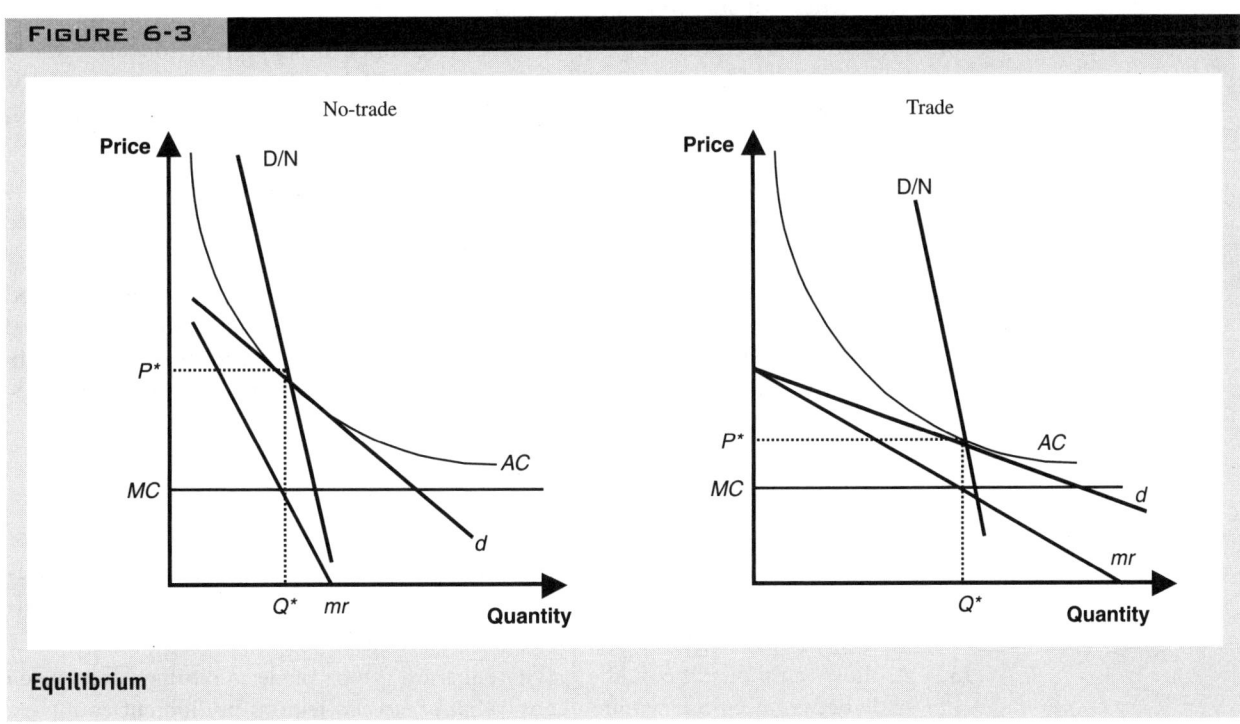

Equilibrium

6b. See the right-hand panel of Figure 6-3.

6c. The D / N curve has shifted to the right. The demand curve d has had its P intercept fall but has also become flatter. The associated marginal revenue curve has moved in a similar fashion. Finally, the price charged by the typical firm has fallen and the quantity sold has increased. In both cases, zero profits are being made.

6d. When international trade is allowed between the two identical countries, the size of the total market doubles, but the number of operating firms in this market, although larger than in each individual country in autarky, is less than twice the number of firms in each market in autarky. Hence, the D / N curve shifts to the right. Because more firms are operating in the integrated world market than in each country in autarky, the demand curve d has shifted down while also becoming flatter. Firms that stay in the market compensate for the lower price they can charge by selling a larger quantity of output so that price continues to be equal to average cost.

6e. The gains from trade include the availability of increased product variety, and these goods have become cheaper. Trade expands the product range available to consumers. This can be seen in the change in the demand curve d. (It is flatter or more elastic because there are more competing varieties.) Demand per firm has increased, however, as can be seen by the shift in the demand curve D / N to the right. Higher demand per firm allows firms to move down their average cost curve and therefore charge lower prices.

6f. The adjustment costs are associated with the closing of some firms and the subsequent dislocation of the employees at those plants. The fact that the D / N curve has shifted to the right indicates that some of the firms in each country must close and so lay off workers.

7a. The larger a market is, the more variety that market will support. The more variety in a market, the flatter the demand curve d and the lower the price charged for each variety. Hence, the real wage should be higher in the large country in a no-trade equilibrium.

7b. The small country gains more from trade because it gets access to the larger number of varieties that are produced in the larger market.

8. No, the monopolistic competition model would not be appropriate for this industry because with so few firms in the industry, the firms are likely to behave strategically. The monopolistic competition model dispenses with strategic behavior among firms by assuming that there are many of them.

9. Yes. Wine is differentiated to some extent merely by where it is produced. In principle, this is enough to generate intra-industry trade: People may consume both wine from California and from France merely for variety.

10. If workers move across industries, then trade between countries is probably motivated by comparative advantage rather than product differentiation, increasing returns, and imperfect information. Trade causes firms to reallocate resources across industries in comparative advantage models and across firms within industries in the monopolistic competition model.

11. Because the Heckscher-Ohlin model does not give rise to a gravity equation, a gravity equation is more likely to fit the data between countries that have similar endowments.

12. Because product differentiation gives rise to intra-industry trade, the index of intra-industry trade is likely to be closer to 100 when goods in that industry are highly differentiated and closer to 0 when goods are homogeneous.

13. As shown in the textbook, the gravity equation can be made to distinguish between trade between regions within a country and between regions in different countries.

The difference in the constant across borders from the constant within borders can be used to gauge the size of the "border effect."

14. As shown in the textbook, the number of goods being exported from Mexico can be used as the smallest reasonable estimate of the expansion of variety available in the United States. Doing the same for Canada would give a crude measure of the expansion in variety due to NAFTA.

15a. At home, $MR = 10 - 2Q$. In Foreign, $MR = 6 - 2Q$.

15b. Setting marginal revenue equal to marginal cost in each market, we find that the amount sold in Home is 4 units and the amount sold in Foreign is 2 units. This translates into a price in Home of 6 and a price in Foreign of 4.

15c. See Figure 6-4. The key feature of the diagram is that the demand curve in the exporter's home market has been drawn steeper than the importing country. The higher price charged by the firm in the exporter's home market is evidence of dumping.

FIGURE 6-4

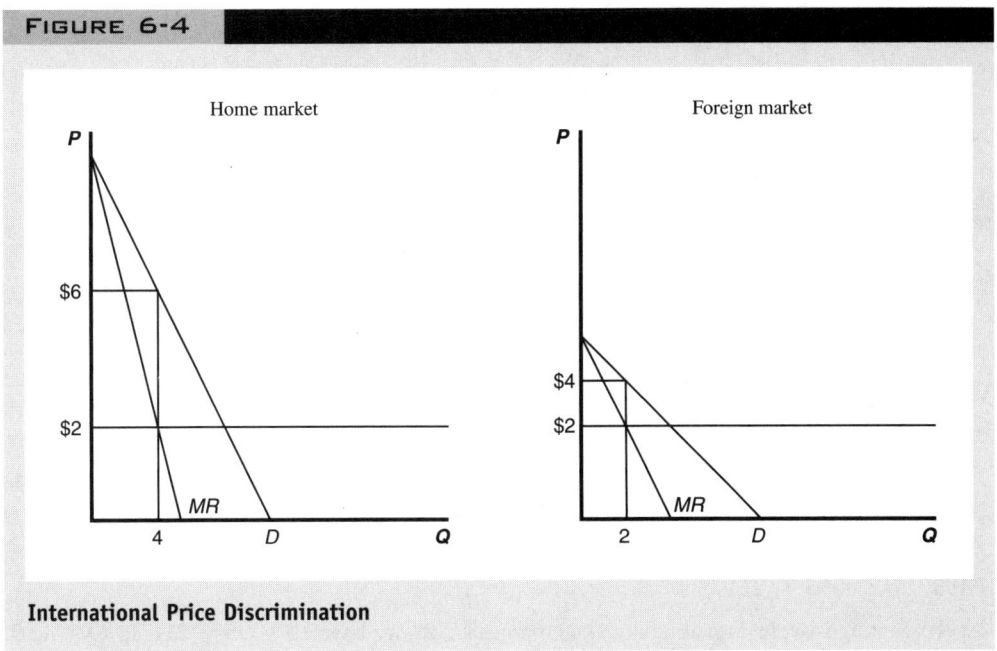

International Price Discrimination

16. Yes. The firm could be accused of dumping if the average cost is greater than $10 (as might happen during a recession) or if the price being charged in the foreign market is not increased above the home price by the amount of any shipping cost incurred.

17a. See Figure 6-5. (Note that the actual level of demand in Foreign has been assumed to be large relative to the amount sold by the firm.)

FIGURE 6·5

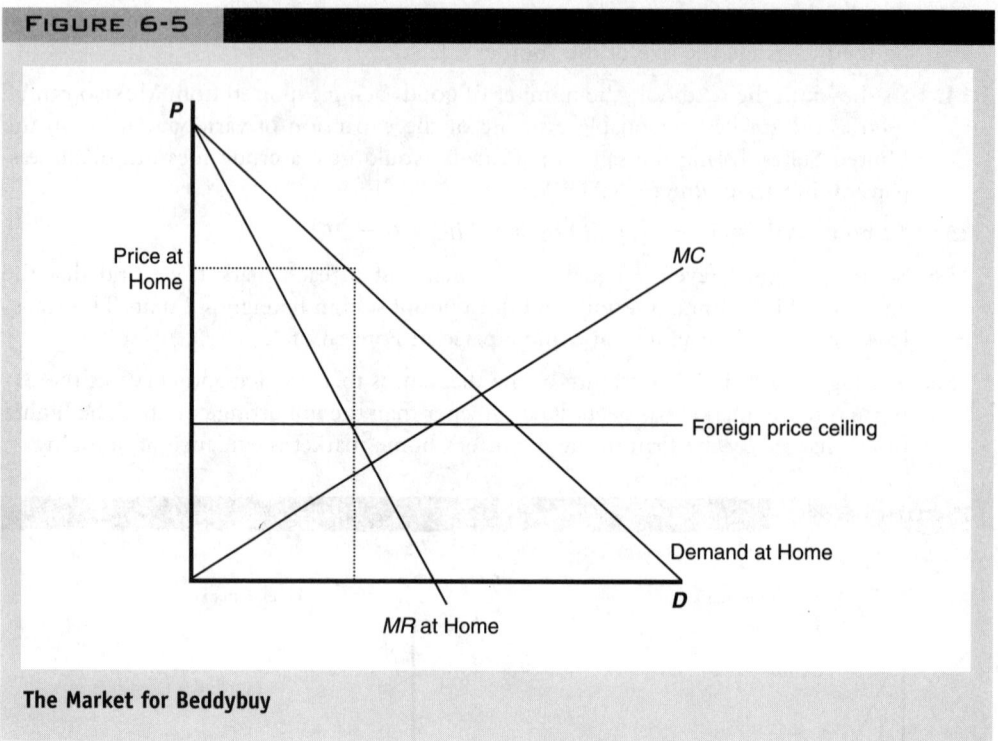

The Market for Beddybuy

17b. If the drug company finds that consumers at Home are buying their product abroad, they may cease to sell their product in Foreign if the profits from being able to charge them the monopoly price at Home are large relative to the profits of supplying both markets when consumers are paying the regulated price.

18. International trade turns a monopoly into an oligopoly. Because international trade allows more firms to compete in the country's market, prices should be lower. This is good for consumers and is a form of gains from trade.

19a. $MR = 95 - 2Q$.

19b. Setting marginal revenue equal to marginal cost, we have $10 = 95 - 2Q$. So $Q = 42.5$. Plugging this back into the demand equation, we have $P = 95 - 42.5 = 52.5$.

19c. Economic profit is ($52.5 - $10) · 42.5 = $1,806.25.

19d. The marginal revenue facing a firm in each market is $MR = P - q$, where q is the amount sold by that firm.

19e. Setting marginal cost equal to marginal revenue in a firm's home market, we have $10 = P - q_H$. Setting marginal cost equal to marginal revenue in the foreign market, we have $15 = P - q_F$. From the demand curve we have $P = 95 - q_H - q_F$ (because sales in each country are due to local and foreign firms). Putting all these equations together, we have $P = 95 - (P - 10) - (P - 15)$. Solving this equation, we find $P = 40. Hence, the firm sells $40 - 10 = 30$ in its home market and $40 - 15 = 25$ in the foreign market.

19f. Although the firm is charging the same price in each market, the export sales have higher costs, and so $5 should be subtracted from the foreign price to make it comparable to the home price.

19g. The profit in a firm's home market is ($40 - $10) · 30 = $900. The profit in foreign market is ($40 - $15) · 25 = $625. The total profit is then $900 + $625 = $1,525, which is lower than the firm's profits when trade was not allowed.

Foreign Outsourcing of Goods and Services

7

1a. First, we calculate the cost of each activity in each country. These calculations are shown in the following table:

	a	b	c
Home	$4 \cdot 1 + $2 \cdot 4 = $12	$4 \cdot 2 + $2 \cdot 3 = $14	$4 \cdot 3 + $2 \cdot 2 = $16
Foreign	$5 \cdot 1 + $1 \cdot 4 = $9	$5 \cdot 2 + $1 \cdot 3 = $13	$5 \cdot 3 + $1 \cdot 2 = $17

In the absence of transport costs, Foreign is the cheaper producer for activities a and b, whereas Home is the cheaper producer in activity c. With transport costs of $2, the gap in costs would have to be at least this large to induce Home firms to outsource the activity to Foreign. Hence only a is produced in Foreign and b and c are produced in Home.

1b. From the table in the answer to 1a, we see that if there are no transport costs, then a and b would be outsourced to Foreign and only c would remain in Home.

1c. Before the transport costs fall, the amount of Home's skilled labor used in the production of a good is 2 + 3 = 5 and the amount of Home's unskilled labor is 3 + 2 = 5, so the ratio is 1. After the reduction in transport cost, the ratio is 3:2 because only c is done in Home. Hence, the ratio increases from 1 to 1.5. In Foreign the ratio is initially 1:4 but rises to (1 + 2):(4 + 3) or 3:7. Hence, relative demand rises in both countries.

1d. No, only the interpretation of the trading pattern would be different.

2. Banning foreign investment may keep the stock of capital in the country low and the rental high. The high rental to capital would raise the cost of performing each production activity and so limit the amount of outsourcing.

3. If only trade in final goods were allowed, then comparing the factor intensities of goods makes sense. However, once activities can be split into pieces, it is only the factor intensities of the activities that matter for the location of production, not the factor intensities of goods.

4a. The actual assembly-line kinds of jobs done by blue collar workers increasingly may have been outsourced to lower-wage countries, leaving primarily white collar jobs in the United States.

4b. The relative wage of white collar workers has risen over this same time. In the Heckscher–Ohlin model this would mean that firms would substitute blue collar workers for white collar workers. But exactly the opposite appears to be happening.

4c. There could have been skill-biased technical change that resulted in the automation of blue collar jobs.

5a. See Figure 7-2. The diagram shows an improvement in the terms of trade for a country with a comparative advantage in R&D. Because R&D activity will buy more components, firm output increases from Y_0 to Y_1.

FIGURE 7-2

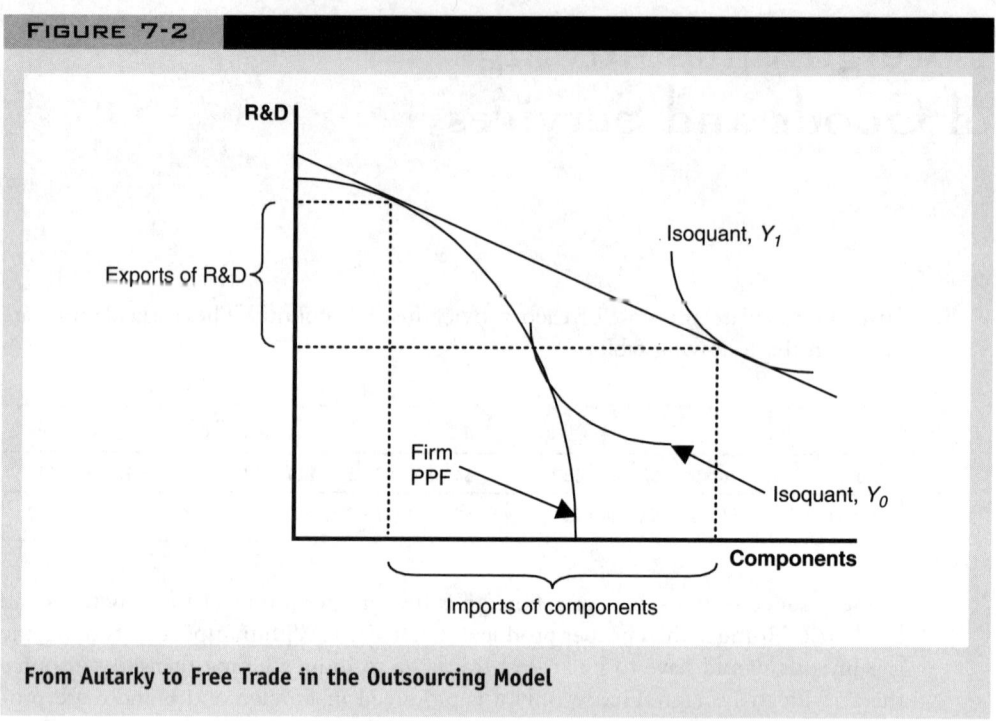

From Autarky to Free Trade in the Outsourcing Model

5b. Home firms export R&D to Foreign firms in return for imports of components that Home firms use (along with R&D that they keep) to produce final goods.

5c. Home firms are able to produce more final output with the same quantity of inputs. Hence, their apparent productivity has increased.

5d. As in the Heckscher–Ohlin model, the increase in the output of the skill-intensive activity (rather than good) increases the relative demand for skilled workers.

5e. See Figure 7-3. An improvement in the terms of trade allows the firm to purchase more components with the same amount of R&D. This change induces the firm to shift resources output of components production into R&D production, expand its trade, and ultimately increase its output from Y_1 to Y_2.

FIGURE 7-3

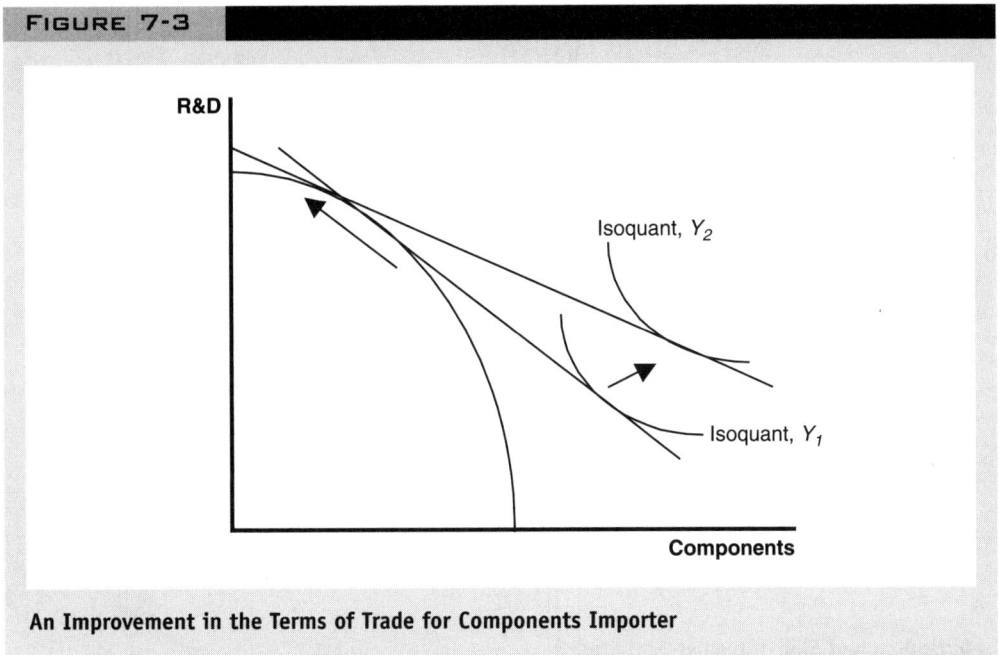

An Improvement in the Terms of Trade for Components Importer

5f. The terms-of-trade improvement increases the amount of final output that the firm can produce with the same quantity of inputs. Hence, the firm appears to be more productive.

6a. Improving Foreign's ability to produce components would help Home if it results in an improvement in Home's terms of trade: A decline in the relative price of components makes Home better off.

6b. Improving Foreign's ability to conduct R&D would hurt Home if it results in a deterioration in Home's terms of trade.

7. According to the study, 14% to 19% of productivity growth can be attributed to outsourcing, whereas less than 7% can be attributed to high-technology capital.

8a. See Figure 7-4. The diagram shows that if transport costs are high for the least skill-intensive activities and low for the most skill-intensive activities, then the slicing of the value chain could be very different.

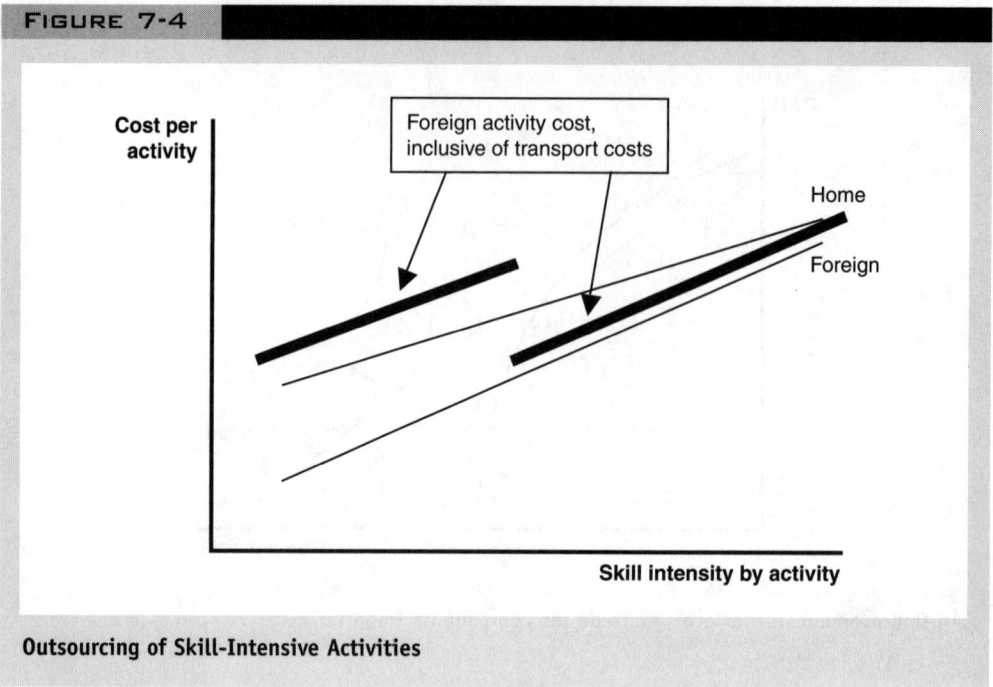

FIGURE 7-4

Cost per activity

Foreign activity cost, inclusive of transport costs

Home

Foreign

Skill intensity by activity

Outsourcing of Skill-Intensive Activities

8b. Yes, once we have nonuniform transport costs across activities, any number of permutations could actually arise. An example is illustrated in Figure 7-5. Transport costs are low for very low skill-intensive activities and for very high skill-intensive activities while being high for activities of moderate skill intensity. As a result, the least and most skill-intensive activities are outsourced in this example while those "in the middle" stay put.

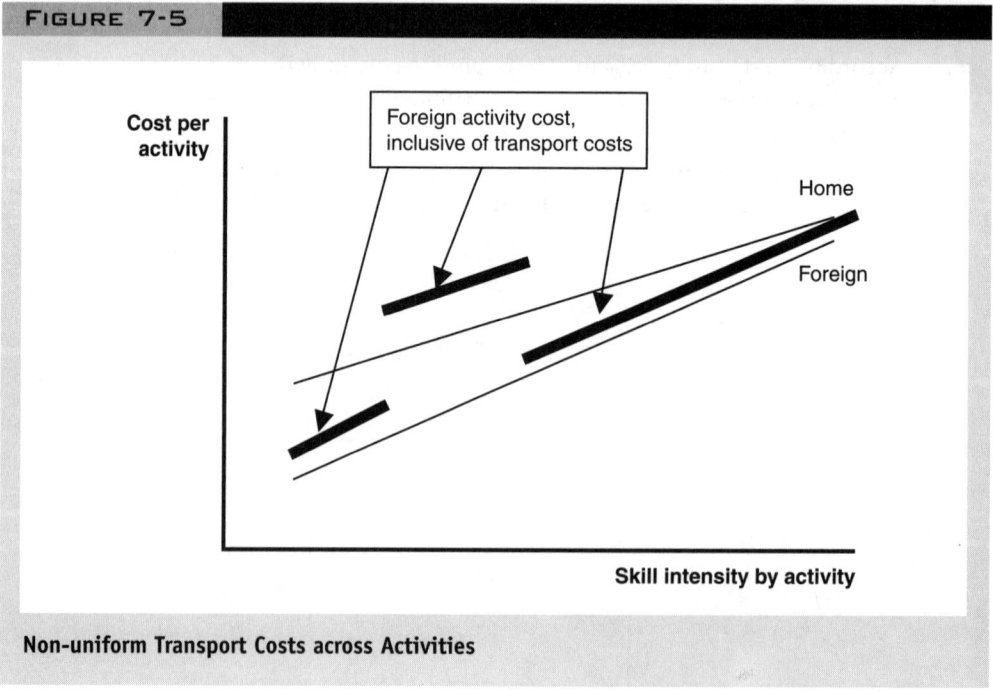

FIGURE 7-5

Cost per activity

Foreign activity cost, inclusive of transport costs

Home

Foreign

Skill intensity by activity

Non-uniform Transport Costs across Activities

9. India's growing output of business services could hurt the United States if it causes a deterioration in the terms of trade for the United States.

10. As services become more tradable, the United States could begin to export a larger volume of them. As output of services expands, factors could be pulled out of manufacturing and into services. This is essentially what is happening in the gains-from-outsourcing example given in the textbook and considered again in problem 5.

8

Import Tariffs and Quotas under Perfect Competition

1a. The firm would be selling its product in your market at less than the normal price. Normal price would mean the price in the exporting country's market, the price in a third country, or the average cost of production.

1b. This is an example of a free-trade agreement, which is allowed under Article XXIV of the GATT.

1c. "Normal trade relations" perhaps better conveys the actual meaning of "most favored nation status," which is the principle of nondiscrimination.

2. Anne's consumer surplus is $1, the difference between the $3 that she was willing to pay for the first tomato and the price of the tomato, $2.

3. Producer surplus is the payment to the fixed factor of production. Hence, the producer surplus in this case is revenue minus the wage bill, or $40.

4a. The autarky price is the price at which the country would not want to import any of the product, or $10.

4b. The triangle in Figure 8-2, with area $\frac{1}{2} \cdot (\$10/\text{unit} - \$6/\text{unit}) \cdot 15$ units $= \$30$, is the gains from trade. This is equal to the difference between the gain in consumer surplus and the loss of producer surplus, which is also a triangle, with a height of $\$10/\text{unit} - \$6/\text{unit}$ and a base of 15 units. See triangle D in Figure 8-2 in the textbook.

4c. See Figure 8-5.

FIGURE 8-5

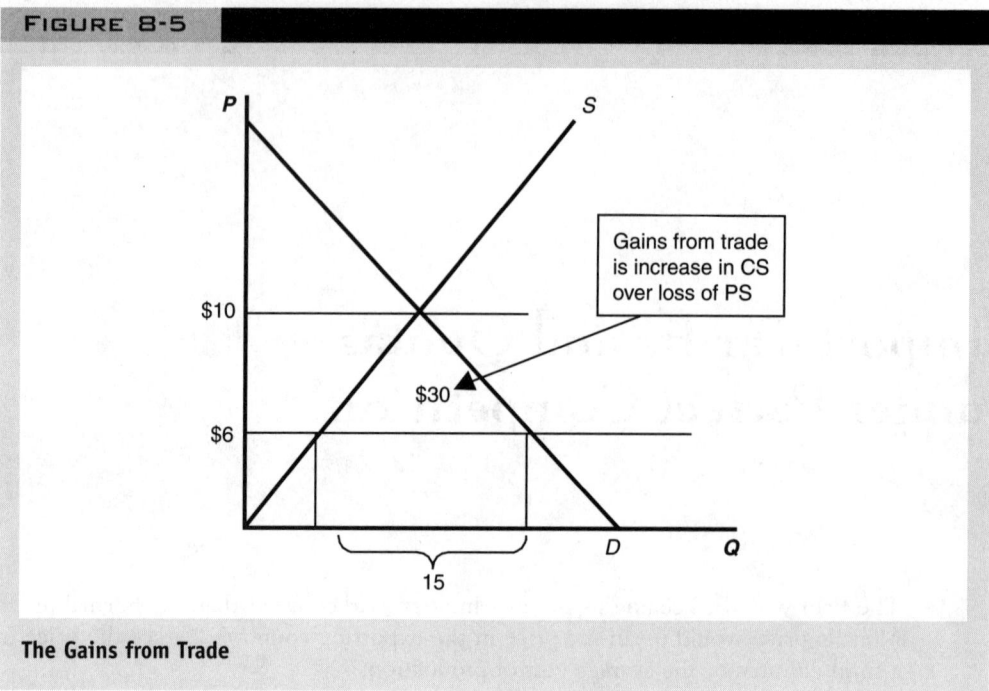

The Gains from Trade

5a. The price at Home rises to $8 (which is $P_W + t$).

5b. The tariff is $2 per unit and 7.5 units are imported, so the total tariff revenue is $15.

5c. The deadweight loss of the tariff is equal to the reduction in imports (15 units − 7.5 units) multiplied by half the $2 increase in price: $1/2(\$2/\text{unit})(7.5 \text{ units}) = \$7.5$.

5d. The change in producer surplus is equal to the difference between the change in revenue minus the change in payments to variable factors of production, or $5.

5e. Consider Figure 8–6. The figure shows the effect of the tariff on the home country. The labeled geometric figures correspond to components of the welfare change that were calculated earlier in the problem. The total loss of consumer surplus is equal to the area $f + g + h + i$. From 5d, the area f is $5. From 5c, the area $g + i$ is the deadweight loss of $7.5. From 5b, the area h is the size of the tariff revenue, $15 as calculated. Hence, the total loss of consumer surplus is $27.50.

FIGURE 8-6

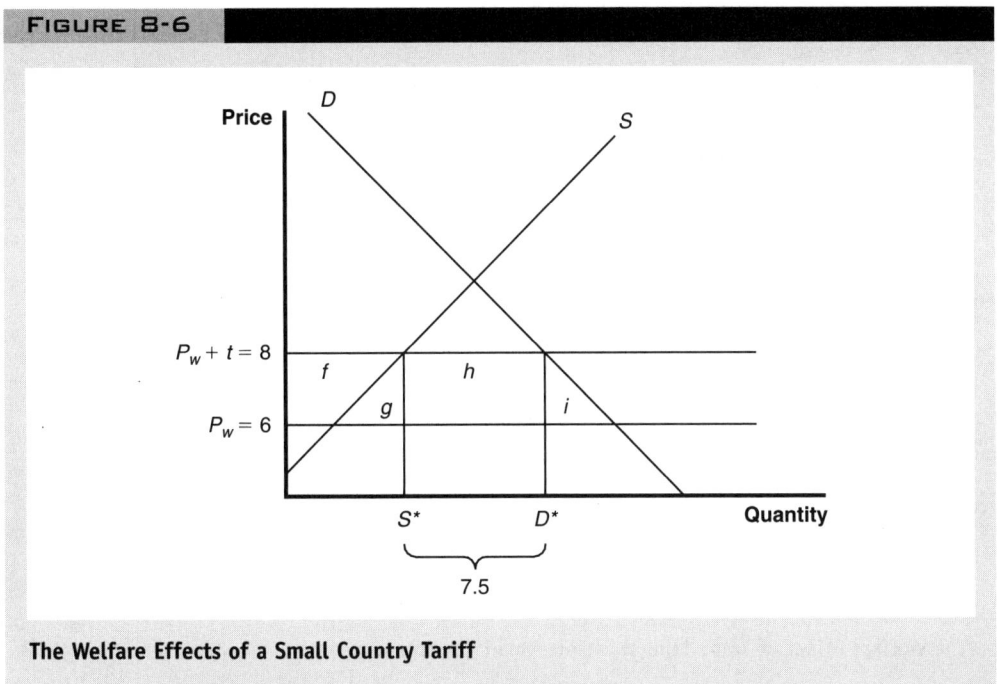

The Welfare Effects of a Small Country Tariff

5f. See Figure 8-6 and the numbers for *f, g, h,* and *i* provided in the answer to 5e.

6a. Producer surplus decreases by $175. This is equal to the reduction in revenue (holding fixed output) of $200 and subtracting the production loss of the tariff 1/2($2)25 = $25.

6b. Consumer surplus increases by $625. Holding fixed the quantity sold, the $2 fall in price raises consumer surplus by $600. Add to this the consumption loss under the tariff 1/2($2)25 = $25.

6c. Tariff revenue falls by $400 = $2(300 − 100)

6d. The deadweight loss of the tariff is equal to $50, and the removal of the tariff gets rid of this deadweight loss, making the country better off.

6e. The information is displayed in Figure 8-7.

FIGURE 8·7

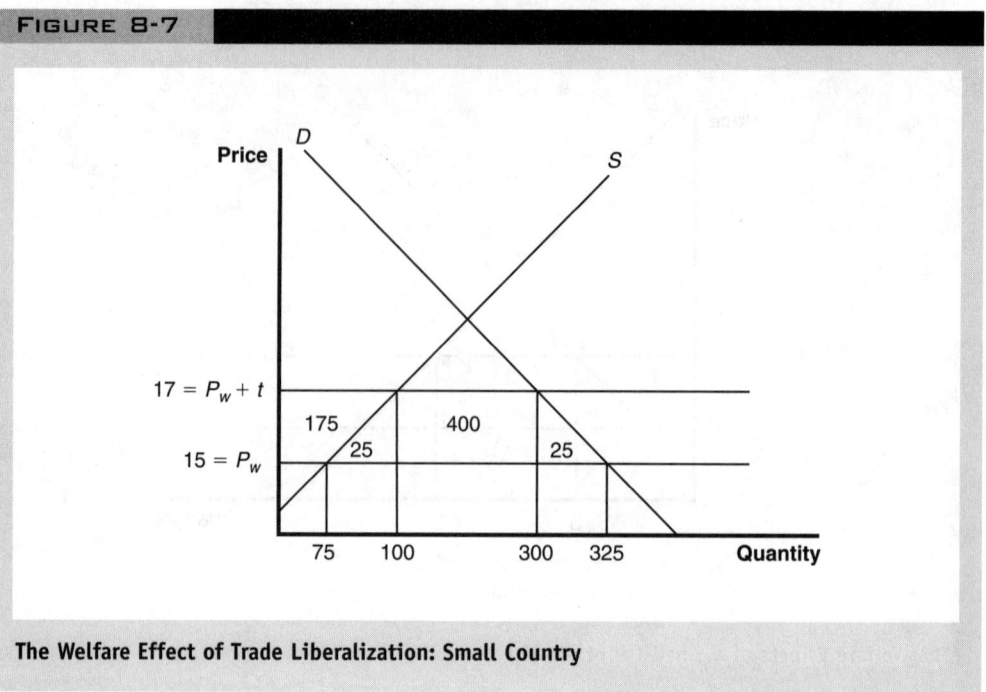

The Welfare Effect of Trade Liberalization: Small Country

7a. Because the home price is $11 and the tariff is $2, the world price with the tariff must be $9.

7b. The revenue raised by the tariff is $2/unit multiplied by 50 units or $100.

7c. Using the deadweight loss formula we have $(1/2)(\$11/\text{unit} - \$10/\text{unit})(100 \text{ units} - 50 \text{ units}) = \$25$.

7d. The total effect on national welfare is the terms-of-trade gain minus the deadweight loss. The terms-of-trade gain is $(\$10/\text{unit} - \$9/\text{unit})50 \text{ units} = \$50$. This is greater than the deadweight loss by $25. Hence, Home gains from this tariff.

7e. The welfare effect on foreign is its terms-of-trade loss (Home's gain) plus its dead-weight loss. The deadweight loss is $(1/2)(\$10/\text{unit} - \$9/\text{unit})(100 \text{ units} - 50 \text{ units}) = \$25$. Hence, the total welfare loss to Foreign is $75.

7f. The effect on world welfare is the sum of the deadweight losses in both Home and Foreign, or $50.

7g. See Figure 8-8.

FIGURE 8-8

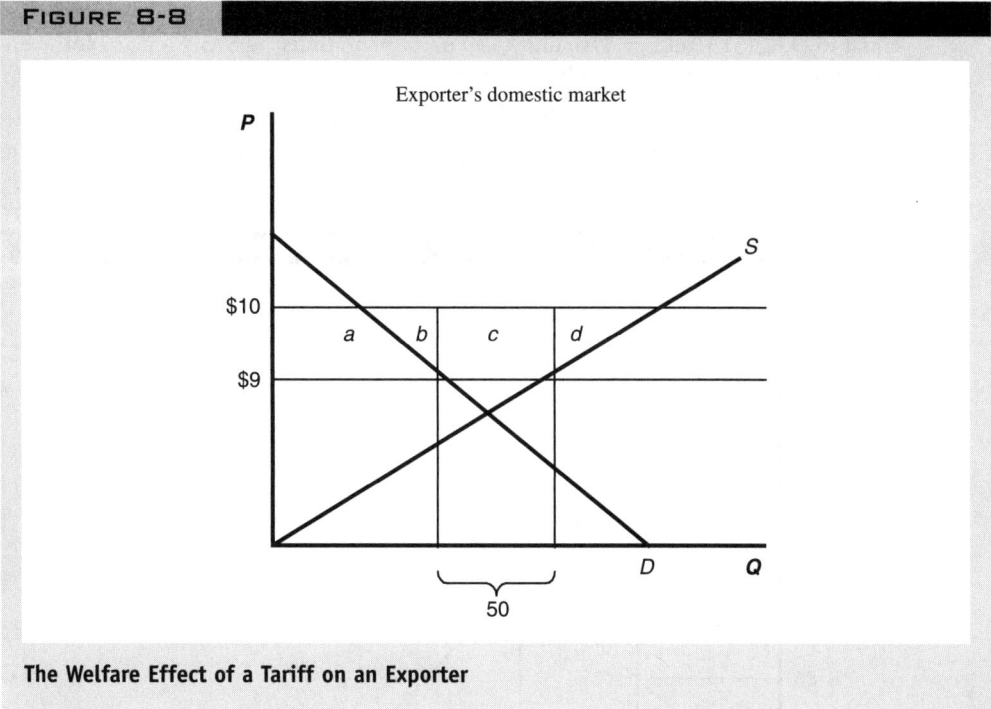

The Welfare Effect of a Tariff on an Exporter

The diagram shows consumer surplus gain a, producer surplus loss of $a + b + c + d$, and net loss of exporting country welfare of $b + c + d$, which is equal in value to the sum of deadweight loss of $b + d = \$25$ and terms-of-trade loss of $c = \$50$.

8. The elasticity of the supply curve is related to its steepness. The steeper the supply curve, the lower the elasticity. When the supply curve is very steep, the more the incidence of the tariff falls on the exporting country. The more of the tariff borne by the foreigners, the larger the optimal tariff.

9a. In the case of perfect competition and quota licenses that are distributed via a perfectly competitive auction, the welfare effect of tariffs and quotas are equivalent. Both raise the domestic price of the good above the world price (and so alter producer and consumer surplus in the same way), and both raise exactly the same amount of revenue for the government.

9b. A producer would rather be protected by a quota than a tariff in this case. In the case of the quota, the domestic price is determined solely by domestic demand, domestic supply, and the size of the quota. Changes in the world price then have no effect on producer surplus. In the case of the tariff, the price at home is equal to the price on world markets plus the tariff. A reduction in the world price would then reduce the home price as well, thereby lowering producer surplus.

10a. The value of the quota rent is the difference between the domestic and world price of the good (\$5/units) multiplied by the size of the quota (50 units). Hence, the value of the quota rent is \$250.

10b. The deadweight loss to the exporting country is equal to $(1/2)(\$10/\text{unit} - \$8/\text{unit})(100 \text{ units} - 50 \text{ units}) = \$50$. In addition, the exporting country suffers the terms-of-trade loss of $(\$10/\text{unit} - \$8/\text{unit})(50 \text{ units}) = \$100$. Hence, the total welfare loss to the exporting country is \$150.

10c. The importing country enjoys the terms of trade gain of $100 and a deadweight loss equal to $(1/2)(\$13/\text{unit} - \$10/\text{unit})(100 \text{ units} - 50 \text{ units}) = \$75$. Hence, Home enjoys an increase in national welfare of $25.

10d. See Figure 8-9. The box of size $100 is the terms-of-trade loss (gain) for the exporter (importer), the triangle with size $50 is the deadweight loss in the exporting country, and the triangle with size $75 is the deadweight loss in the importing country.

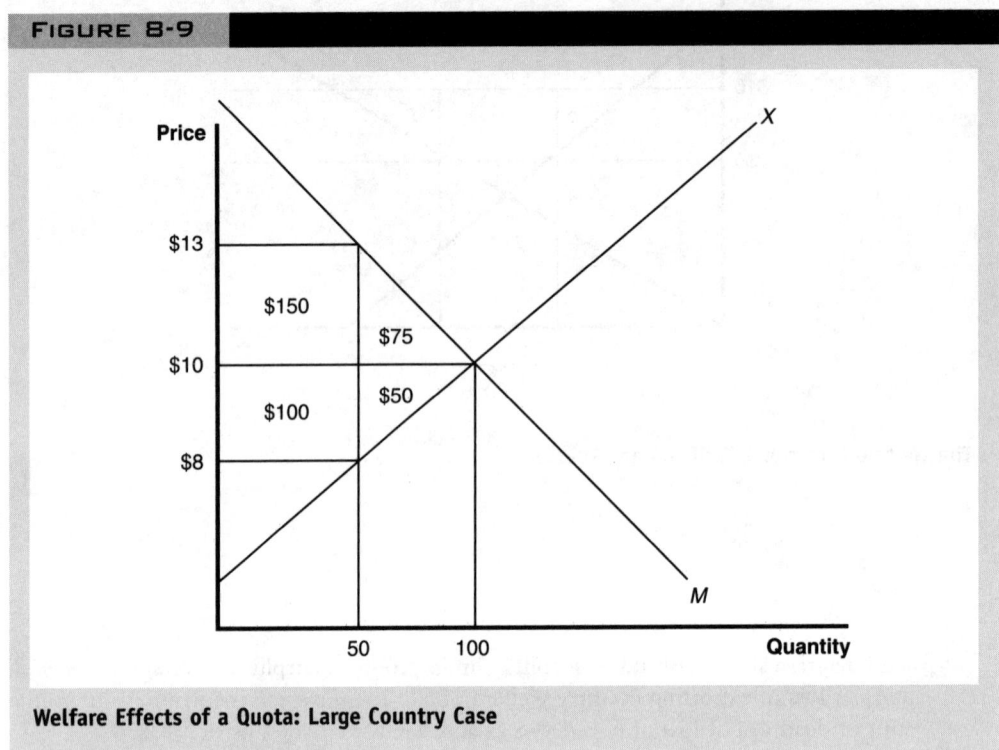

FIGURE 8-9

Welfare Effects of a Quota: Large Country Case

10e. If the importing country were to give the quota rents to the exporting country, then the exporter would see the quota raise its welfare by $100 = $150 − $50, whereas the importing country would see its welfare fall by $225 = $150 + $75.

11. By giving the quota rents to the exporting country, the importing country reduces the incentive for the exporting country to retaliate or seek redress from the WTO. As we found in the last question, the exporting country can actually be made better off. In fact, the case study on Japanese automobiles is consistent with this hypothesis.

9

Import Tariffs and Quotas under Imperfect Competition

1a. See Figure 9-2. When international trade is not allowed, the firm is a monopoly and therefore chooses its quantity so that marginal cost is equal to marginal revenue (Q_1). This level of output implies a monopoly price of P^M.

FIGURE 9-2

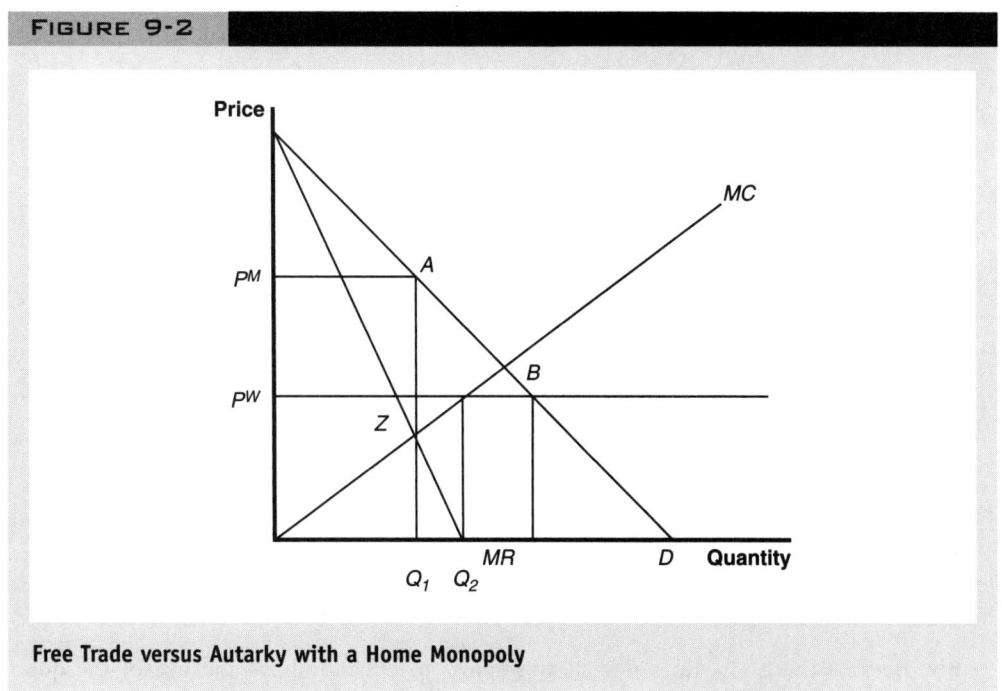

Free Trade versus Autarky with a Home Monopoly

1b. International trade forces the firm to lower its price to P^W.

1c. When the firm is exposed to international trade, the best it can do is choose the quantity that sets the world price (its new marginal revenue curve) equal to its marginal cost (Q_2). Given the way that the diagram is drawn, this actually implies an increase in output.

1d. The international market constrains the monopoly power of the firm and so lowers its producer surplus.

1e. The price charged by the monopolist in autarky (P^M) exceeds the world price, so free trade improves consumer surplus.

1f. Consumers gain the trapezoid, $P^M A B P^W$. This gain in consumer surplus contains within it the lost monopoly profits (the rectangle $P^M A Z P^W$). Hence the country is better off with trade.

1g. If the world price were below the intersection between the marginal revenue and marginal cost curve, then the monopolists' output would fall rather than rise.

2. Yes. Consider Figure 9-2. Suppose that P^W were above the intersection between the demand curve and the marginal cost curve but below P^M. In this case the monopolist would be willing to satisfy all domestic demand at that price. The fact that the country could import at that price is all that is needed to force the domestic price down.

3a. See Figure 9-3. Note that the marginal revenue curve has been omitted to avoid cluttering up the diagram. The result is very similar to the perfect competition small-country case. The tariff increases the price, expanding the producer surplus by the area a, and decreasing consumer surplus by $(a + b + c + d)$. The tariff collects revenue c, so the total impact on national welfare is $-(b + d)$.

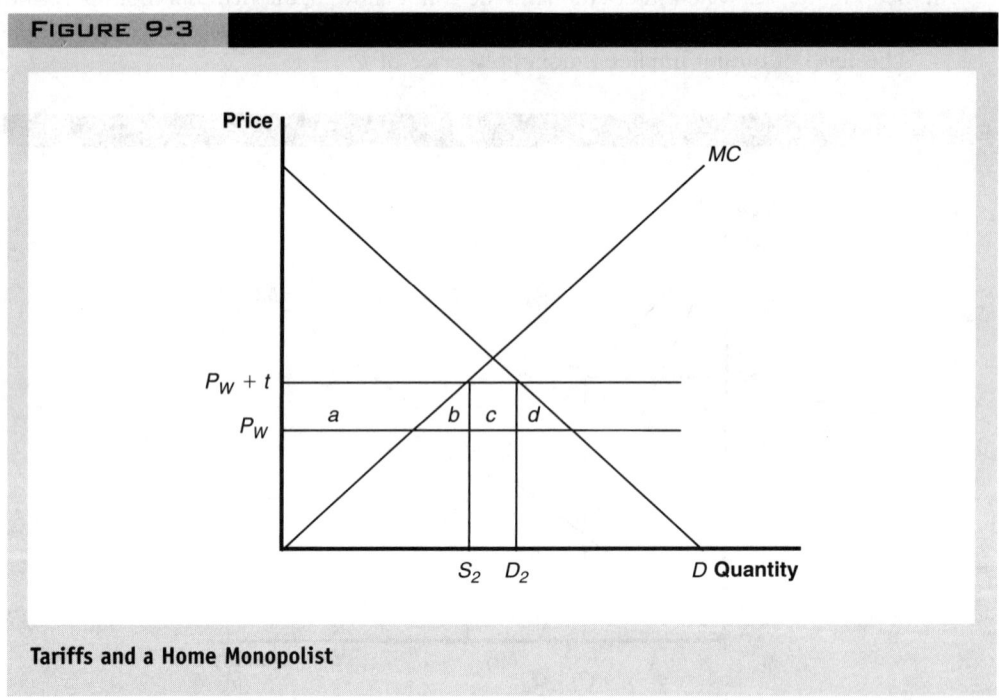

FIGURE 9-3

Tariffs and a Home Monopolist

3b. Because the quota does not allow imports to expand above the size of the quota when the price on the domestic market rises, the Home firm has monopoly power. As shown in Figure 9-4, the quota that under perfect competition would lower imports by the same amount as a tariff of size t has the effect of shifting the demand curve and marginal revenue curve facing the monopolist to the left. The firm charges a markup over its marginal cost that exceeds the size of the tariff t. As a result the domestic price with a quota P^Q exceeds the domestic price with a tariff $P^W + t$, so consumer surplus is lower under a quota than it is under a tariff.

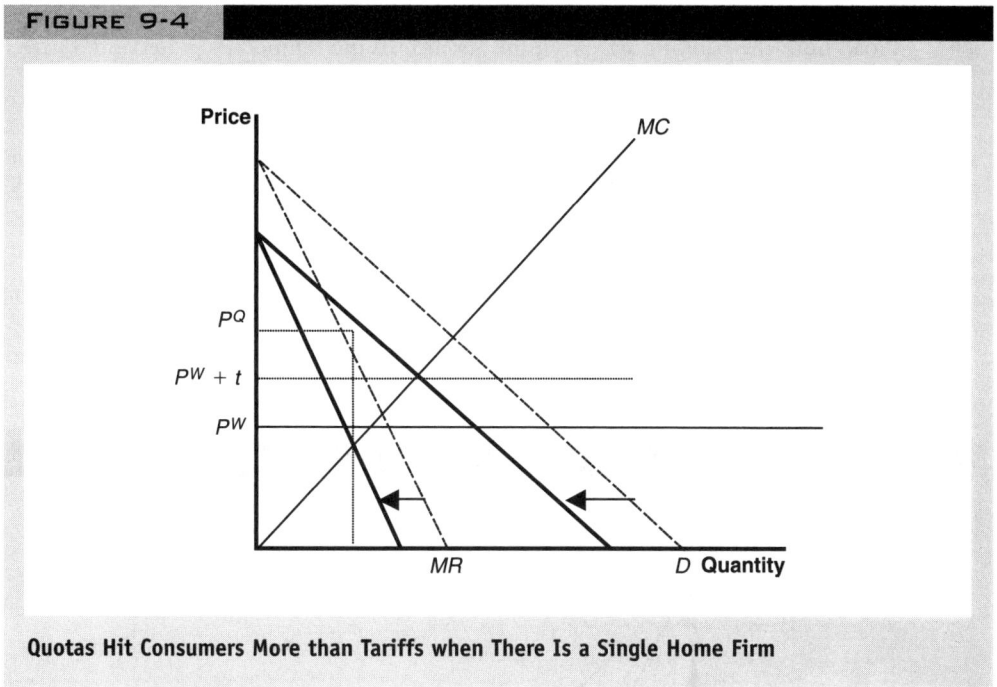

Figure 9-4

Quotas Hit Consumers More than Tariffs when There Is a Single Home Firm

3c. Suppose a tariff t resulted in M units imported. The tariff revenue would be $t \cdot M$. A quota of size M would imply quota rents of $(P^Q - P^W) \cdot M$ because each quota license allows the owner to buy at the low world price of P^W and to sell at the high domestic price of P^Q. Because $P^Q - P^W > t$, it follows that the quota rent associated with imports of M exceeds the tariff revenue associated with import with imports of M.

4a. By raising the price of cucumbers above the world price, the tariff would lower consumer surplus in every year that the domestic price is above the world price.

4b. In order for infant industry protection to be appropriate, P must be below the average cost of production for the home cucumber firm now but must be no less than the average cost of product for the home cucumber firm in 5 years.

4c. If capital markets were perfect in Home, then one argument for infant industry protection would not be valid. A firm that will eventually be competitive should be able to borrow against future earnings if these earnings are to materialize. An argument might still be made if there were positive externalities in the cucumber industry.

4d. The existence of positive externalities, such as knowledge spillovers, could justify infant industry protection, but in the cucumber industry that might be a hard sell.

5a. If the reason for infant industry protection were purely that capital markets were imperfect, then it would make no sense to offer the protection. This is because the producer surplus accrues to the foreign multinational rather than to a domestic firm.

5b. If the argument were that this is an industry with knowledge spillovers, then domestic entrepreneurs might benefit from having the foreign multinational. These spillovers would lower the cost of domestic firms and so might justify the tariff. The application to China's auto industry suggests that multinationals may have played a role in getting the auto industry started in China.

6. From the application in the textbook, it appears that Harley-Davidson could not get a loan from the banking system in the absence of the temporary protection. There is no suggestion that it had to do with any positive externalities.

7a. See Figure 9-5. If there is no tariff, then the marginal cost of serving the market is $10. Setting marginal cost equal to marginal revenue ($10 = 100 - 2Q$) and solving, we find that the optimal quantity to sell is 45 units. Plugging this number into the demand function ($P = 100 - 45$) gives us a price of $55.

7b. See Figure 9-5. The tariff raises the marginal cost of serving the market to $20. Setting marginal cost equal to marginal revenue ($20 = 100 - 2Q$), we find that the optimal quantity to sell is now 40 units. Plugging this number into the demand function ($P = 100 - 40$) gives us a price of $60. Here is an example of a tariff that is not fully passed on to consumers. A $10 tariff increased the price by only $5.

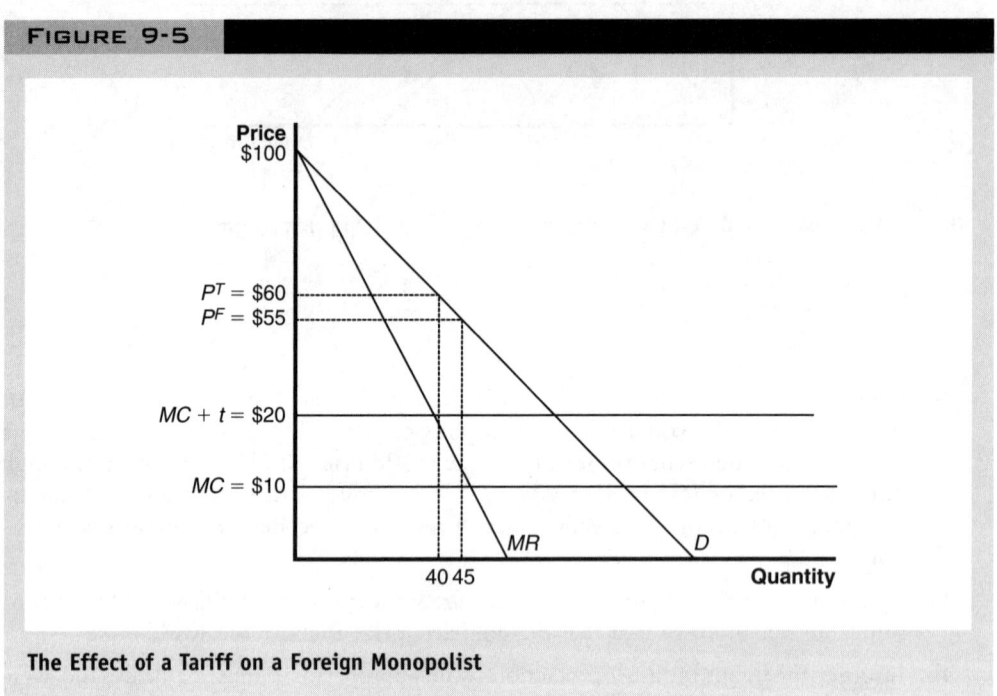

FIGURE 9-5

The Effect of a Tariff on a Foreign Monopolist

7c. Using the formula for the area of a triangle, consumer surplus is equal to $1,012.50 with free trade ($1/2 \cdot [100 - 55] \cdot 45$) and $800 with the tariff ($1/2 \cdot [100 - 60] \cdot 40$). Tariff revenue collected by the government is equal to 0 without the tariff and $400 with the tariff ($10 \cdot 40$). National welfare is the sum of consumer surplus plus tariff revenue, so the tariff made the country better off.

8a. See Figure 9-6. The key point is that the marginal revenue curve is not as steep as the demand curve and so the domestic price rises by more than the tariff. Before the tariff is applied, the foreign monopolist sells quantity Q_1 where the marginal cost (MC) of serving the market is equal to the marginal revenue (MR). This quantity implies a home market price of P_1. The tariff increases the marginal cost by t per unit ($MC + t$) and so induces the monopolist to cut back supply to Q_2, which implies a price of P_2. Because the demand curve is steeper than the marginal revenue curve, the price increase $P_2 - P_1$ is larger than the size of the tariff t.

FIGURE 9-6

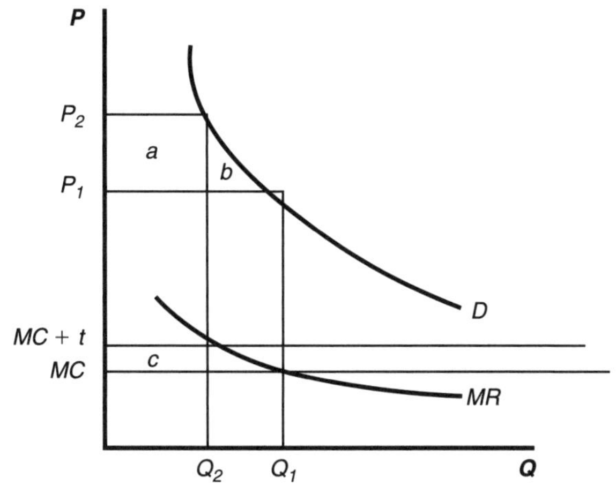

Demand Curve Steeper than the Marginal Revenue Curve

8b. No, in this case the loss in consumer surplus (area $a + b$ in Figure 9-6) must exceed the increase in government revenue, which is equal to $t \cdot Q_2$ (area c in Figure 9-6). This must be so because $P_2 - P_1 > t$.

9. As pointed out in the text, the mere threat of antidumping tariffs can induce foreign firms to raise their price in the importing country. Hence, the government official's statement is potentially misleading because foreign producers may have been induced to change their behavior even if no antidumping cases are filed.

10. It is relatively easy to file a dumping case, and there is a good chance that the government will find in favor of a dumping claim. Even when a dumping case is not fully prosecuted, the threat of dumping duties is often enough to induce foreign firms to increase their price.

11. For antidumping tariffs to be applied, there must be evidence of "material injury" to domestic producers. If there are no domestic producers, then there can be no evidence of material injury.

Export Subsidies in Agriculture and High-Technology Industries

10

1. By increasing the supply of food, the aid drives down the price of food on world markets, a phenomenon that hurts developing-country exporters of food. A more helpful policy is to provide aid in cash.

2. A tax credit on fertilizer would lower the cost of agricultural producers and so may be construed as a production subsidy.

3. An export subsidy increases the price of the good in Home to a level above the world price. This would allow arbitragers to buy a good at the low world price, import the good, and then request the export subsidy. Hence, the government must put an import tariff in place to prevent this possibility.

4a. The country exports 120 units and the government pays $1 for each unit, so the total cost to the government is $120.

4b. Because this is a small country, the effect of the subsidy on national welfare is the deadweight loss. This is equal to one half of the increase in exports multiplied by the increase in the Home price of the good, or $10.

4c. See Figure 10-4. The deadweight loss is equal to $10, and the total cost of the subsidy is $120.

FIGURE 10-5

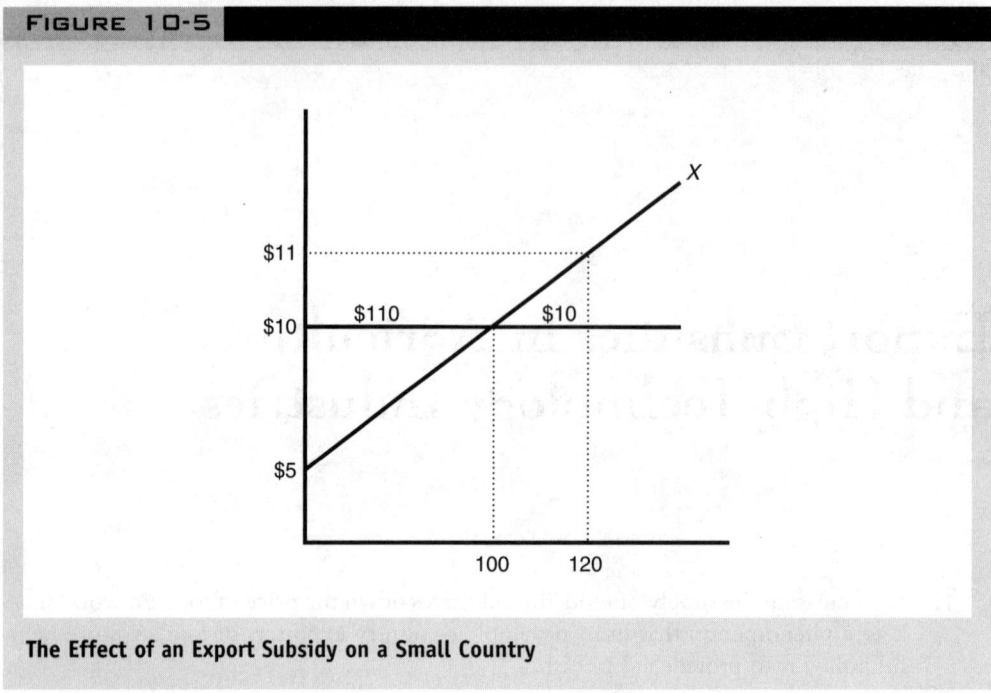

The Effect of an Export Subsidy on a Small Country

5a. The cost of the subsidy to the government is the area $(b + c + d)$.

5b. Producer surplus increases by $(a + b + c)$.

5c. The size of the consumption loss is equal to $s \cdot (D0 - D1) / 2$. This is the formula for the area of a triangle.

6. For a high enough price in the Home market, producers will be willing to supply even more than consumers demand. A large enough export subsidy (combined with a tariff) can raise the price above the autarky price in Home and induce the country to export.

7a. The cost of the subsidy is the volume of exports multiplied by the subsidy per unit exported: ($10/unit) · (150 units) = $1,500.

7b. Home suffers a terms-of-trade loss = ($100/unit − $95/unit) · (150 units) = $750 and a deadweight loss equal to (1/2) · ($105/unit − $100/unit) · (50 units) = $125. Hence the total loss of welfare to Home is $750 + $125 = $875.

7c. The subsidy raises Foreign's national welfare because consumer surplus increases more than producer surplus falls. However, Foreign's gain is not as large as Home's terms-of-trade loss. In Foreign, there is deadweight loss = (1/2) · ($100/unit − $95/unit) · (150 units − 100 units) = $125. The deadweight loss accrues because Foreign's producers make too few units and consume too many relative to free trade. Foreign's gain is then Home's terms-of-trade loss less Foreign's deadweight loss, or $625.

7d. See Figure 10-5. Consumers gain $a + b$, while producers lose a.

FIGURE 10-5

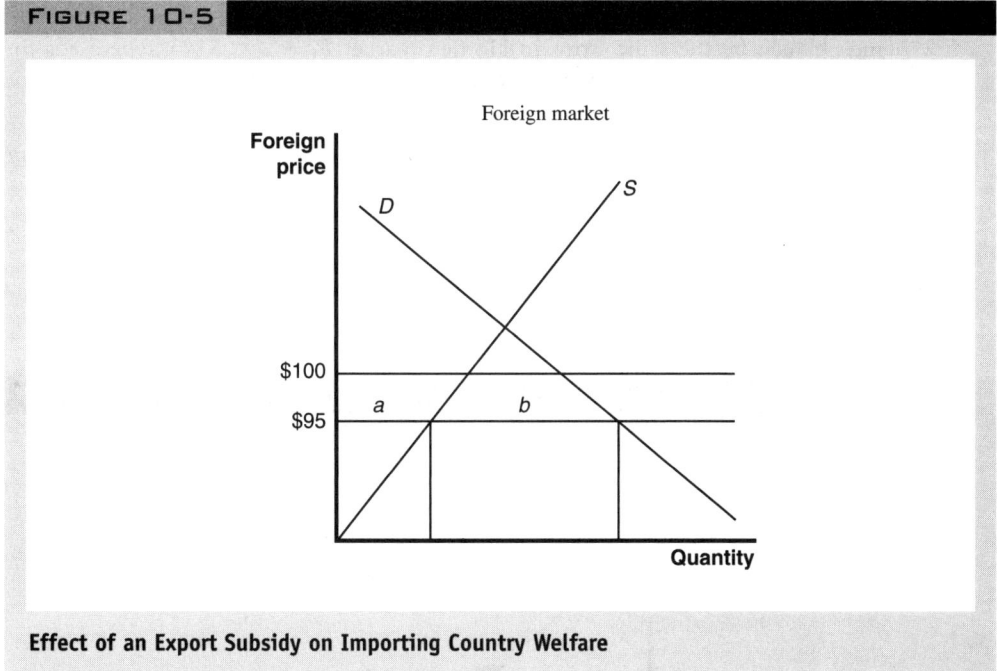

Effect of an Export Subsidy on Importing Country Welfare

7e. See Figure 10-6. Home losses include its deadweight loss *d* and its terms of trade loss *a* + *b* + *c*. Foreign enjoys terms-of-trade gain *a* + *b* + *c* but suffers deadweight loss of *c*.

FIGURE 10-6

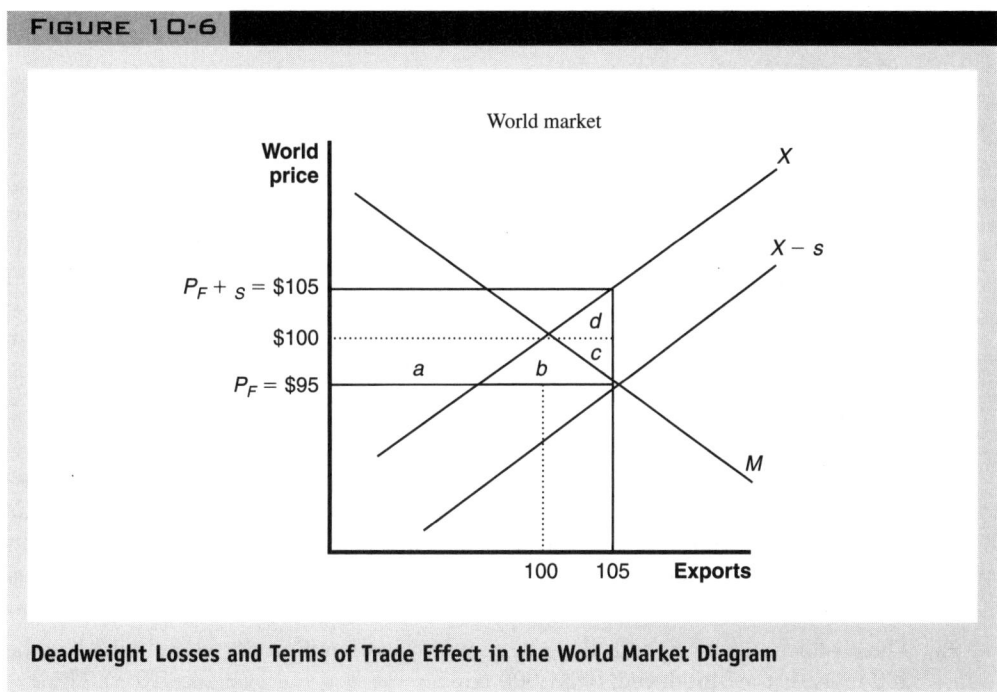

Deadweight Losses and Terms of Trade Effect in the World Market Diagram

7f. Yes. The price being charged by firms in their own market is $P_F = \$95$, and the price being charged by the same firms in Home's market $P_F + s = \$105$, where s is the subsidy of \$10. Because the price charged by these firms is lower in their domestic market than in Home, the criteria for dumping are satisfied.

7g. The importing country could impose countervailing duties to offset the effect of the subsidy.

8a. See Figure 10-7. The export tax lowers supply on the world market from Q_1 to Q_2 and therefore drives up the world price from P_1 to P_2. The price in the home market is the world price less the export tax (because the tax does not need to be paid on domestic sales). Exports drop.

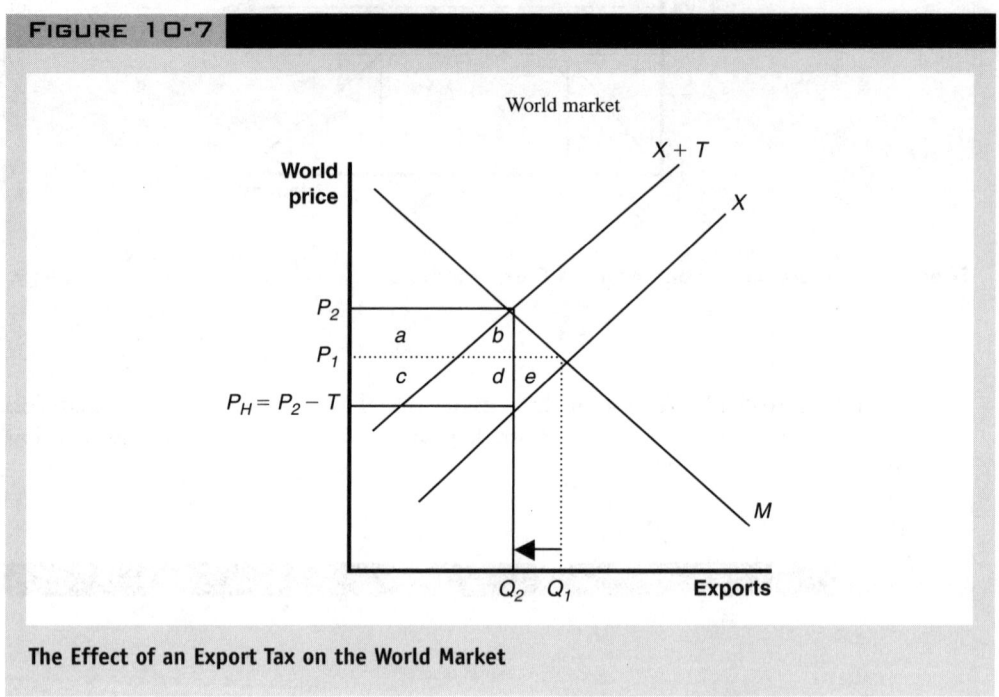

FIGURE 10-7

The Effect of an Export Tax on the World Market

8b. Because Home's price falls from P_1 to P_H, its producers are made worse off while its consumers are made better off. The loss of producer surplus exceeds the gain in consumer surplus by the area $c + d + e$ in Figure 10-7. The government collects tariff revenue on exports equal to $T \cdot Q_2$, which is equivalent to the area $a + b + c + d$ in the figure. Some of the tax revenue is paid by foreign consumers $(a + b)$ because the export tax improves the exporter's terms of trade.

8c. The export subsidy unambiguously reduced the exporter's welfare. In addition to the deadweight loss, a loss is associated with a deterioration of the terms of trade. The export tax also creates deadweight loss, but it causes a terms-of-trade gain. If the terms-of-trade gain is large relative to the deadweight loss, the country is better off with the tax. If an export subsidy is favored over an export tax, it must be that governments seek to increase producer surplus because the export subsidy increases producer surplus whereas the export tax reduces producer surplus.

9a. The production subsidy costs the government \$5 per unit produced multiplied by the 200 units that are produced, or \$1,000 (area $a + b + c + d$ in Figure 10-8). The export subsidy costs the government \$5 per unit exported multiplied by the volume of exports of 150 units (200 − 50), or \$750 (area $b + c + d$ in Figure 10-8). Hence, the production subsidy costs the government an additional \$250.

9b. In both cases the production distortion is given by the area d in Figure 10-8, which can be calculated as $(1/2) \cdot (\$15/\text{unit} - \$10/\text{unit}) \cdot (200 \text{ units} - 150 \text{ units}) = \$125$.

FIGURE 10-8

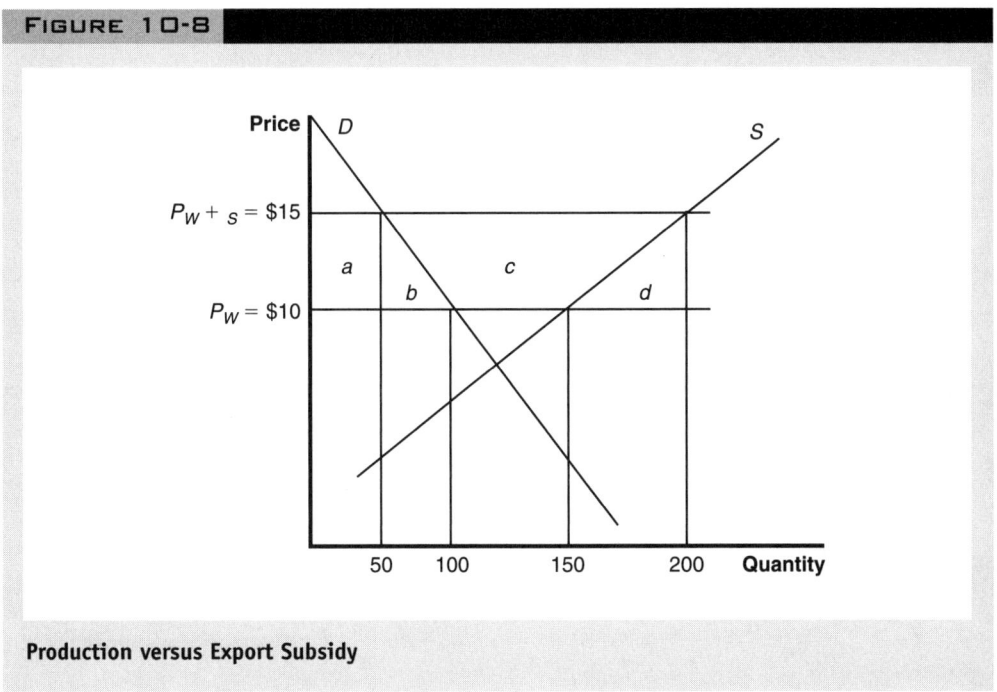

Production versus Export Subsidy

9c. The consumption distortion in the production subsidy case is zero because the price facing consumers has not changed. In the case of the export subsidy, the consumption distortion is given by the area b in Figure 10-8, which can be calculated as $(1/2) \cdot (\$15/\text{unit} - \$10/\text{unit}) \cdot (200 \text{ units} - 150 \text{ units}) = \$125$.

9d. In Figure 10-8, the effect of the export subsidy on national welfare is $-(b + d)$ and the effect of the production subsidy on national welfare is $-d$. Hence, the export subsidy reduces national welfare by \$125 more than the production subsidy because of the consumption distortion $-b$.

9e. If Home is large, the export subsidy has a bigger impact on the country's exports because it reduces consumption and increases production, whereas the production subsidy only increases production. Because exports are less affected, the export supply curve shifts by less and the impact on the terms of trade is smaller.

9f. If Home were a large country, its production subsidy would reduce the world price. The reduction in the world price increases Home's consumer surplus.

10. Yes. If the subsidy is sufficiently large, producers can be induced to produce more than consumers demand and the country will then become an exporter of a good that it would otherwise import.

11a. Assuming that there is no retaliation or asymmetry of production so that only one country is producing the good, there is no deadweight loss. The subsidy simply results in the transfer of a fixed amount of profit from one country to another.

11b. If the United States were to retaliate against the European Union, then plausibly both countries would end up producing and so there would be no profits. In this case, both countries would be worse off than if neither were offering subsidies.

11c. The two countries might have found themselves in an international prisoner's dilemma. Their efforts to increase their own well-being could have made the two countries collectively worse off. The 1992 agreement might have been an attempt to get out of this situation.

11

International Agreements:
Trade, Labor, and the Environment

1. The multilateral agreement will only work if there are mutual gains to the parties involved. If only one country is large, then that country may have no incentive to agree to tariff reduction.

2. If many small countries join a customs union, they may collectively become large on international markets. Because large countries are better off with restrictions on imports and small countries are better off with free trade, these countries may raise the tariff on outsiders.

3. This odd possibility is possible. Suppose that marginal costs of production are constant in Home and outside the free-trade area. It could be that Home's external tariff is low enough that countries outside the free-trade area have a lower marginal cost than Home and so supply the Home market. Now suppose that another country (Foreign) in the free-trade area has very high tariffs. Because there are rules of origin, Home producers get better access to Foreign's market than countries outside the area and so are the lowest-cost producer for the Foreign market while being a high-cost producer for their own market.

4. See Figure 11-2. Let the marginal cost of production for a country within the free-trade agreement be C. The free-trade agreement lowers the cost for this country to supply the domestic market and so trade rises. This is nothing different than we saw in Chapter 8.

FIGURE 11-2

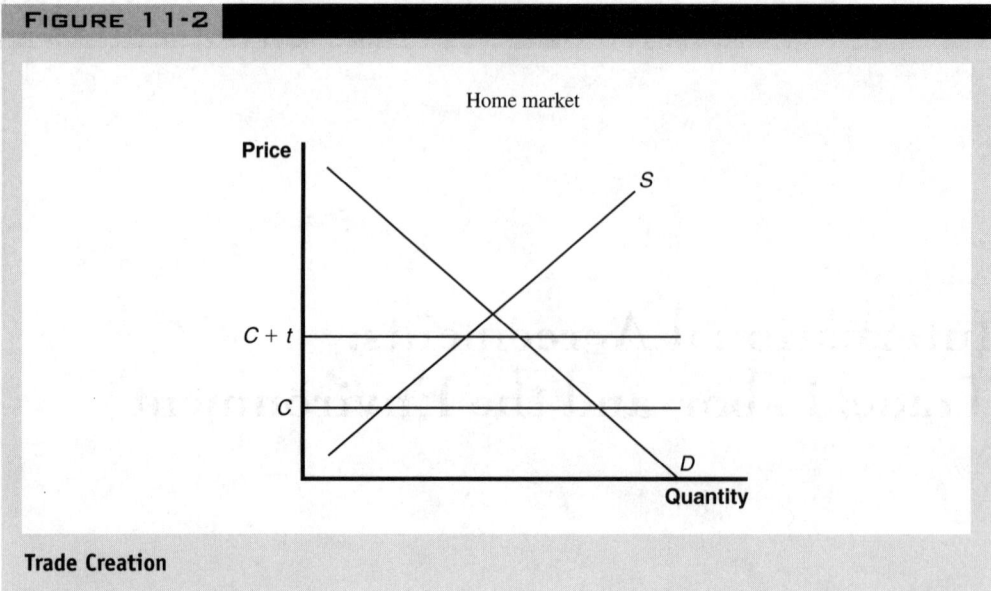

Trade Creation

5a. There can be no trade diversion in this example because country A has the lowest marginal cost of the three countries. It would be the supplier before and after the agreement.

5b. An RTA with country B could lead to trade creation if the initial tariff was high enough that home did not import the good from either country A or B.

5c. See Figure 11-3. Before the regional trade agreement, a tariff t is applied to imports of both A and B so that the marginal cost of A serving Home is $C_A + t$ and the marginal cost of B serving Home is $C_B + t$. Because $C_A + t < C_B + t$, the low-cost country A is the sole supplier when the tariff is equally applied to each country. Now suppose that country B joins a regional trade agreement with Home and the tariff is sufficiently large that country B is now the lowest cost supplier. Because $C_B < C_A + t$, trade is diverted from the low-cost producer A to the high-cost producer B.

FIGURE 11-3

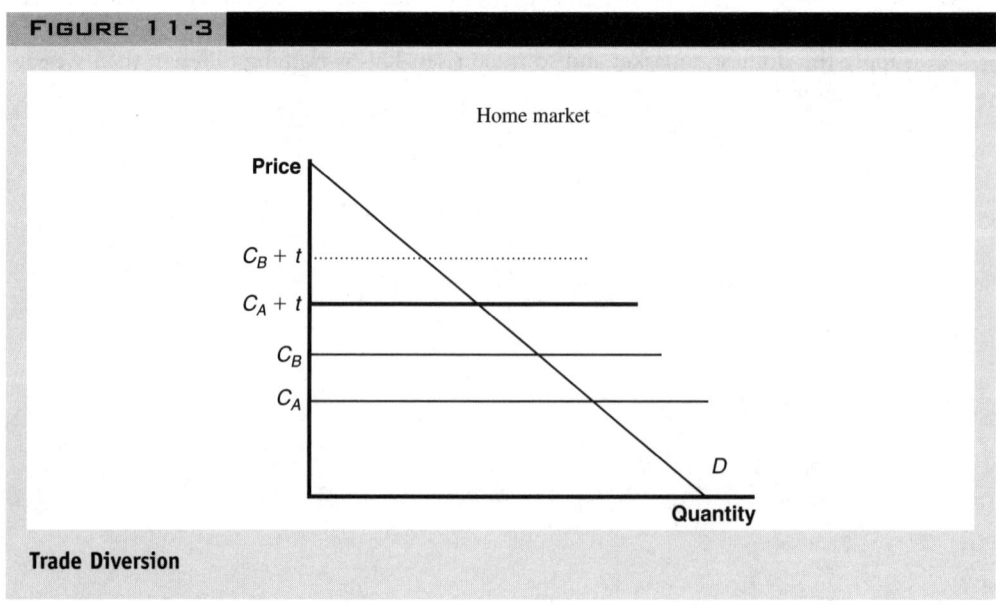

Trade Diversion

5d. Yes. Before the RTA, the price in Home was $C_A + t$. After the RTA, the price fell to C_B. It is true that tariff revenue has been lost, but it is also true that consumer surplus has risen because the price does fall.

6. Fair Trade Coffee, which is discussed in Chapter 3, is an example of an NGO that has had some success raising living standards. Consumers pay extra for coffee made under appropriate circumstances.

7. They worry that this is a form of disguised protectionism intended to raise the cost of production in low-wage countries.

8a. This question describes a specific-factors–type framework. If the wage rises in the formal sector, then the value of the marginal product of labor must rise as well. This means that employment in the formal sector must fall.

8b. Labor pushed out of the formal sector finds employment in the unregulated informal sector. As labor employed in that sector rises, the value of the marginal product of labor falls and so too does the wage paid in the informal sector.

9a. As in the tuna-dolphin case, there is a strong chance that the WTO will rule against Home because it is imposing a production process method on Foreign.

9b. No. As long as the reporting is nondiscriminatory, this would be fine with the WTO.

10. Rich countries will have tighter regulations on pollution than poorer countries. If these regulations raise the cost of highly polluting industries more than less-polluting industries, then tariff reduction could cause highly polluting industries to move to poorer countries. Pollution could increase as a result.

11a. If the pollution is primarily local, then an international prisoner's dilemma is less likely to arise because one country's pollution does not affect another.

11b. If the marginal costs of all producers rise, then the global supply curve for these goods shifts inward, resulting in a higher price for sneeds. The exact amount of the price increase depends on the shape of the demand and supply curves.

11c. Your country's sneed industry benefits from the higher price for sneeds on world markets while its marginal cost curve stays the same. Therefore your country's producer surplus rises.

11d. There is a free rider problem. If all other countries sign on to the agreement, your country gets the benefit of less global pollution from its actions and it benefits in terms of producer surplus because the price of sneeds has risen.